T0353075

On
Gold
Hill

On Gold Hill

A PERSONAL HISTORY OF WHEAT, FARMING, AND FAMILY, FROM PUNJAB TO CALIFORNIA

⊰ JACLYN MOYER ⊱

BEACON PRESS
Boston

Beacon Press
Boston, Massachusetts
www.beacon.org

Beacon Press books
are published under the auspices of
the Unitarian Universalist Association of Congregations.

Many names and identifying characteristics of people mentioned in this book
have been changed.

This book is printed on acid-free paper that meets the uncoated paper ANSI/
NISO specifications for permanence as revised in 1992.

Library of Congress Cataloging-in-Publication Data is available for this title.
ISBN: 978-0-8070-4530-5; e-book: 978-0-8070-4531-2
audiobook: 978-0-8070-3521-4

For Gurmeet Kaur Saund

CONTENTS

AUTHOR'S NOTE

The following is a work of nonfiction. Some names have been changed to respect the privacy of individuals. Though I've relied upon historical and scholarly sources, I come to the page not as a historian, nor an agronomist, political scientist, cerealist, or expert of any kind. I come instead as a student attempting to puzzle her way through the funhouse of history and science, family lore and memory. What ensues is a personal account of my ventures into these tangled corridors.

❧ PROLOGUE ❧

A Saturday farmers market. Midsummer. Morning. Woven baskets and canvas shopping bags. Nylon canopies flap-flapping in the breeze. The tang of overripe melons and a trace of chill in the air.

I walk with my sister toward the bustle. We're on the shady side of the street and goose bumps pimple my bare arms. But I know it won't last, this coolness. I've spent enough summers here in these parched Sierra foothills to be sure of that. By the end of the hour, the heat will shoulder in and everything will go sluggish, drawing back from the sun as best it can—birds hunkering in the cover of oaks, rattlesnakes slipping under rocks, squash blossoms crumpling inward. Now, a steady breeze sharpens the chill and I glance at the sunny side of the street where honeyed light pools across the asphalt, then step toward it.

Back when I lived in this region of Northern California and spent my days farming vegetables not far from this town, I'd have stayed in the shade. I'd have let the chill sink deep into my skin, tried to store it there in my flesh, a reserve against the coming heat. In those days, too, I'd have been on the opposite side of the vendor tables. Filling bins, counting change, smiles and thank-yous and recipe suggestions. But it's been more than three years since I stopped farming: today, I'm just a visitor here.

I'm drifting through the market, enjoying a visitor's cheerful indifference, when I see the words *Gold Hill* inked on a banner above a table of vegetables. I know I've stopped moving because my sister nudges me, asks, "What?" When I don't answer she follows my gaze. "Oh, they're here," she says. "The farmers who took over your old place."

I shouldn't be so surprised. My sister had told me that the latest tenants, the third set of eager organic farmers to lease the land since my partner Ryan and I had left it, were from her town.

"Come on," she says now. "I'll introduce you."

⊸

The new farmers are as surprised to meet me as I am to meet them. Like Ryan and me when we arrived on Gold Hill, they're a young couple thrilled for the chance to farm those ten acres of loamy soil. They wear dusty jeans and work boots, hats sweat-stained at the brow. After our introductions, the man resumes stocking produce while the woman and I talk. She tells me of their plans in sentences that bump into each other, the crops they intend to grow, their commitment to creating a more socially just and ecologically resilient food system. Her enthusiasm is contagious, her aspirations familiar. Soon I, too, am talking fast, eager to recall those particular ten acres, the stretch of land I know better than any on earth.

We discuss the intricacies of the irrigation system Ryan and I had designed, the stubborn patch of Bermuda grass by the parking lot. She tells me she's still getting acquainted with the microclimate of Gold Hill. "It's a banana belt," she says and I nod, remembering the way the morning light poured over the fields, how it seemed to gather there in that small basin. I remember, too, that I'd planted sapling fruit trees on that land, trees I knew wouldn't bear much of a harvest for close to a decade. How I'd hung a swing from the mulberry near the farmhouse and imagined my future children spending long afternoons there.

As we talk I begin to feel a familiar unsettledness rising, some slumbering thing stirring inside me. I look away from the young woman, focus instead on her produce. A smudge of dirt interrupts the smooth shine of an eggplant, and I rub it away with my thumb. More jolts of memory: sticky resin blacking my hands after a morning harvesting tomatoes, the hollow plunk of peppers tossed into a bucket, the scent of irrigation water on sun-warmed soil.

"Where are you living now?" the young woman asks. It's just small talk but I feel my throat tighten. I answer in a voice as breezy as I can muster, tell her we live in Oregon, it's very green, *lush*. No, we're not farming anymore. Yes, we have a big garden. I go on about our garden, how nice it is to be able to take time with everything, tend to each plant, nothing like working with the kind of ruthless efficiency farming demands. I don't mention how much I miss stepping into the greenhouse on a winter morning, those tables filled with thousands of seedlings—slender needles of onions, frilled blue broccoli, meaty zucchini cotyledons. Or the fall squash harvest, loading truck bed after truck bed with globes of color. Or the way it had once felt to say those words: *I'm an organic farmer.*

I begin to look for a way out of this conversation, a way to move my body away from this stall before I smack into the question I imagine she'll ask next: *What happened?*

What's so hard about that question anyway? We'd simply chosen to leave, to let it all go and move on. I'd typed up the letter terminating our lease, sent it in. And yet, there were those tired questions, bubbling up again in my mind: What if we'd only stayed another year, what if I'd been a shrewder businesswoman, a harder worker, a better farmer? Would things have been different? Had I made a mistake, was farming the good life and I'd given it up? Had I chickened out? Gotten out? Sold out? Dropped out? Failed out?

A customer steps up, ready to pay for his bag heaped full of leafy greens. Beautiful produce, he tells the farmer. And it's true, her display is stunning: all bright colors and broad leaves. She smiles at this compliment, and I watch as she adds up the total. Her hands are calloused and strong, dirt staining the creases of her fingers. Her stall buzzes with shoppers. She chats warmly, grins easily. Here, a hardworking organic farmer, diligent and prosperous, doing the good work, bettering the world while living out wholesome, worthwhile days. She plays the part well, I think. Maybe she *is* the part. I watch her and wonder, *Why wasn't I?*

I look down at the pepper in my hands and see it is trembling, so I put it back on the pile, tell myself it doesn't matter. All that is in the past now. I'd done those years on the farm, nearly four, and lost nothing. Ryan and I had transformed a fallow field, dust and star-thistle, into ten verdant acres, a productive organic farm, and we'd left happily, ready for something new, unscathed.

Another customer approaches the farmer. My hands have stopped shaking, and I'm feeling better, fine. I'll wave goodbye, mouth "good luck!" and walk away. I turn to do just that, but the woman lifts a finger, *wait a minute*, and motions for me to come over. She finishes the transaction, steps away from the register, and leans toward me across a heap of squash.

"I wanted to tell you," she says, "we've had a pretty impressive stand of volunteer grain come up this spring."

"Volunteer grain?" I repeat.

"Along the west edge of the farm, all the way to that back corner near the creek."

When I don't respond she adds, "We think it might be wheat."

The back of my neck goes hot. "Oh?"

She waits for me to say more, then prods, "Didn't you and Ryan grow wheat? There's that mill stone still in the barn? We heard you were doing some kind of heirloom grain thing?"

I nod. Ignore the heat spreading down my spine. I haven't talked about our wheat for a few years, have tried to put it out of mind since the day I poured the last handful of flour into a mixing bowl, then stared at the empty ziplock bag dusted faintly yellow. That bag sat on my counter for days before I finally threw it out, the last trace of my wheat clinging to the plastic.

"We tried," I say, making a sound I hope comes out like a casual chuckle. "It was just an experiment. It didn't really pan out in the end. Anyway," I add, "that was years ago."

"Well," she says, "we've asked around. As far as anyone knows, none of the other farmers grew grains."

The west edge. That would be the place we'd last planted the wheat.

"How tall is it?" I ask.

"Pretty tall, four, five feet maybe."

"Blond?"

"Yes."

"Beardless?"

The woman falters. "I'm not sure," she says. "I don't really know much about grains."

✧

When I arrived on Gold Hill, twenty-five and brimming with ambition, I, too, knew hardly anything about growing grains. Ryan and I hadn't planned to grow wheat. We intended to grow vegetables—ten acres of certified organic produce. At the time, the "farm" was only a weedy field, thistle and ryegrass. There was an old hay barn and a long-abandoned spring-toothed harrow half buried in the baked earth. There was no irrigation, no greenhouse or tractor. There was no farm stand, no washing stations, not even a stray shovel. All those things Ryan and I would need to build or buy. But we found none of this daunting, only laden with possibility.

It was one afternoon that first summer, a few months into the rush of all the building and planning and gathering, that a baker friend of mine came sauntering up our driveway, a loaf of bread in hand. The loaf, he explained, was made with a grain I'd never heard of: Sonora wheat. The wheat had been grown on a farm not far from my own. "Seems like it would do pretty well here," he said, fanning out an arm in the direction of our newly leased fields. "Maybe you should plant some."

I shook my head. "I don't know anything about growing wheat."

"Well," my friend said after a moment, "you could look into it."

I turned toward my fields, tried to imagine them filled with wheat. Though I'd never spent any time on a wheat farm, I found I had no trouble conjuring an image, a cereal box vision of amber stalks gleaming in the sun. I shrugged and told my friend I'd think about it.

I assumed I'd do some halfhearted research, an hour of googling maybe, an email to an acquaintance who had experience with wheat. The search led to a phone call with a seed supplier. I asked some basic questions and nearly stopped there—nearly hung up the phone and forgot all about the idea of growing wheat. I might have done just that if not for the words that came at the end of the conversation, a detail offered casually, the woman's voice crackling over a bad connection: "The grocer told me Sonora makes flatbreads just like the ones he remembers eating when he was growing up somewhere in northern India. Punjab, I believe."

I didn't tell the woman on the phone, not that day, that my family was from northern India. I didn't tell her I was Punjabi. In fact, I don't think I'd ever said those words—*I'm Punjabi*—to anyone. Though the statement was true—my mother was born in Punjab, as were both her parents, and their ancestors as far back as anyone knew—it seemed equally false. At the time, I'd never been to India, knew little about Punjabi customs or traditions, didn't speak the language. I knew only that my mother had left that place and come to America with her family when she was fifteen, and at some point thereafter lost her Punjabi accent. To me, her voice had always sounded just as Californian as my own, with one exception: the *v* and *w* sounds had gotten irrevocably switched in her mind, so that windshield wiper often came out vinshield viper; wisteria, visteria. It was the one remnant of India my mother had failed to shed. The rest of it she'd seemed to have sloughed off long before I was born. Once, I heard my mother refer to herself as a "nonpracticing Indian," as if she'd simply chosen to opt out of this facet of herself like one might a religion or a profession.

I can't recall a moment when I first began to wonder about my mother's past, to look for a sense of my own cultural roots, or when I noticed these things were nowhere to be found. As far back as I can remember I felt a kind of cavity in the place where I imagined this sense of heritage might otherwise have lived. As a child I believed this vacancy would shrink as I became an adult and other forms of identity filled in the space, but instead it only grew. By the time I spoke with the wheat seed supplier that summer morning, it had become an aching hollow, and her words—*flatbreads just like the ones he remembers eating when he was growing up somewhere in northern India. Punjab, I believe*—landed there with an echoing thud.

After hanging up the phone, I replayed the conversation in my head. The seed supplier had given me plenty of compelling reasons to grow Sonora—it was drought tolerant and didn't require any irrigation, it produced a distinctly flavorful flour and tender dough, it was among the first wheats ever grown on North American soil and one of the oldest varieties still in existence. But it was, of course, the link between this wheat's history and my own that I found most irresistible. The coincidence struck me as an opportunity: Might this obscure wheat contain within it a door to my own heritage? If I could manage to grow Sonora—plant the seed, harvest a crop, mill flour from the berries—might I, in turn, reclaim a piece of the inheritance I'd lost?

Ryan and I planted a two-acre field with Sonora wheat that first fall. We grew the grain for three years, encountering a new obstacle with each attempt, until, at last, I held in my arms a sack of flour. I'd done what I set out to do. And yet I felt no closer to understanding my roots. Instead, I was less certain than I'd ever been of what constituted my heritage and what it could meant to "reclaim" it, of why I'd wanted to become an organic farmer and how that conviction had unraveled, and what wheat had to do with any of it. The one thing I'd learned enough to feel sure about was that it did, in fact, have something to do with it.

I left the farm with all I could carry of our final harvest—a bin of onions, two crates of winter squash, a scant twenty pounds of flour—and a gnawing confusion. I couldn't shake the notion that Sonora wheat was entangled with my family history, with my own ambitions, and with the fate of my farm, but I couldn't then make sense of the ways these things were bound up. For months I picked over memories, attempted to stitch them together into something I could understand. But then a sudden wash of regret would pour over me, or a scorching sense of failure, or the blinding frustration of being so unable to find any meaning in the tangle. Eventually I gave up, pushed the questions aside. The wheat, the farm, all that, I assured myself, was behind me now, just a youthful endeavor, nothing to dwell on. By the time the last remnants of my farm produce had been used up, I'd laid my questions down to rest.

❧

Now, at the farmers market, the young woman is still looking at me as if waiting for a reaction I haven't yet supplied.

She clears her throat. "What I mean is," she says, "your wheat, it's still there."

I feel my heartbeat pulsing in my temples. Resist the urge to rub at them. I can't quite wrap my mind around this, can't think it through—how many seasons had it been since we'd tilled under the last crop? Could enough of those seeds have germinated, grown tall, set seed, been tilled under again?

"No," I say flatly. "I don't think so. My wheat, those seeds are long gone by now."

The farmer and I look at each other for a wordless moment before another customer steps up ready to pay. We exchange smiles, great-to-meet-yous, then I turn and walk quickly out of the market.

❧

Back home in Oregon, I can't get the woman's words out of my head: *Still there.* From a shelf near my desk, I pull out a wooden box of keepsakes I've collected over the years and dig through its contents. Old letters. A few smudged photos. A river stone. It doesn't take me long to find what I'm after: a thimble-size bundle of fabric, bound with thread. I set the bundle on my desk and gently work at the knot until the thread slips and the fabric falls open. There, in the cupped depression, a mound of wheat. Thirty or forty grains in all, enough to fill a teaspoon.

I haven't looked at these seeds, haven't unbound the bundle of fabric since the day I tied it up a few weeks before we left the farm. Now, I peer closely. Half of the grains are plump and butter-colored, my own Sonora seeds. These were the last of them, I'd thought—kernels I'd rubbed loose from an ear of our final harvest. And then there are the other grains. Longer and narrower, their hue a dusty auburn. These seeds don't really belong to me at all—I'd stolen them from a rooftop in Punjab where they'd been dumped from a dustpan and left for the birds.

I pinch up one of the auburn seeds. It's nothing special, no traditional heirloom—just a modern variety, high yielding and conventionally grown. I roll it between my fingers and recall the morning I'd picked it out of the dust pile: a lone kite overhead, scent of wood smoke, the slap of my cousin's chappla sandals on concrete steps. One memory leads to another—the taste of a raw wheat berry chewed to a gummy pulp, then stretched thin to test the strength of gluten; the rattle and ping of a combine; a flock of drought-starved geese grazing a field of knee-high stalks; yields per acre, dollars per pound; the warmth of just-milled flour seeping into my palm; an empty fertilizer bag stuffed with scraps of fabric—and with the memories, that familiar feeling, a blend of vexation and yearning, like trying to untangle a mess of yarn, if I could only find the right strand to tug. *Still there.*

I study the seeds, line them up to inspect each one as if I might find some insight among the kernels. The seeds, of course, yield no such answers so I wrap them up again, drop the bundle back into the box, and turn instead to my bookshelf where I find my copy of *The Wheat Plant* by John Percival. I thumb through it until I land on the page with the photo of the Sonora stalk. I don't really need to look to know what's there. By now, I've memorized the page. It hangs in my mind alongside a collection of other facts and images, information accumulated over those four years on the farm, a fragmented history of this plant. What I want now is the rest of the story. Because knotted up with it, I suspect, I might find a piece of my own.

I don't imagine, not on this day, just how far into history I'll wander, or where the threads I tug will lead me—to times of gold miners and seed hunters, into colonial India and through Partition, to the beginnings of the modern organic farming movement and past the unfolding of the Green Revolution. On this day, I've no idea where I'm going at all.

I know only that I need to go, need to start somewhere. So I examine again the page in the book, squint at the photo, reread the words, then turn back to chapter one and begin at the beginning:

Among the world's crops wheat is pre-eminent both in regard to its antiquity and its importance as a food of mankind.

Part 1

ORIGIN STORIES

❧ 1 ❧

If you try to trace a story back to its beginning, to locate a point of origin, as I've been doing, chances are, you'll never find it. The further back one looks, the further every story goes. All beginnings, then, are fictions, invented dawns, origin stories.

This one starts here:

One spring morning around the year 8000 BCE, a gust of wind careens across the hillsides of what is now Damascus. The soil here in the Fertile Crescent is rich; there's plenty of sun and ample rain. Wild emmer covers the landscape: four feet tall, bright green, and flowering. Each stalk carries at its highest point a string of florets, pale yellow anthers dangling, delicate stigmas tucked inside. On this day some of the flowers, already fertilized, drop their anthers and begin to swell into seeds, each one a capsule of genetic information for the creation of a new plant. The majority of these seeds are the product of self-pollination, and therefore will produce plants that carry a genetic makeup very much like their parents'. But on this morning, in the interior of one of these developing seeds, a shift occurs—a mutation, a glitch, a fluke, a breakthrough, a mistake. Whatever it is, it will alter the fate of everything to come.

Spring turns to summer and the grasses go coppery, the stalks crisp. The ear carrying the mutated seed, now fat with grain, ripens under the sun until, like all the others, it becomes so brittle it bursts, sending spikelets of seed scattering into the air. The spikelets fall to the ground where their arrow-shaped points drive them into the soil, planting them deep enough into the earth to root when, a few months later, the fall rains arrive.

By the time spring comes again these seedlings have grown tall, have become towering grasses themselves, and the hills are once again flushed green. Summer nears and these plants grow heavy with seed. Heat browns the stalks, and again the ears shatter apart when ripe, sowing a new generation of seed. Soon, all the grain is dispersed and the stalks stand empty. All but those of one plant.

Atop the stalks of this plant, each ear holds tight to its spikelets of seed. Weeks go by but these ears don't shatter, don't fling their contents into the air—they only nod slightly downward with the weight of all they carry. Look close enough and you can see that the place where the spikelets are attached to the ear is misshapen, so it does not break apart when brittle. This misshapenness appears, at first glance, to be a malfunction, a morphological mutation that fails to serve the plant. The seeds, held inside the ear, are unable to effectively disperse and embed themselves into the soil. It seems they'll remain trapped high up in the head of the stalk until the rains come and pummel them down. Then, tangled in the mess of rain-flattened straw, too far from the soil to take root even if they manage to germinate, the seeds will rot. They'll decompose back into the earth and this odd mutation will vanish just as quickly as it appeared.

But this is not what happens. For on this day, a human is walking through this field of ripe wild emmer. She bends to the painstaking work of gathering up scattered seeds from the ground, one spikelet at a time. The food she'll get from these seeds is nutritious, but the work of gathering is slow and tedious, allowing little time for anything else. From across the field the woman notices these ears, still intact and held aloft like small flags over the landscape of emptied stalks. She walks closer, peers at this peculiar plant, snaps off one ear, and confirms that it is still full of seed. In that one quick snap, she's collected forty grains. She snaps the other ears from their stalks then brings what she's found to her family. There she rubs the ear between her palms and watches the spikelets of seed fall into a tidy heap. These humans save this precious seed—seed that will produce ears that don't shatter when ripe but hold their grains snug—and they sow it when the fall rains arrive. The following summer, there is more. This goes on and on until the humans are no longer gathering up wild emmer seed by seed, but are harvesting with great efficiency the heads of their cultivated strain: domesticated emmer, *Triticum turgidum*, subspecies *dicoccum*.

Both plant and human have something to offer in this new relationship, and something to gain: For the emmer, ineffective at dispersing its own seed, the human dutifully threshes the grain free of its ear and sows it into the ground. For the human, the emmer provides a source of sustenance that can be harvested efficiently and stored for years. The relationship blooms, and the lives of the two species become further intertwined each year. Soon, this plant and its progeny are providing humanity with a fifth of its calories, enabling civilizations to settle and grow, industry and arts to develop. In turn, as the years, centuries, and millennia pass, humans begin felling forests, bringing water to the most formidable of deserts, developing poisons to wipe out competing plants, building machines capable of splitting apart nitrogen molecules for fertilizer—all to ensure the successful proliferation of this plant. And proliferate it does, until it has reached nearly every corner of the earth.

⇜ 2 ⇝

By 2012, the lives of humans and wheat had been entangled for 10,000 years in a relationship that had shaped much of the world. Midway through this year, on a bright May morning, lies another beginning. At least that's how I saw it at the time, sitting with Ryan in the office of our soon-to-be landlord, readying a pen to sign my name on a lease agreement: ten acres of weeds and a derelict two-bedroom farmhouse in exchange for $10,400 a year. A moment passed—scratch of ink on paper, shuffle of pages—and it was done, the land was ours to farm. We shook hands with the director of the land trust, then straightened our copies on the desktop. When I recall this moment now, all those pages tapping against the oak, I hear the sound of a dealer shuffling cards and wonder, Did it sound that way to me then?

Ryan and I stepped out of the office that day into the kind of late spring morning when everything seems to brim with potential: Apple boughs dripping with clusters of marble-size fruit. Ribbons of pollen riding the breeze. Zinnia buds swollen with the pressure of so many petals curled inside. Even the hue of the sunlight glinting a vow of all the heat to come. But we didn't dally on all this. Instead, we drove straight to the property. Ryan started digging up the old water line to the house to replace with a new one—the first step in making the house livable—and I left to go to town for a quick grocery run. But on the way I noticed tents set up on Main Street, a farmers market. I parked and headed toward the bustle.

At this market—seven years before and fifty miles south of that other market where I would later meet our replacements—I wandered through the aisles, still giddy with the thrill of my name inked on the lease. Since I'd first stumbled across the ad months before—a land trust seeking proposals from farmers interested in leasing a portion of a historic ranch and restoring it to a working farm—I'd been awaiting this day, plagued with anxiety dreams about the whole thing falling through, the conservancy backing out, the property catching fire, the lease going to someone else instead. But after so many months of revising proposals, attending interviews, negotiating details, it was, at last, final.

I eyed the vendor stalls, my head thrumming with visions of the similar displays of carrots and beets, baskets of snap peas and bouquets of bachelor's buttons that would fill my own farm stand the following spring. In the center of the market, a heap of red fruit gleamed in the sunlight and, even from yards away, I could smell the resiny musk: tomatoes, the first of the season. I hadn't had a fresh tomato in the better part of a year and imagined lifting one from the pile and eating it right there like an apple. But I wanted to wait, to take the tomatoes back to the farm where I'd slice them into thick slabs and sprinkle each with salt. Ryan and I would sit on our new front porch, our ten acres spread out below us, and eat them together. It would be a celebration.

I was reaching for a tomato when I noticed an older woman a few yards away, walking toward me. Unlike the other patrons who wore jeans and tank tops, flowered skirts and sun hats, she was dressed in a teal green salwar kameez. The silky tunic fell down past her knees over the matching pair of billowing pants. Where the pants cinched together at the ankles, the fabric draped over itself, hanging down the back of her heels and cascading across the tops of her feet. Only her toes peeked out, strapped into black sandals that, like the rest of her outfit, looked just like the ones my grandmother always wore. The familiarity made me smile. A sheer chunni nestled around her neck and even before she stood next to me and the scarf slipped from her shoulder to brush against my arm, I knew exactly how the fabric would feel on my skin. I was still smiling when the woman looked up. "Sat Sri Achall," she said. *Hello.* It was one of the handful of Punjabi phrases I could then understand, and I replied with the same greeting—softly enough, I hoped, to hide my awkward pronunciation.

The woman eyed the pyramid of plump tomatoes, lifted one after another to turn the fruit over, squeezing the flesh ever so slightly. I did the same, placing those that were too firm or too soft back atop the stack. When we reached for the same tomato—a squat fruit striped red and orange—our fingers touched, and we both laughed. The woman placed her hand on my wrist as if we were old friends and said something to me in Punjabi. I caught only the word for tomato: *tamater.* She repeated herself.

But I could offer only a shrug. I felt her fingers lift from my wrist. "You do not speak Punjabi?" she said in English. I shook my head. "Hindi?" I shook my head again. "Oh, I'm sorry," she said, "It's just that you look so much like my daughter, I thought you might."

And with those words I was seven years old again, inside the dimly lit Indian market a short drive from my grandmother's house in Los Angeles where she and I have come to buy a gnarl of ginger root. My grandmother wears a burgundy salwar kameez with a delicate floral pattern across the sleeves and neckline, a matching scarf. She chats in Punjabi with the store owner while I wander the aisles, tracing my fingertip over a spine of okra and examining a sack of coriander seeds. When my grandmother calls to me, I look up to see her standing next to the proprietor, the two of them smiling broadly in my direction. She motions for me to come over and I know she wants to introduce me. I set the sack of seeds back on the pile and look down at my dusty Converse sneakers and yellow socks pulled up over my ankles, my skinny legs poking out from jean shorts, my bright blue T-shirt with a leaping dolphin on the front. The store owner is dressed in a spotless cream-colored linen shirt and matching white turban. I feel cartoonish in my outfit, as if I'm wearing a Halloween costume on the wrong day, and I keep my eyes on the floor as I walk.

When I reach her, my grandmother wraps her arm around my shoulders and pulls me into the gauzy folds of her scarf. The fabric smells of cardamom and boiled milk. The store owner squats so his eyes are at the level of my own and says something to me in Punjabi. I look back at him blankly and watch his smile wither into a question mark, his brow wrinkle in confusion. Looking into this stranger's face, I realize that Punjabi, the language of my ancestors, one that had been passed from each generation to the next, carried across continents from India to Kenya to California, has ended here, with me. I've dropped the baton. And this language, it is suddenly smackingly clear, is the key to the world in which my grandmother lives. A key I do not possess. Shame burns my cheeks and I want to run out of the store, the thick scent of spices turned suffocating. Instead I press my face into my grandmother's chest, burying it in the silk of her scarf.

With no such chest to hide my face in that morning at the market, I attempted to smile at the woman who was peering up at me awaiting some kind of explanation. I mumbled a murky story about how, though I couldn't speak the language, she had guessed correctly—my grandmother was in fact from Punjab, my mother too. "Ah!" the woman said, grinning. "You *are* Punjabi!" I didn't qualify her statement and for a moment it seemed she might place her fingers back on my wrist. "And where is your family from," she asked, "which part?"

I slipped my hand away, turned back to the tomatoes to avoid the look I was certain would slip across her face when I answered, the same look I'd been turning away from with flushed cheeks since I first watched it transpire upon the store owner's face decades ago. That slow morph of a smile into an expression altogether different, a mix of disappointment and surprise, of pity and gotcha.

Because the truth was, I couldn't answer even this most basic question: *Where is your family from?* I could understand barely a word of Punjabi, had never been to India, didn't own a salwar kameez, hadn't the slightest idea how to make achar, the spicy pickled lemon my grandmother ferments in gallon jars that I carted home from visits and ate on toast for lack of the accompanying Indian meals.

I hadn't yet answered the woman, hadn't uttered the only thing there was to say—I don't know—when a friendly vendor interrupted with a tray of tomatoes. "Sample?" she offered. I looked at the slices, each one dripping wine-colored juice: Cherokee Purples, I'd bet. Desperate to put something in my mouth to displace the words waiting there, I snatched one from the tray and slipped it between my lips. The slap of flavor was sharp, cutting. All acid.

The woman reached for her own sample and I ducked away, merged into the crowd of shoppers perusing potatoes a few tables down, then hurried toward the register to pay.

In line, I felt a tap on my shoulder. Behind me, the woman in the teal kameez held her arm outstretched. In her palm rested the striped tomato we'd both reached for.

"Take it," she said. "It's yours."

↜ 3 ↝

Whenever my mother talked of her life before my sister and I were born, the stories she told reached only as far back as one spring night in 1971. On this night, in the dark April sky above the city of Los Angeles, an airplane angles downward toward the still hot tarmac of LAX. At one of the plane's small windows, a fifteen-year-old girl presses her forehead to the glass. Nearby, her parents and three younger siblings sleep, but her own eyes are wide open, taking in the sight below: lights. More numerous than she'd thought possible, the lights chart out long straight lines and grids of rectangles, snaking curves and shapeless masses. They appear endless and she feels as though she's looking down upon another universe. A universe into which she is descending.

When the plane lands, this young girl and her family step out into a balmy California night, and her new life begins: high school classes, a scholarship to UCLA, then pharmacy school in San Francisco. A summer job at a company owned by the father of a young white man who didn't know not to ask an Indian girl out for a date. An engagement, strictly forbidden. A winter wedding anyway. A house and five acres in the country six hours north of LA. Daughters, a swimming pool, a career as a pharmacist. Spaghetti dinners and pet sheep in the backyard.

I always knew, of course, that something had come before all this, that my mother had lived out an entire childhood and the better part of an adolescence in another culture, in faraway places—first India, then Kenya. These facts were never hidden or secret, just unimportant. A kind of preamble to get out of the way before my mother's real story got going, necessary logistically but fundamentally irrelevant. Still, I always felt like I'd picked up a series one volume in, like there was another whole book that came before the place where I'd begun reading. I'd caught plenty of glimpses: the Indian meals my mother cooked a few times a year, simple flatbreads and dal made with the kind of effortless efficiency that comes only with having done something a thousand times before; the way, every once in a while, a Punjabi word would slip out of her mouth in place of the English equivalent; how she sang American songs in a key different than I'd ever heard anyone else sing them. Mostly, though, my windows into this past were offered up by my grandparents.

Every year or so over the course of my childhood, we visited with my mother's parents. Sometimes my parents, sister, and I would pack into our car and drive south to LA. Other years, my grandparents made the six-hour trip up Highway 5 to our house. When they came to see us, I'd watch the road from my bedroom window until I saw the hood of an old Camry sedan nose up the hill and turn into our driveway. I'd watch the car slow to a stop, Nanaji in the driver's seat where, I knew, his thick fingers were wrapped around the wheel, gold rings glinting. In the passenger seat Naniji would be worrying a string of prayer beads through her thumb and forefinger. When they rang the bell, I listened for my mother's footsteps, for the scrape of the door swinging open, the flurry of Punjabi. Only then would I creep down the hall, stand at the edge of the living room, and wait for my grandmother to notice me. When she did, her face would erupt in a smile, she'd ushed me near, pull me close, then ask if I was hungry. I'd wait for her to settle in, have tea, unpack her things in our spare room, and then—as she never failed to do—call my sister and me one by one into her room to present us each with a gift.

"Jackie," she called from her door at the end of the hallway on one such visit. "Come. Please, I have something for you." I stepped into the room and my grandmother swept the door closed behind me. Though it was just the spare room of my parents' house, edged with mundane clutter— extra blankets, piles of file folders, boxes of wrapping paper—my grandparents' presence transformed the space. Folded shawls were draped over the back of a chair. A book of prayer lay atop the neatly made bed. A small framed painting of a man with a long beard and a white turban, his face serene, palm raised, sat atop the nightstand. Even the air felt different, laced with cardamom and black tea.

My grandmother sat cross-legged on the floor with her bare feet tucked into the folds of her salwar kameez. A suitcase spread open in front of her. I was eight or nine, dressed in my usual leggings and cotton T-shirt. I lowered my body onto the floor and crossed my legs too, trying to sit exactly like my grandmother. She pulled a garment from the suitcase and handed it to me. "Jackie, you like?" I unfolded the shirt, laid it flat on the carpet. A hundred button-size mirrors reflected back a distortion of my face. Between the mirrors, orange threads wove a tight pattern against black linen. The sleeves were finished at the wrists with gold embroidery. By the time I got a good look at the shirt, my grandmother had already laid out two others. One of the shirts was pink, my least favorite color, with complicated embroidery covering the chest like a bib, the sleeves made of mesh. The other was cherry red and long enough to reach my knees. "From India," my grandmother said. "You like?" She looked at me, eager for an answer, the thick lenses of her glasses magnifying her eyes.

I picked up one of the long shirts, the red kameez, though I didn't then know to call it that. "Yes," I said. "They're pretty."

"Haanah, very pretty." My grandmother beamed. "You take them all then, haanah?" When she leaned forward to speak, I could smell the coconut oil she rubbed into her hair.

I scooped up the pile of shirts. I knew I'd never wear these clothes, never be caught dead in them at my very white rural elementary school. Instead, I'd keep them folded on the top shelf of my closet. On rainy afternoons I'd pull them down and run my fingertips over the plastic mirrors. I'd press the fabric to my face and take a breath: cloves, warm milk, dust.

When I stepped into the hallway with a bundle in my arms, there stood my mother, shaking her head. "You know Jackie doesn't wear that stuff, Mom. You have got to stop bringing her gifts like that, it all just sits in the closet." My grandmother cast her eyes away and murmured something in Punjabi. I clasped the bundle tight to my chest, waited for my mother to return to the kitchen. When she did, I looked up at my grandmother. "Thank you," I said to her downturned face, then ran to my room.

⦦

During their visits with us, I watched my grandparents with a kind of distant wonder. I coveted the scent that lingered on everything they touched. I put my ear against the wall separating my bedroom from the spare room and listened to the Sikh prayers they murmured every morning, believing that if I listened hard enough I might wring some meaning from the words. Mostly, I sat on a chair in the kitchen and watched my grandmother cook.

She fried okra and simmered dal, blended cilantro and coconut into chutney. She rolled out flat circles of dough, cooked them atop a curved steel pan, then flipped each over an open flame until the bread ballooned with hot air and blisters speckled the surface. When the first roti was done, she tossed it onto a dish towel–lined plate, where it deflated onto itself. Then, using the back of a spoon, she rubbed a dollop of butter into the bread, folded it in half, and, smiling broadly, placed the hot roti into my ready hands.

Once, my grandmother waded into my parents' pool fully dressed while I sunbathed nearby in my swimsuit. I watched as she lowered herself slowly onto the first step. She didn't appear to care that the water soaked the hem of her pants, and for a moment I mistook her behavior for a streak of boldness. Once my family and I, on a drive in the mountains, had spontaneously pulled over at a lake. My sister and I didn't have swimsuits on but, unable to resist the water, we plunged in wearing our jean shorts and T-shirts. For the rest of that drive we couldn't stop giggling with the exhilaration of having defied a norm.

But that afternoon, watching the pool water tug at the hem of my grandmother's pants, I didn't dare giggle. She stepped down onto the next stair and the water reached her knees, I guessed, though it was difficult to know where exactly her knees were amid the billows of her pants. She continued into the pool until the water rose to her chest. The tails of her crimson chunni floated to the surface, tinting the water red as if the pool were filled with wine. With her back to me, my grandmother leaned slightly forward and cupped her hands together to splash her cheeks, then patted a wet palm across her forehead. When at last she turned to walk back toward the steps, I lifted my towel to cover my own bare shoulders.

Another visit, I sat at our kitchen table doing my homework—long division. It was a hot afternoon and I thought everyone else in the house was napping, but after finishing a page, I looked up to find my grandfather standing across the kitchen with a screwdriver in hand. His hunched back faced me so that I could make out each notch of his spine beneath his white linen shirt. He moved around the kitchen making hardly a sound, opening cupboards, pulling out a teakettle, two pots, and a large pan. Only the pads of his slippers whispered against the tile floor. I held my breath and kept my pencil hovering over the page, afraid of ruining the quiet. I watched him examine the cookware, turning the pots over in his large hands, gently wiggling their wobbly handles back and forth. He bent brackets and tightened screws until each piece was firmly in place; he did not allow the tools a single bang as he worked, nor the pots a single clank. At last my grandfather turned a screw one degree too tight and it released a tiny squeal. I let out my breath.

⊷

For most of my childhood, a square of slippery fabric sat folded on a shelf in a spare closet otherwise filled with sleeping bags and half-finished sewing projects. If spread out smooth across the floor, the fabric was wider than I was tall and nearly spanned the length of a room. It was cherry red at the top hem, deep blue at the bottom. The color morphed across the spectrum in between so that the cloth resembled a clear sky at sunset.

When we were kids, my sister and I often pulled the fabric from the closet and draped it over chairs, crawled into the space below and imagined we were camping beneath an open sky. I called it the sunset sheet. I didn't call it a sari. I didn't know what a sari was.

Once, I pulled it off the shelf and asked my mother about it. "What is this thing, anyway?" I might have said. She stood with her hands on her hips and traced the length of cloth with her gaze as if sizing up an opponent, as if she'd never seen it before and was trying to discern its function. Then she straightened, shrugged. "Oh that," she said. "That's just something I've been meaning to give away."

↫ 4 ↬

Perhaps we need to go back, start the story of wheat again, this time at a different point of origin. Because before wheat can spread across the world, another pivotal moment must occur. This one comes in the late Stone Age, a few thousand years after the fateful mutation in 8000 BCE. On this day, in the southwestern corner of the Caspian Sea belt, two species of grass find themselves growing side by side for the first time. One, a wild plant now called *Aegilops squarrosa*, has long thrived here. The other, a newcomer to the region, is our *Triticum turgidum* subspecies *dicoccum*: that nonshattering domesticated emmer.

The two species have come to rub shoulders thanks to Neolithic humans who've carried their cultivated emmer seeds east, into the range of *A. squarrosa*, and planted them here. On this day, both grasses are in flower and something—a strong wind perhaps, or an animal's fur, or the brush of a human hand—carries pollen from one species to the other. The plants cross, resulting in the birth of a new species: *Triticum aestivum*. Bread wheat.

Owing to the genes handed down by its wild grass mother, *A. squarrosa*, this new wheat can withstand not only its native mild Mediterranean climate but also severe winters and humid summers. It spreads with its human cultivators across the far reaches of Europe and Asia. Over the ensuing millennia, farmers select and save seed from the plants that best suit the particular cultural needs of their communities. The combined forces of natural and cultivator selection produce thousands of unique varieties adapted to a range of environmental conditions, growing practices, and culinary uses. These distinct varieties make up what we now call landraces, or, less commonly, folk varieties. Their vast genetic diversity has enabled wheat to thrive in nearly all of Earth's climates. Today, more land is devoted to wheat production—of which bread wheat comprises 90 percent—than any other crop on Earth.

It's not only wheat's ability to thrive in a range of climates that accounts for its widespread prominence, but also its dietary and culinary attributes. Compared to most other cereals, such as corn and rice, wheat contains superior nutrition due to its high ratio of protein to starch. And this protein—which we now call, with varying degrees of fondness or disdain, gluten—exhibits a unique quality: when ground into flour and mixed with water, gluten can form a distinctly elastic dough, unmatched in its ability to stretch without tearing. This has enabled the creation of a myriad of foods produced from its flour: hearth breads, bagels, croissants, communion wafers, naan, noodles, cookies, cakes, baguettes, dumplings, pies, pizza, pasta, pita, and on and on.

"It is not surprising," write the researchers Daniel Zohary and Maria Hopf, experts on the origins and spread of cultivated plants, "that in numerous cultures food has been equated with bread."

⤾ 5 ⤿

Roti—the name for the simple flatbreads my grandmother cooked and served with nearly every meal—is among the handful of Punjabi words I understood as a child. It's a word I learned not by first translating it to English, but in the way a native speaker would learn: "Do you want a roti?" someone would ask—my mother, an aunt, my grandmother—before folding a still-hot bread slick with butter into my outstretched hand. What I didn't know until recently is that roti can also mean, simply, "food."

A few times every year over the course of my childhood, my mother made roti herself. I'm not sure what prompted her, on those occasional afternoons, to pull on an apron and dig out her steel tuva from the back of a cupboard. Did she miss this food, a bread she'd eaten nearly every day for the first eighteen years of her life? Had something provoked a memory, a flicker of nostalgia? Or was roti just the easiest thing to make, something she could still do without thinking, the motions stored in her muscles?

My mother usually served the flatbreads with a bowl of simple black dal and aloo matar gajar subji. My sister and I ate this food the way we'd watched our grandparents eat, the way my mother did: we tore a piece from the roti, then used the bread to scoop up a bit of vegetables, a dollop of yogurt, a pinch of pickled lemon. My father, however, did not abide this method. Instead, he pronounced roti "road-y," laid the bread flat across his plate, heaped it with vegetables and yogurt, then rolled the whole thing up and ate it like a burrito. He made no attempt to correct his pronunciation or his technique. And though we were not usually a family to let one another get away with much, no one gave my father a hard time for this behavior. For who, in light of everything, could blame him?

Before my parents were married, my father, a hippie from Los Angeles with long blond curls and a mustache, decided to call my grandfather to ask for permission to marry his daughter. My mother told him she didn't think this was such a good idea. Though the couple had been dating for a few years, my grandparents knew nothing of their eldest daughter's relationship. They expected my mother to have an arranged marriage to a suitable Indian groom, not a white Californian who wore bell-bottoms and talked of such nonsense as "true love." My grandparents had already facilitated introductions between my mother and potential husbands—they'd gone so far as to send her to England to meet a prospective match. And though she had no intention to follow through with any of the arrangements, my mother had been amiable, willing to placate her parents by attending the introductions. I'm not sure how or when my mother did plan to break the news to her parents, had my father heeded her warning and given up on calling my grandfather to ask for his blessing. But my father brushed off my mother's caution, assured her that he'd simply explain the situation: "We're in love. Who wouldn't understand that?"

My grandfather did not understand. Instead he replied, "We don't do that," hung up the phone, gathered his car keys and the machete he used in his backyard, and drove north to San Francisco, where my parents lived, pledging to kill my father. When my mother's sister called with a warning, my parents fled both their homes, hiding with friends for a few days, until my mother knew her father had given up his search—lost his resolve or perhaps been talked down—and returned home to LA.

I heard this story countless times growing up. The tale had become a kind of legend, our family's origin story, told often to wide-eyed guests: My father, chuckling at his own naïveté, his Summer of Love brand of idealism—"I was sure once I explained our love for each other, everything else would sort of just cease to matter," he said. "But it turned out, I was wrong"—here my mother rolled her eyes and shook her head as if she chalked up everything to the idiocy of two foolish men and had long ago washed her hands of the whole ordeal.

I laughed along, imagining my father as a young man, full of earnestness, head swimming with John Lennon lyrics and love for my mother, a pacifist eager to stand up to a man he'd never met in defense of his ideals. I imagined the speech he might have delivered to my grandfather, the ensuing silence, then those words, *We don't do that*, the clicking of the phone line going dead. What I never could quite picture was my grandfather's face pressed against the phone at the other end of the line. Not the face I knew, anyway—those two eyes shrouded in wrinkles, squished into grinning crescents, hair tucked meticulously into a cream-colored turban, silver beard rolled under his chin. I couldn't equate the man in the story to the thin body of the grandfather I saw every few years, those hunched shoulders and bony limbs, that soft voice hardly speaking at all.

Nor did I ever give much thought to the rest of the story: Who had my grandfather been before that day, holding a plastic phone against his ear while a stranger's words about love and possibility poured from the line? And what had transpired in the days and years from that phone call to the afternoons I spent watching my grandmother cook, or peering over a page of homework as my grandfather carefully tightened all the handles on my mother's pots?

❧ 6 ❧

One afternoon when I was seven or eight, I stood with the other second-grade students outside of our classroom waiting for the teacher to arrive to unlock the door. Everyone was still buzzing from lunch recess, giggling in clusters or darting about playing games. A boy sidled up to where I stood chatting with my three best friends. "Hey, what are you anyway?" he asked. His tone wasn't unkind, only curious, but I flushed red and looked away. "Are you Black?" he offered when I didn't answer. My public school, like the rural Northern California town where I lived, was predominantly white. I didn't have any Black friends, and the white kid questioning me, it appeared, didn't either. Neither did I have any Indian friends. The only other Indian people I then knew in our town were the family who owned a convenience store not far from my house. The father wore a turban like my grandfather, his sons called my mother Auntie-ji, and he always gave my sister and me free ice cream. Years later, in the days after 9/11, the windows of his store would be smashed in.

"No," I answered the boy, wishing I hadn't spent the last few weeks of summer on vacation at the beach, where my skin had tanned from nut brown to deep mahogany. "I'm not Black."

"Then what are you?"

I glared at the boy but could come up with nothing to say. I looked back at my friends, hoping to return to whatever we'd been talking about and ignore this kid until he gave up and went away. But now all my friends' eyes were on the boy.

"What are you?" he asked again. I stared at my feet, then glanced back at my friends who were now also looking at me, waiting for an answer. I wished our teacher would arrive and unlock the door. A hacky sack landed a few feet away, but no one bent to pick it up.

"I don't know," I blurted out at last, then spun around and walked down the hall to the bathroom.

When I returned a few minutes later, my teacher stood at the open door, and the last few students were filing into the classroom. I joined them, and class began. My friends and the boy seemed to forget all about the exchange, and no one brought it up again. Still, I spent the rest of that day replaying the incident in my mind, trying to figure out what I should have said, as if the boy's question were a riddle I might yet solve. I found no solution. Though I'd responded out of a panic to escape the boy's questioning, I knew the answer I'd given was the best I had: I didn't know.

What I did know was that I wasn't white. That fact was clear enough, or I wouldn't have found myself under this line of questioning in the first place. I also knew, of course, that my grandparents were Indian, but my interactions with them mostly affirmed just how little we had in common. The only conversation I could recall having with either of my parents about race or ethnicity consisted of my father telling me in his gentle way: "There's only one race, the human race." I understood what he was trying to say, and I believed him. But this notion did little to help me make sense of my own identity. What I knew, I'd cobbled together instead from a set of found facts: (1) I spoke only English, except for a handful of Punjabi phrases. (2) My skin was brown. My hair and my eyes, too, were brown. (3) My family didn't practice religion; I'd never been to church. (4) My mother was born in India, my father in Los Angeles, and I in Northern California. The only home I knew was here, the granite-studded slopes of the Sierra foothills.

The house where I grew up sat on five acres, surrounded by other five-acre parcels with single-family homes on all sides except one. To the west, thousands of acres of rolling hills studded with live oak and gray pine tumbled toward the central valley forty miles away. This land was part of a cattle ranch, though we rarely saw cows and only occasionally caught sight of a rancher on a four-wheeler. To me, it was just open space.

Only three strings of rusty barbed wire separated the ranch from my family's property, and I spent my childhood roaming these hills with my sister and our friends, easily climbing through the fence by pressing a toe down on the lowest wire and gripping the middle wire between barbs to pull it up. In summer, the sun-bleached slopes prickled with foxtails and burrs. Rattlesnakes roped through the grass, and the midday heat slackened our limbs. We waited for the cool of evening before venturing out to listen to frog song and owl calls and the low moans of cows. In fall, the hills turned gray and we collected acorns and smashed them into mush on granite boulders. The pines dropped pineapple-size cones and bundles of needles that we fashioned into brooms for sweeping the floors of our stick-and-rock forts. In winter, the dry creek beds filled with rain-water and we searched for gold and turtles in granite pools, never finding either. At the start of spring, the oaks unfolded new leaves, tea-green and velvet-soft against our cheeks, and we assembled wildflower bouquets of buttercups and lupine, fairy lantern and shooting stars. In the distance, the blue spine of the Sierras emerged from beneath the winter snowpack.

Open ranchland like this characterized the landscape of the foothills during my childhood years. Visitors didn't always appreciate the beauty of this terrain. They often found the hills too hot, too dry, too brown, and when I return to them now from the deep-green forests of Oregon, I too can see it that way if I try. But for me, these ranches—their billowing slopes and granite outcroppings, their oaks and gray pines and lupine—defined the topography of home, and I loved them fiercely, a love sharpened by the fact that they were swiftly shrinking.

In the years of my childhood, as the Bay Area blew up and Sacramento sprawled farther east, our county—scenic and commutable—began to grow rapidly along with those places. Many of the local farming and ranching families found themselves "land-rich but cash-poor," and they sold their acreage to developers who swiftly erected shopping centers and housing developments. In 1995, the year I turned eight, a developer acquired 3,500 acres of ranchland along the western edge of my home county and commenced construction on what was then one of the largest master-planned luxury communities in California. The curves of hill-tops were graded flat, roads built, and a community of 5,000-square-foot houses with swimming pools and five-car garages was erected where herds of cows had once gathered under oaks. At the time, the average value of ranchland in California was $2,225 per acre. A single house on half an acre of that land is now worth upwards of $2 million.

This trend was not unique to my hometown. During the years I was growing up, California lost approximately one square mile of farm-land to urbanization and real estate development every four days. Neither was this kind of ruthless transformation unique to the time of my childhood—since the inception of the state, no landscape in California has gone unchanged for long. As a kid, of course, I didn't consider the ways my beloved foothills had been so thoroughly altered before they were mine. Instead, I watched the changes subsume my surroundings with a child's righteous outrage. Each time a new chunk of ranchland was graded and paved, oaks bulldozed, barns flattened, and cattle sent who knows where, I tightened my allegiance to the disappearing land-scapes and, in turn, to a pastoral ideal I then imagined went hand in hand with these spaces.

❧ 7 ❧

Despite this hearty childhood romance with an imagined agrarian life, I never considered, back then, actually becoming a farmer. I wanted to be a film director or a veterinarian or maybe a scientist—an archaeologist or a canopy biologist. I wanted to go to Antarctica and study penguins. At school and at home, I'd always been told one thing in regard to what I should do when I grew up: whatever I wanted. The same sentiment was reiterated grade after grade: work hard and follow your dreams. *Be anyone, do anything, live anywhere.* The possibilities, I was assured, were limitless. This seemed true, in part. By the time I reached middle school in the late 1990s I could send a message to someone on the other side of the world and have it answered immediately via the World Wide Web. This same technology allowed me to instantly retrieve nearly any piece of information I desired.

But amid this bounty of possibility lurked a mirrored sensation of scarcity, of depletion. In elementary school book reports I dutifully recounted stories about lost rainforests and vanishing panda bear habitat. Via shoebox dioramas and unwieldy mobiles, I depicted the threats facing green sea turtles and the near extinction of California condors. Even before I could read, I studied the worrying illustrations in children's books. In *The Little House*, I watched a personified country cottage and the pastoral hills surrounding it become enveloped by the monstrous smog and roaring highway of a growing city. I glared at the Onceler as he cut the last truffle tree in the pages of *The Lorax*, and willed the man in *The Great Kapok Tree* to leave his ax and let the rainforest grow. Like most of my generation, I'd never known a world not filled with news of global warming and finite resources: rising seas and disappearing coral reefs, oils spills and spare-the-air days. Nor had I ever been unencumbered by the notion—reiterated on bumper stickers and advertisements, on shopping bags and brands with names like "If You Care"—that the fate of the natural world rested squarely on the shoulders of each consumer choice my family and I made. Paper or plastic? Bleached toilet paper or unbleached? Free-range eggs or local eggs, or organic eggs, or animal-welfare certified eggs, or no eggs?

Then came the hanging chads of George W. Bush's election. I was in my last year of middle school then, sitting among thirty other thirteen-year-olds straining to follow our teacher's valiant attempt to explain the electoral college. We watched as she filled the whiteboard with numbers and amoeba-like district shapes and words like *gerrymandering*. When the bell rang for lunch, we rubbed our heads and filed out of the classroom, hoping we wouldn't be tested on the subject and feeling quite a bit less sure about the concept of "democracy" than we'd been before.

Next, of course, came September 11th. On that morning, I sat atop my usual lab stool in freshman life sciences class, but we didn't bother to set up our microscopes or open our textbooks. We took a break from studying toxin-related birth defects in frogs—examining photos of amphibians with their hind legs fused together, others with no legs at all—and instead spent the morning watching the twin towers fall over and over again on the classroom television, the word *terrorists* marching across the bottom of the screen.

By the time I graduated high school in 2005, America had for the last four years been entangled in a war no one seemed able to explain. Magazines ran articles listing the top ten places to visit in the next few decades before they disappeared beneath rising seas. A plastic gyre twice the size of Texas floated in the Pacific Ocean, and traces of agricultural pesticides were being found in the bodies of all newborn babies. Scientists told us that 161 species of birds had disappeared over the course of the last 500 years and predicted my generation would see the extinction of 20 percent of all living species before we turned forty. Despite all this, at my graduation ceremony the commencement message remained the same: *Be anyone, live anywhere, do anything.*

These opposite sensations—boundless possibility and overwhelming collapse—afflicted me with a particular kind of confusion, a feeling like trying to force two magnets of the same charge to sit on top of one another rather than repel. I stood on the brink of adulthood, filled with youthful ambition, but I could find no traction. The traditional pursuit of a middle-class American life—a good job, a nice house—now seemed all wrong: resource-guzzling and exploitive, dependent on employment by morally bankrupted corporations, greedy, lonely, monotonous. But if not that then what, exactly, was I to aspire to? I wanted something that embodied a refusal of all this: a kind of work that rejected the hollowness of a corporate job, that could help repair our environment and support social justice. But I'd no idea where to find such a path. Nothing felt trustworthy, everything slippery, threatening to buckle. Everywhere I looked, things seemed undependable—the economy, the weather, the relative peacetime, politicians and CEOs, the very land beneath my feet.

❧ 8 ❧

For most of my life, my grandparents lived in a tract house in LA's San Fernando Valley. Theirs had a swept cement driveway, prickly stucco siding, and a low-pitched roof, all exactly like the next-door neighbors'. But if you were to accidentally step into the wrong house, you'd realize it the moment you took a breath. The cupboards in my grandparents' house smelled as though they'd been battered in cumin and fried. No amount of scrubbing could rid the wood of the scent of my grandmother's cooking,

One morning, when I was thirteen or fourteen, I woke early in the small guest bedroom of this house. My mother and sister were both still asleep, one on a twin bed, the other on the mat on the floor beside me. I stepped out of the room and crept down the hall to the bathroom. The house's blinds were all drawn tight and the hum of LA traffic murmured through the walls, as it did night and day without pause. I'd no idea what time it was, but when I emerged from the bathroom again into the tiled hall, I saw a pool of light spilling from the kitchen. My mother was usually the first up in the morning and I headed toward the light, assuming I'd find her in the kitchen starting to brew her usual green tea. Instead, it was my grandmother who stood in front of the stove in a rose-colored kameez, a matching chunni hung over her head with one tail spilling down her back to the floor. I didn't need to ask to know what she was doing. First thing every morning, using dishes reserved solely for this purpose, she made two paratha and a pot of cha, then carried them into her temple room where she performed a series of rituals and read from the sacred Sikh text, the Guru Granth Sahib. After this daily ceremony, the food would be blessed and she and my grandfather would eat it together.

I stood silently at the edge of the kitchen, considered turning and walking back to the guest bedroom. Adolescence had made me even shyer around my grandmother—acutely aware of the mismatch of our languages, ashamed when I couldn't understand her words, sometimes unable to decipher them even when she spoke in English because her accent was so thick. Before I could turn around my grandmother looked up to see me there at the end of the hall. "Ah, hello Jackie!" she said, waving me over. She pulled me to her side, patting my bare shoulder, and I wondered if my spaghetti strapped nightshirt was the wrong thing to be wearing. "Are you hungry?" I shook my head. "No? I make paratha now, for Babaji. Then, I make for you. OK?"

Without waiting for an answer, my grandmother released me and pinched a hunk of dough from a mixing bowl. She spun the dough in her fingers, flattening it into a thick disk, then began rolling it smooth with a slim wooden beilna. She went about her work silently and I stood across the counter, mesmerized by her nimble fingers and strong hands, her seamless and utter competence.

When the first two paratha were cooked, my grandmother covered the remaining dough with a plate and turned off the stove. She pulled her scarf up over her head and arranged the cooked paratha onto a plate, then poured steaming tea into a porcelain cup. I watched her carry the offering across her living room toward the sliding glass door that led to the temple room, fashioned from the old back porch. When she slid open the door, lamp light poured from the room. I could see garlands hanging across the ceiling, shiny and brightly colored like something hung for a birthday celebration, paintings of gurus in gold frames on the walls. My grandmother slid the door shut behind her and I listened from the kitchen, hoping to catch a bit of her murmured prayers. I'd been inside the temple room a handful of times, instructed by my mother on how to cover my head, how to place the dollar bill she'd given me atop the altar. I'd studied the bed-like platform, covered in intricately crocheted draperies, and glanced at the holy book that rested upon it. The Guru Granth Sahib, larger than a telephone book, held the sacred Sikh scriptures in its many pages—more than 2,000, I'd been told—and was regarded with great reverence as a living guru. I'd longed to climb up onto the platform, to sit in the place where my grandparents sat when they read from this book, to fan the corners of all those pages and feel their wind on my cheek. But I never lingered long in the room.

That morning, I heard nothing—not the lilt of my grandmother's voice or the ruffle of a page turning—until, many minutes later, the swoosh of the door sliding open and the soft slap of chappla slippers across the tile told me the ritual was over. My grandmother returned to the kitchen, brushed the chunni off her head and turned on the stove to resume making paratha. This time, while the tuva heated, she dug a burly daikon root from the fridge and shredded it with a cheese grater. She sprinkled garam masala, a minced serrano pepper, and a few good pinches of finely chopped ginger over the shredded root. After rolling out a circle of dough, she loaded the surface with this mixture and dashed it with salt. Careful not to tear the dough, she folded it around the filling, then pressed the package into a flat square between her palms before tossing it on the hot tuva. Sometimes my grandmother folded cauliflower or mashed potatoes into the flatbreads, sometimes thinly sliced onions or just plain butter. But muli paratha—the flatbreads filled with spiced daikon—were my favorite, and I knew she remembered this. I watched the first paratha blister and bronze against the heat. When it was finished my grandmother flipped it onto a plate and placed it in front of me. I pulled pieces off the hot bread—butter-shined and flaky like a croissant—and dipped each bite in fresh yogurt and pickled lemon. My grandmother said little but smiled broadly watching me eat. Before I finished the first paratha she brought another, and then another, filling my body with her food as if she might impart something of herself into me this way. I ate until I felt like I needed to lie down.

↤ 9 ↦

W hen my grandmother was not cooking or sitting cross-legged in her temple room with her chunni draped over her head, I remember her often on the sofa. At her own house she sat with her legs pulled up onto the cushions, one hand clasped around an ankle, watching Indian soap operas. At my parents' house, however, the TV only received the free channels—news shows and sitcoms about American life like *Full House* and *Friends*. So on visits to our house, my grandmother simply sat in front of the closed wooden cabinet that held the TV. Sometimes my mother joined her and the two women talked. Sometimes my grandmother closed her eyes and let her head lean against the upholstery. Other times she just rested her gaze on the carpet and sat quietly.

If my sister or I entered the room while my grandmother sat awake on the couch, she'd perk up, nudge her glasses up her nose, and call us over. When I was still small enough to fit in her lap, she pressed the silks of her salwar kameez smooth across her thighs and helped me climb onto her legs. I lay my face against her shoulder where the layers of her scarf folded into one another like a nest, the silk slippery and cool against my skin and the smell of cooking oil and masala so thick it would linger in my own hair for days. My grandmother rubbed her hand in slow circles across my back and asked me to learn Punjabi. "Please," she said, "so we can talk, haanah?" With my eyes closed and my face hidden in silks, I promised I would. I wished I could absorb my grandmother's language through my skin in the way I felt I could absorb the scent of her. But when she'd leave a few days later, I always forgot my promise.

The first time I remember my grandmother asking me to learn to speak Punjabi I was just five or six. As I grew older she continued to hold me in her lap until only my head could fit on her legs, the rest of my body curled across the couch, and she continued to ask me to learn her language. And though I always said I would, I never did.

Eventually, she stopped asking. I don't know if she gave up or lost interest, but by the time I neared the end of high school, she no longer bothered to mention it; as I watched her roll out roti dough or slice lemons for achar I found myself wondering what she'd have told me if I'd learned to speak Punjabi all those years ago. What closeness would we have shared without the mismatch of our languages always between us like a curtain, what knowledge of my origins might have passed down to me, an inheritance that instead vanished into the fissure between generations? I began to feel the absence of what I might have gained like a phantom limb—an ache that struck me at unpredictable moments, a regret I couldn't shake. And this particular personal loss rose to the top of a catalog of other losses that, though I hadn't meant to be keeping a tally, shadowed my consciousness: The ranchlands once surrounding my hometown. The old-growth forests and coral reefs. The polar ice caps and coastal wetlands. All those birds.

⇜ 10 ⇝

Afte high school, I left the foothills for the coast to attend the University of California, Santa Cruz. In this breezy beach town on the northern tip of Monterey Bay, I first encountered what I'd later learn to call the alternative food movement. In Santa Cruz, a lively weekly farmers market took over much of downtown every Wednesday. Booths sprawled across several city blocks and shoppers swarmed, loading their baskets with local tomatoes and organic strawberries, sun-warmed peaches and heaps of leafy green vegetables I'd never heard of, glowing jars of raw honey and bags of mushrooms that looked to me more like something found in the sea than grown on damp logs. Every public elementary school in the city had a funded school garden program. Restaurant menus listed the names of the farms that supplied their ingredients. Books by Alice Waters and Michael Pollan were displayed prominently in bookstore windows. Around the corner from my freshman dorm room, a student-run food co-op reeking of mildew and dried sage offered carob bars and yerba mate tea, locally grown dried beans and bottles of apple cider vinegar with the stringy "mother" floating inside.

At the center of campus, a thirty-acre organic vegetable farm called the Center for Agroecology and Sustainable Food Systems spread across the curve of a hill. The farm was used for research and to host an organic farmer training program, and its produce was incorporated in offerings at the university dining halls. A bike path ran adjacent to the farm and I often stopped there on my way to class, to eat a snack or finish an assignment at a picnic table between fields. From the farm I could look west and, on a clear day, see the great expanse of the Pacific Ocean shimmering in the distance. Or I could turn east and watch turkey vultures and red-tailed hawks circle above the tops of the redwoods that forested the hills behind campus. Jasmine vines twisted up graying barns, and rows of brassicas I could not then identify traced the contours of the land.

Meanwhile, my undergraduate classes in sociology and environmental studies affirmed that the industrial food system was at the root of many of the environmental catastrophes and social injustices of our time. It was poisoning ecosystems and warming the planet, exploiting workers and creating herbicide-resistant super-weeds, inducing "obesity epidemics" while keeping 10 percent of the world's population hungry. The more details I learned, the more bewildered I felt, paralyzed in the face of all this and at the same time rattled with a sense of urgency, the need to *do* something—but what could be done?

One day, riding my bike to class, I stopped at a picnic table at the university farm and pulled out a book to finish some reading. No one else was in sight. I gazed out over the shining Pacific, then scanned the tidy fields surrounding me. The purple flowers of a pollinator row—though I wouldn't have known to call it that back then—thrummed with bees, and lines of beefy broccoli plants abutted rows of red-stemmed chard. Just then, a group of student apprentices emerged from behind a barn. Some began harvesting beets, pulling up the fat globes and stacking them into bulb crates. Their movements were quick, efficient, but I could hear laughter amid the rhythmic slap of greens and the rattle of crates. I watched the bins fill, one after the other, while other farmers began scuffling hoes along rows of carrots, skillfully ridding the field of weeds. Here, I thought, were people *doing* something, taking action.

I started spending more time in the orbit of the alternative food movement. I interned with a garden-based education nonprofit, joined work parties where I learned to build compost piles through a student-led community agroecology program, sowed a bed of beets in the organic garden co-op behind my dorm building. The people I met talked about the evils of Monsanto and vast honeybee die-offs; they read dog-eared copies of *The One Straw-Revolution* by Masanobu Fukuoka and Wendell Berry poetry. None of us wanted to take any part in the industrial food system, and it was easy to believe, back then, that we didn't have to.

Instead, we volunteered at local farms in exchange for boxes of vegetables, which we diced up into murky soups. We bought five-dollar pints of organic strawberries at the farmers market, paying with school loans or money our parents sent us for groceries. We went on night runs to the local bakery and loaded our bike baskets with bags of day-old bread pilfered from the dumpster outside. We tore out the weedy lawns of our rented houses and planted kale and Swiss chard. We swapped foods we'd produced ourselves: homemade kombucha and sourdough bread, closet-grown oyster mushrooms and, once, jerky someone cured from a road-killed deer. On these small farms and organic gardens, in our back-yards and moldy kitchens, we believed we might cast aside the dictates of the industrial food system and chart out a better path.

⟿ 11 ⟾

During these years in Santa Cruz, I learned the popular origin story of the modern organic farming movement. Though I can't pinpoint a particular instance when I first heard the tale, by the time I left that town I'd encountered it enough times to take it for fact. The story begins with a man named Sir Albert Howard.

In the wake of the industrial revolution, Howard, a British botanist by training, grew disillusioned with contemporary Western agriculture and its increasing emphasis on chemical-intensive methods. So he left his contemporaries in their British research institutions and journeyed instead into the agrarian villages of Asia to become a student of the local cultivators. There, Howard got his hands dirty working alongside traditional farmers, studied their ancient agricultural methods, and acquired a newfound reverence for "Nature's farming." He then went on to refine and codify the methods he'd learned into a system of farming based around a holistic view of plant health and "The Law of Return"—the idea that, in nature, all plant and animal matter returns to the soil to replenish fertility via decomposition. At the center of his system was the practice of using the plant waste products of agriculture to manufacture compost, which was then added back into the fields. Howard gave talks and wrote books and magazine articles describing and promoting his philosophy. His ideas spread around the world and he was soon deemed the "father" of organic farming.

It's a catchy story, and an internet search will furnish you with plenty of retellings. Its themes—the renegade hero, the return to ancient wisdom, the nobility and wholeness of the traditional farmer, the hands-in-the-dirt ethic—were echoed in much of the popular organic farming literature I was reading during my college years, and they were threaded through the mission statements and promotional materials of alternative food and organic farming organizations.

But outside of the basic outline of this story, I didn't know much of anything about Sir Albert Howard. I'd only encountered references to his work and quippy one-line quotes in the pages of other classic organic farming texts—Wendell Berry's essays, Michael Pollan's writings, Eliot Coleman's manuals. I recall once picking up a copy of one of Howard's most well-known books, *An Agricultural Testament*, from someone's college coffee table and flipping through the pages.

In those days I didn't linger long on the details of this origin myth, nor did I stop to consider the historic context. It didn't cross my mind then to wonder what might have been left out of the story. After all, it was just the kind of tale I was then eager to hear.

❧ 12 ❧

I graduated college in June of 2008 and walked into the financial collapse that would trigger the Great Recession. Six million American households lost their homes while our government hastened to bail out banks. Meanwhile, flames ravaged the West, marking the worst wildfire seasons on record, a phrase that would be repeated nearly every year thereafter.

With a liberal arts degree in something called Community Studies and no plan, I spent the summer working fire camps, getting paid to spray out the mobile shower units the firefighters used and wondering what to do once the gig was up. The company I worked for had made millions providing showers for rescue workers in the aftermath of Hurricane Katrina, and I spent those blistering summer days squinting in the murky orange glow of the smoke-obscured sun, wondering about the future: Is this what it looked like? An economy feeding on disaster, a few getting rich on the demise of others, everything burning and flooding? I had no plan beyond the next few weeks. How could anyone make plans in a world so precarious?

At the end of summer, I took the money I'd made at fire camp and bought a plane ticket to Edinburgh. From there, a friend and I rode our bikes across western Europe, stopping occasionally at internet cafés to make halfhearted efforts at coming up with something to do once winter arrived—googling English teaching positions abroad, browsing WWOOFing (World Wide Opportunities on Organic Farms) options in warm places. I sent in applications. Eventually, my choices narrowed to two internship positions I'd been offered. One was a part-farming, part-teaching job with a nonprofit educational organic farm on the coast of Marin County. The other was an editorial role with a Peace Corps–like organization in Ahmedabad, India. I oscillated between the pull of each, unable to make up my mind. They seemed opposite in many ways: One was in a familiar place, offering a serene rural setting and outdoor, physical work. The other was in a foreign city unlike any I'd ever experienced and involved travel and many hours in front of a computer. At the time, I saw only the contrast of the two opportunities. But looking back, I can see that the same impulse drew me to both: a yearning for a sense of roots. Via one path, I might cultivate this elusive quality. Through the other, I might unearth it.

Eventually, it was an accident that made the decision for me. While riding my bike down a quiet street back home in California, I collided with another bicyclist going the wrong way and broke a bone in my hand. The bone healed quickly, but scar tissue prevented me from moving my index finger. To regain mobility, I needed surgery. If I left for India and postponed the operation until I returned, the doctors said, my hand could end up permanently disabled. So I accepted the position at the farm in Marin, and settled in.

Slide Ranch was a dreamy manifestation of idealized Northern California culture. I, along with six other "teachers-in-residence," lived in tiny individual cabins made of reclaimed wood perched together on a bluff over the Pacific Ocean. There were composting toilets, a shared bathhouse, and a giant horse trough lined with a wooden grate that, when filled with water and set over a firepit, became a hot tub. A handful of slightly larger homes housed other staff members, and everyone shared one large communal kitchen stocked with bins of granola and dried beans, gallon jars of local honey and cases of organic peanut butter. What produce we didn't grow on site was purchased from the weekly farmers market, and we rotated cheese-making duties to ensure a constant supply of fresh goat cheese in the fridge. Everyone ate meals together around one long dining table.

The farm consisted of organic gardens, dairy goats, chickens, ducks, sheep, a composting system, and miles of coastal wildlands and tide pools. I spent my days milking nanny goats and bottle-feeding their kids, weeding between rows of kale and Swiss chard, gathering and washing eggs, learning to slaughter chickens and ruminants, making compost heaps, and leading agricultural education programs for school-age children, families, and adults. Participants helped milk goats, harvest from the gardens, and collect eggs. In doing so, they ostensibly learned about where food comes from.

✿

At Slide Ranch, I met Ryan. He lived in a ramshackle cabin set apart from the teachers' housing and spent his days maintaining the ranch's many buildings. He'd grown up in Texas, in a landscape not entirely different from the one where I'd spent my childhood, and we talked longingly of warm summer evenings, something that did not exist on the coast of Marin, where we wore down jackets against the biting wind and daily fog. I took him to the Sierras, leading him along wilderness trails I knew by heart to the high alpine lakes I loved. I showed him the American River in the foothills where I'd grown up, and we laid in the scorching summer sun until our bodies could take no more heat and we plunged into the frigid water. He introduced me to woodworking, showed me how to run an old fir two-by-four through a planer to reveal the wood's honey-colored flesh, how to recognize black walnut by its smell, how to laminate scraps of curly maple and oak together to make a cutting board, how to rub oil into the surface until the grain shone. Together we wandered the fancy neighborhoods of Mill Valley with Felco pruners in our pockets, clipping cuttings from the flowering plants that overflowed residents' yards—pineapple sage, trumpet vine, passionflower, butterfly bush. We brought the severed stems back to the ranch and poked them into pots filled with soil. Some of the cuttings shriveled, but others began to grow. New leaves emerged from each node and, when I turned the plants upside down and shook them loose from their pots, I could see webs of new roots winding through the soil. This never failed to amaze me, the emergence of a root system where there had been none, the transformation of what was once just a severed stem into a whole new plant.

Ryan had found his way to agriculture more or less by accident. After spending his undergraduate years at art school in Rhode Island, he'd found a job as a field hand on an organic vegetable farm nearby. He liked the work for many of the same reasons I did—the inherent relationship with the natural world, time spent outside, physical challenge, community—and stuck with it for two years. Then he left the region to head west to California, where he landed at the farm in Marin. When my year-long residency was up, we left the farm together, our cars packed full of plants.

❧ 13 ❧

Ryan and I spent a handful of years moving around the western United States. We stopped for stints in Bozeman, Nevada City, Austin, and Santa Cruz. In each place we stayed long enough to plant a garden from our collection of rooted cuttings, taking a round of fresh cuttings when it was time to move on. You could trace our trajectory by mapping out the trail of plants left behind, clones of one another blooming across the West.

I took a variety of jobs along the way, sorting amaryllis bulbs at a flower farm, working in school gardens or as a substitute teacher, pouring espresso. Ryan found farm crew positions and short-term carpentry jobs. In Santa Cruz I managed an elementary school garden program and Ryan worked as the assistant manager for the Center for Agroecology and Sustainable Food Systems, the university farm where, several years prior, I'd first considered becoming a farmer.

We didn't stay in Santa Cruz long, however, due to the severe gap between the cost of living near the money-drenched Silicon Valley and the salaries of two people working in agriculture education. In fact, this gap persisted in most of the places we explored, and eventually we landed in a twelve-by-sixteen-foot cabin on the edge of the Eel River outside the tiny town of Covelo, a remote community deep in the Mendocino Mountains. A friend had offered us the chance to live here rent-free in exchange for turning what had been a small hay barn into a livable cabin, and the surrounding field into a productive vegetable garden. We moved in the spring and spent our days working on the cabin, shoveling horse manure into garden beds, swimming in the river, and taking walks under the twisting limbs of madrone and oak. I taught garden-based science and nutrition at the local public school. Ryan built cabinets for the town's one coffee shop, a desk for a neighbor, a porch for another. Our stay in Covelo was in many ways idyllic, a reprieve from trying to figure out where to live, what to do for work, how to pay rent, but it was only temporary, and when winter arrived we began making plans for the fast-approaching spring.

One morning that winter, Ryan and I sat beside each other in plastic schoolroom chairs at the town library, where we had access to the internet. We were browsing the web in search of a future. I checked job-posting sites, internship programs, graduate schools. I didn't know what I was looking for. It seemed like everyone I knew at the time either worked for a tech company in the Bay Area, or cobbled together an assortment of part-time jobs ("gigs," as this kind of thing would later be called): tutoring in the morning and freelance copyediting in the evening, building decks and painting houses in the spring and summer, selling firewood in the winter, pouring espresso three days a week and teaching at a community center the other two, trimming pot in the fall and selling pottery on Etsy year round.

Via websites with names like "Sustainable Food Jobs" or "Opportunities in Ecological Farming," I looked for work on farms or in agriculture education programs. Most positions turned out to be "internships" or "apprenticeships"—a.k.a., unpaid. Often, farms offered some kind of seasonal housing (think canvas tent, room in a shared house, trailer) and free produce in exchange for labor. The few paid positions I found offered minimum wage, no benefits, and seasonal employment, which meant a worker either had to live off savings or find another job to support herself during the winter months.

At the time, I found the proliferation of organic farming internships annoying, as it often took a bit of reading and research to determine that a "job" posting was actually a listing for an unpaid position. But I did not, at the time, pause to consider what the ubiquity of such labor arrangements suggested about the state of organic farming in America. Ryan and I were young—we had few bills and, thanks to the help of our parents, no student debt. We were not yet thinking about long-term financial stability or accumulating savings or providing for children, and we weren't considering unexpected expenses that might arise, a health emergency or dental care. We were thinking of crisp spring mornings and ripe, fresh-off-the-vine watermelons, of days spent outdoors and deep sleep earned from long hours of physical challenge. We could afford to squeak by financially in order to do work that didn't feel like meaningless drudgery, that aligned with our ideals. And, by means of a flawed sort of logic, the very fact that the work was underpaid seemed to validate its virtuousness, to provide proof of its opposition to capitalist ethics.

Rain pattered the library roof. Ryan and I didn't talk much, but I could hear him clicking and clicking, so I knew he hadn't found anything intriguing enough to spend much time on. I scanned the list of available farmland posted on California FarmLink, a website designed to match farmers seeking land with landowners seeking farmers. A listing near my hometown caught my eye—ten acres for lease. I clicked the link open and read the property description. I recognized the land immediately: it was part of the old Veerkamp ranch.

A short drive from my childhood home, the Veerkamp ranch was one of the few large chunks of open space that had remained intact despite the widespread residential and commercial development. The 272 acres of oak woodland and grassy pasture had been owned by the Veerkamp family since 1871. Stretching across the Gold Hill region, the ranch occupied a sunny banana belt of fertile soil that remained warmer than much of the surrounding landscape during the cold winters and, I would later learn, had once been the agricultural heart of the county. At one time or another the land had grown vegetables, pears, tea, silk, cattle, walnuts, and grapes. Before the Veerkamps the ranch had for a brief two years been the site of the Wakamatsu Tea and Silk Colony, the first Japanese settlement in North America. And before that, the land was home to the Nisenan people. The last agrarian enterprise on the ranch—a small-scale dairy—had shut down in 1987, the year I was born. After that the place grew increasingly vacant; only a few cattle grazed the hills on and off over the years.

A few months before that morning in the library, I'd heard from my parents that the Veerkamp ranch had been sold. A developer must have snatched it up fast, I'd assumed, planning to subdivide the property into tidy five-acre parcels, build a residential community of mini-mansions, and name it after the landscape it would displace—something like Rolling Hills Estates or Oak Meadow Village.

The property flanked the main road that led from town to a popular river spot. In high school I'd driven past the place often on summer evenings in a car full of friends headed to the river to swim, or to dance at a café near the water that hired salsa bands on weekends. Once, we pulled

over into the driveway leading to the abandoned Veerkamp place. Someone had a can of malt liquor and a badly rolled joint and we tumbled
out of the car and walked toward the old barn, giggling when someone
pushed on the door and the hinge released an eerie creak. I wandered
through the barn and out a back door. Up the hill sat an old dairy building and, past that, a small vacant house tucked beneath the canopy of a
mulberry tree. The sun hung low on the horizon, shellacking everything
in amber light: the rusted metal roof of the dairy, the bronzed summer
grass, the small farmhouse. I wondered who had once lived there, why
they'd ever left.

I hadn't been surprised when I heard the Veerkamp property had
sold. Every time I returned home to visit, one more chunk of open space
was gone. Still, the thought of that house and those barns torn down—
the land subdivided, driveways asphalted, lots landscaped with oleander
and petunia—turned my stomach.

But that day in the Covelo library, I learned that the new owner was
not a developer. Instead, a local land trust had purchased the ranch and
placed it under an agricultural conservation easement to preserve the
open space. The trust was now requesting proposals from farmers interested in leasing ten acres of the property to restore to a working farm.
I'd heard of such arrangements before, intended to preserve open space
while also keeping farmland accessible to farmers. But mostly these
things seemed to occur around the Bay Area, or in other progressive
and moneyed communities—I'd never thought this would happen in
my home region of El Dorado County, a middle-income county with
a largely conservative, libertarian-leaning population. I nudged Ryan's
elbow. "Check this out," I said, clicking through the photos of the property. A few weeks later, under the guise of visiting my parents, Ryan and
I drove the five hours from Covelo out to the Veerkamp ranch to take a
walk around.

↩ 14 ↪

An aluminum gate bearing a *No Trespassing* sign blocked the entrance to the ranch. We parked in the gravel turnout in front of the gate, and climbed out of the car. Sinewy clouds stretched across the winter sky. A gust of wind shook two leafless sycamore trees, and the branches groaned and rattled. I spread open the barbed wire fence so Ryan could climb through. The motion, so familiar from my own childhood, set loose a swell of nostalgia. From the other side, Ryan then held the wire open for me.

The place looked mostly as I remembered it: rolling green pasture grayed in places by matted remnants of dried summer grass. Oaks stretching muscled limbs over the hillsides. An old livestock-loading chute collapsed into itself. Sheets of rusted tin peeled off the old barn's roof. I wondered if high school kids still snuck in there to drink gas station liquor beneath the cobwebbed rafters. Only the cows were missing.

Ryan and I followed a trace of a dirt road past the vacant dairy building, two derelict houses, and an old walnut orchard carpeted in cracked shells. We walked under the naked limbs of oak and buckeye until we reached a large pond formed by a stone dam that blocked the flow of a seasonal creek. In the years before the county water lines were built to reach this ranch, the pond would have provided a valuable source of irrigation during the region's long, dry summers. Now, it floated a flock of geese. Along the banks of the creek leading into the pond, piles of granite rubble lay in heaps, vestiges of the 1850s gold rush still strewn plainly across the landscape.

I imagined how this place might have appeared to those miners and pioneers, having just traversed the brutal Sierras to descend at last into these foothills and their promise of fertile soil, of reinvention, of gold. The sight might have provoked a sensation for these early California dreamers not unlike the one I felt now, gazing out over that same landscape and allowing a version of that same dream to take hold in my own

imagination: a dream of starting fresh in a place brimming with potential; of working hard and reaping bounty; of jettisoning the past to create
a life of one's own invention.

Ryan and I continued around the perimeter of the ranch before returning to the buildings near the road. The only signs of new ownership
we found were two freshly painted kiosks detailing the history of the
property and some recent repairs to the main house, which appeared to
have been made into some kind of museum. I cupped my hands around
my face and peered through the windows. Inside, informational posters
hung from walls and relics of different eras sat displayed on tables and
shelves.

The Veerkamp ranch stretched across both sides of the road. On
the opposite side from all of the houses lay the ten acres available for
lease—a stretch of open land cradled in a rim of hills, treeless except for
one giant oak marking the southwest corner.

Ryan and I crossed the road and stepped out onto the land. In the
center of the field, I knelt and pulled up a clump of grass, dug my fingers
into the ground. The soil here was dark and sandy, unlike the red clay
we'd found across the street. The land looked like it had once been part of
an alluvial flood plain, rich in sediments washed from the surrounding
hills and deposited here over centuries by the adjacent creek. A corrugated metal barn sat along the roadside. Its sliding door was locked shut,
but on the back side a window had been cut into the wall. Ryan gave
me a leg up so I could look inside. The barn was mostly empty: a sloped
cement floor, bits of straw caught on the framing, the steel tines of an old
cultivator bound in cobwebs.

I turned back to look at the land and envisioned long rows of tomatoes and melons. A half-acre of flowers. Blueberries, maybe. I imagined
spreading dark compost over the field, sowing cover crop in the fall.
I imagined early mornings harvesting snap peas and heads of lettuce
in the quiet of dawn. A greenhouse filled with seedlings. Tidy rows of
carrots and cut salad mix. Pollinator rows thick with beneficial insects,
the soil growing darker and richer each season, the field transforming
into an oasis of biodiversity and productivity. Though I certainly wasn't
thinking of Sir Albert Howard that day, the ideas he'd promoted—farming in nature's image, balancing cycles of growth and decay to build soil

fertility, the wholeness found in a life of traditional agriculture—were no doubt kindling my vision.

On the drive back to Covelo, Ryan and I didn't talk much. I'd made up my mind, and I could tell that he had, too. The next week we put together a proposal and applied to lease the land.

When we sent in our proposal, in the early months of 2012, the average age of farm operators in the United States—those in charge of day-to-day management of farms—had crept up to nearly sixty. For decades, the children of farmers had been leaving rural regions to pursue better opportunities outside of agriculture. In recent years, however, a countertrend had begun to gain momentum: Young, middle-class people from nonagrarian backgrounds—like Ryan and me—were abandoning white-collar career paths and urban lifestyles to take up small farming. Organic farms run by thirtysomethings with advanced degrees in unrelated fields were popping up in cities and towns around the country.

After months of meetings and interviews, the land conservancy accepted our proposal. By then, my imagination was swimming with dreams of how Ryan and I could transform the land. Here was my chance to *do* something, to enact my agency in the face of such bewildering catastrophes as climate change and gaping inequality. On the farm, I imagined, I could read about the devastation wrought by industrial food systems—swaths of dead zones blooming across the oceans, miles of mono-crop fields, exploitation of farm workers, pesticide poisonings, honeybee die-offs, soil loss—and say *not here*, not on these ten acres. The farm, I believed, would be my bulwark against that welling sensation of personal powerlessness, of bewilderment in the face of so much wreckage.

And in the beginning, it was.

❧ 15 ❧

Ryan and I moved to our newly leased land in the middle of May. We left Covelo just after dawn for the long trip, our cars loaded with belongings. I drove my old Honda Accord with our cat howling from a cardboard box in the back seat. Ryan followed in our flatbed pickup. It was a good time of year to arrive. Though that winter had been dry—the first year of what would become an unprecedented four-year drought—the hillsides were green, oaks bright with new leaves, air clear and warm. As we neared Placerville, the Crystal Basin range of the Sierras swung in and out of view. Still snow-capped, the mountains gleamed white against a cloudless blue. I'd looked out at that same range nearly every day of my childhood, could have sketched its silhouette with my eyes closed.

Our lease didn't officially begin until fall, but the conservancy had allowed us to arrive early so we could begin setting up the infrastructure we'd need to farm and fixing up the old house where we'd live. The building was infested with nearly every ill a house could host: rats, mold, rot, lead paint, asbestos. All the water lines and electrical wires needed to be replaced, the septic system had long ago caved in, and rotten siding fell away from the exterior with a nudge. The 800-square-foot farmhouse had been built sometime in the 1940s and had lain empty since the last occupants left fifteen years prior to our arrival, apparently tossing out all their trash into the yard and the adjacent ravine before departing. Under the tangle of blackberries and matted oak leaves, we found carpets and televisions, beer bottles and prescription drug vials, bed sheets and plastic of all sorts.

Wearing masks against the cocktail of hazardous dust created in the process, we ripped up moldy carpet and peeling linoleum and sanded away layers of brown paint until at last the original honey-colored pine floor shone through. We replaced three of the windows—all we could afford on the limited budget the conservancy had provided for repairs. We vacuumed trash cans worth of rat shit and walnut shells out from inside the walls and beneath the bathtub. We ran new water lines and painted everything with a creamy shade of white paint, Glass of Milk. We scavenged supplies from Craigslist: floor tiles, a kitchen sink, and a 1950s Wedgewood stove. When our allotted budget ran dry, the house remained in a state of disrepair—the kitchen sink drained into a bucket, missing window trim revealed fleshy pink insulation, the exterior remained unpainted, mosquitoes buzzed in through gaps above old windowpanes that had separated from the walls as the foundation settled. It wasn't exactly the stone farmhouse of Helen and Scott Nearing, but it was ours and it was livable, so Ryan and I moved in.

By then, the dry heat of summer had arrived. The hillsides surrounding the farm turned gold with dried grass. The only plant still clinging to any hint of green was the yellow star-thistle, *Centaurea solstitialis*, an invasive weed with bumblebee-size flowers ringed in spines sharp as needles and distinctive blue-green stalks. Yellow star-thistle thrived in non-irrigated land and outcompeted many native grasses—the plant invaded some 12 million acres in California. That summer, when the foxtail and ryegrass dried up, a blue-green wash spread across our ten acres, and I could see for the first time that the land was blanketed in star-thistle.

Beneath the thistle, the soil was already baked solid. We wouldn't be able to begin cultivating until the fall rains softened the ground, so in the meantime we focused on building the farming infrastructure we'd need. The land trust had agreed to pay for three permanent improvements to the land: a parking lot, perimeter deer fencing, and the below-ground irrigation pipes. To cover everything else that we would need in order to begin farming that first year—greenhouses for starting seedlings and extending the growing season, a walk-in cooler for cold storage, miles of drip tape irrigation (plastic tape perforated with a hole every eight inches) and aluminum sprinkler systems, produce-washing stations, a retail space built into a corner of the barn, harvest bins, tractor implements, hand tools—we borrowed $32,000 from family and planned to live off our savings for the intervening seven months until we could begin selling Community Supported Agriculture (CSA) subscriptions. These prepaid farm shares would help cover the upfront costs of the growing season (seeds, compost, water, fuel) to get us through to the spring, when we would finally have produce to sell and could open our farmstand and start making deliveries to restaurants and grocers. Ryan had his grand-father's 1979 Ford tractor shipped out from Texas, and we purchased the attachments we'd need: tiller, disk, cultivators, mower. With string lines and a field tape we divided the land into fifteen half-acre fields, each with its own irrigation header. We plotted out a crop plan for the coming year, calculating the number of row feet we would need to plant for each veg-etable, the amount of seed to purchase, the yields we could expect. We painted signs and built wooden produce display boxes, created a website, filed the paperwork to officially open a business.

That first summer I grew accustomed to star-thistle spines pricking my ankles, stinging my fingertips, and embedding themselves in my socks, in my boots, in the cuffs of my jeans. The spines worked their way into our house—I found them in the dust piles I swept up each evening, at the bottom of the drum of the laundry machine, between the sheets of our bed.

❧ 16 ❧

One week that summer, I drove with my mother from Placerville, down the Central Valley, to LA. It had been a few years since I'd last seen my grandparents, and I was eager to visit them before our farm went into full swing and it would be harder to get away. It was near dinnertime when we reached my grandparents' house, but regardless of the time I knew a meal would have been ready for us. We were hardly out of the car before my grandmother asked if I was hungry, then began describing all the dishes she'd prepared while ushering us inside and toward the kitchen. There, my aunt was already heaping food onto plates and my grandfather sat at the table.

When hugs had been given and plates served, the five of us sat around my grandparents' table to eat the feast my grandmother had cooked: Black dal. Rice with onions and cumin. Okra and bitter-melon subji. Saag. A freshly made pot of yogurt, still slightly warm, and a stack of buttered roti.

That night, I was digging through my bag for a toothbrush when I heard my grandmother call for me. I found her in the sitting room, reclined atop the slick cushions of her faux-leather couch. A lone lamp cast an orange glow across the tiled floor. She straightened when she saw me, offered her usual nod of welcome, and waved me into the room. In the murky light, something seemed different about her face, unfamiliar somehow. I took a step closer but couldn't quite put a finger on what had changed until, a moment later, she opened her mouth to speak and there, where her teeth had always been, was only darkness. A hollow outlined by an oval of plum-colored lips folding in over gums.

"Sit," my grandmother said, patting the space next to her. "Please, you can sit." I looked quickly away as if I'd walked in on her undressed. But my grandmother seemed unaware of her vanished teeth. "Please, sit down, OK?" Her voice came out nearly unchanged, only the slightest mushing of a syllable here and there, and I lowered myself onto the couch beside her.

Later, when I asked my mother about this—*When did Naniji get her teeth removed? Why didn't anyone tell me?*—she looked at me for a moment, cupped her hand briefly over her mouth as if holding in a laugh, and said, "Because you weren't around. You've never seen Naniji's real teeth—those were taken out years before you were born."

In the sitting room I scanned the framed photos hung on the wall: My aunt in a graduation cap. My grandfather in a turban and suit beside my grandmother in a red kameez, both faces stern, jaws set. Me and my sister as kids, all toothy smiles and big brown eyes. The only white person on the wall is my father. He stands tall and blond between my cousins in a goofy group photo taken some summer afternoon in the backyard of my childhood home.

My grandmother lifted her right hand toward me, an upturned fist. "For you," she said, "I have something." I glanced from her closed fingers to her face and thought: *toothless*. The word came to mind unbidden, but I couldn't get it out of my head. *Toothless*, we say, when we talk about something lacking force. *Toothless*, we say, when what we mean is powerless.

For a moment the room was silent. My grandmother's arm outstretched, my eyes on her face. Then the sudden rush of a faucet in the kitchen across the hall broke the quiet. A splat of water wrung from a rag, the squeak of a spray bottle.

Earlier that night, after dinner, my aunt had spotted a cockroach in the corner of the kitchen. She'd squealed, then squared her shoulders. "Oh no you don't," she'd said, lifting a can of achar and smashing the insect before summoning my mother to the kitchen. Together the sisters embarked on a rubber-gloved crusade against the vermin.

My grandmother and I had remained at the dining table as they emptied the overstuffed kitchen cabinets, piling their contents on the counters to lay bare the hoard of food: Plastic bags of partly eaten snack mixes, gone stale. Open boxes of rusk and vermicelli. An assortment of powders and granulated substances. Jars of cardamom pods and cans of pickled mango. They dumped long-expired foods into the trash, scrubbed at the sticky layer of greasy dust coating the exterior of forgotten jars and plastic bottles, wrinkled their noses at a whiff of rancid corn oil, muttering profanities not-quite-under their breath at the sight of another cockroach, and directing a battery of questions toward my grandmother. *How old is this jalebi? This chivda? And this? Does anyone even know what this is?* My grandmother said nothing, offered only a slight nod here and there until she seemed to have seen enough, stood up, tidied her scarf, and shuffled away.

Now, with one hand still closed into a fist, she lifted the other and motioned toward the sounds coming from the kitchen where her daughters were scrubbing years of grime from inside the cabinets and puzzling the remaining food back in. "I don't say anything to them, haanah? They don't listen. I know they don't listen to me. They want to throw away my food? OK, they will." She shrugged, then whispered, "They don't know."

I leaned closer and, afraid my voice might shatter this sudden intimacy, nodded once. My grandmother's lips were pursed tight; I'd almost forgotten about the missing teeth when she parted her mouth to speak, and there again was that hollow.

"You know, I don't drive?" She turned toward the sitting-room window. Though the pane was covered with a plastic blind, her eyes were fixed hard as if she could see through it. "Maybe I can learn? Maybe not so hard?" She didn't say, not on this day, that even if she learned the mechanics of driving, the roads signs would remain indecipherable, written in a language she couldn't read. "So, you see, I cannot just go to store whenever I want. If my kitchen empty, where is the food?" She placed her free hand on my knee. "Everyone who come here, I always have something to give, no? I make for them roti, I make paratha. Dal, subji. Maybe your mom, maybe her cabinet she keeps empty? Maybe this is OK for her? Not for me. If someone come here, and they hungry, and I have nothing? Then what? What can I do with empty cabinet?"

Her eyes were on mine again, waiting for an answer.

"I don't know," I offered. I'd meant about the cabinets, what to do with an empty one, but my grandmother looked puzzled by this response and I wished I'd said instead, *Yes, I do know. In your house, I have always been fed.*

"No?" My grandmother asked. She smiled, and I couldn't tell if it was an embarrassed smile or a pitying one. I glanced away. We'd come up against the curtain of our mismatched languages. When I looked back my grandmother's mouth was slightly open, and without thinking I ran my tongue along the backs of my own teeth as if to make certain they were still there.

Later, I'd read that much of what we know about human history has come from the study of our ancestors' teeth. Harder than bone, teeth persist in the archaeological record for millennia. Patterns of wear reveal the way a mouth was once used: to grind seeds, to descale fish, to crack open a shell. A difference between the chemical makeup of a first molar and a second can indicate migration. Remnants of food encapsulated in dental plaque show what once sustained us: fish, nuts, wheat.

The details of our own lifetimes, too, are scribed upon our teeth. A person fluent in the language of dentine, of enamel, can gather from our mouths the facts of our daily existence: where we've lived and for how long, what ailments we've suffered, how we've fed ourselves. Our history, calcified.

My grandmother lost her teeth the year she turned forty, my mother will later tell me. This would have been eight years before my birth, and eight years after my grandmother moved to America: the midpoint between her arrival in California and my own. The circumstances are muddy now, no one quite remembers. Probably an incompetent dentist, my mother posits, or a greedy one, a man who told my grandmother her teeth were ruined. Best to simply pay him to extract them all and furnish her instead with a set of dentures.

Or perhaps that's not how it happened at all. Maybe my grandmother stormed into the dentist's office one bright LA morning with an aching tooth. Maybe she stood at the front desk and demanded it be removed, and all the rest as well. *Get rid of them*, she might have said. *They're rotten. I'm done with so much ache.*

And what, I wonder, might the dentist have said? Did he say, *Yes, better to throw out those old things and start fresh*? Did he tell her that teeth are the most lasting parts of the human body, harder than bone? Did he tell her that sometimes, long after a tooth has been removed, after a whole mouth of teeth have been extracted and replaced with shiny new prosthetics, even then, the old ache can persist, disembodied, a phantom pain?

⇌

My grandmother lifted her palm from my knee and placed it beneath her other hand, still curled into a fist. "In India," she said, "we have many cockroach. Kenya, same. You? You, have cockroach where you live?" In truth, I didn't know if there were cockroaches around my farm in the foothills. I hadn't noticed any, but I lied and said yes. Yes, I assured her, I too have cockroaches. If I told her the truth—I'd never seen any in my house—it would have been one more wedge in the chasm between us.

All I knew about cockroaches was that they had been around a long time, that their species survived more than one mass extinction. I wanted to say this to my grandmother that evening. I wanted to ask her if she had heard about the cockroach's famed resiliency, if she thought this made them strong, admirable, or just lucky.

Instead, I repeated, "Yes. We have cockroaches, I'm sure we do."

"Aahcha," my grandmother said. She dropped her gaze down into her lap and at the sight of her closed hand resting there, brightened.

"For you," she said, and extended her upturned fist toward me. Then, knuckle by knuckle she unfurled her fingers until I saw, cupped in her palm, a pile of cream-colored nuggets—her teeth.

We both stared, silent, until my grandmother let out a satisfied *hmm*. "Very beautiful, haanah?" When I didn't respond, she added, "*Moti*. You know *moti*? I don't know how you say in English."

I leaned forward. Lamplight streamed over my shoulder and I saw that I'd of course been mistaken: they were not jagged like teeth, but perfectly round. A string of pearls.

"Aahcha, yes, *pearl*. Real pearl, you know, not fake. Real pearl from India!" She lifted the strand toward me. "You take."

I'd never before held real pearls, never felt their surprising weight or rubbed at their uncanny luster. I'd never paid much notice to them at all, never longed to wear them or considered them especially beautiful. And yet, on that night with the necklace in hand, I found I knew their genesis story well: It begins with a single grain of sand or a tiny parasite, something so small it is almost nothing, that works its way through the shell of an oyster to reach the tender flesh inside. There, it irritates, cuts, until the oyster wraps it in nacre, transforming it coat by coat into a luminous orb, an emblem of beauty and wealth. It's a story of prying prosperity from adversity, of turning a speck of dirt into a fortune. It's a California story. Though I didn't know it then, it was also the story of the moment unfolding in that room: the fifth child of landless Punjabi peasants, born on the dirt floor of a mud-walled home, finding herself seven decades later reclined on a couch in the tiled sitting room of an air-conditioned house in the San Fernando Valley, offering her granddaughter a fine pearl necklace.

I draped the strand over my fingers and marveled at this feat of transformation, sand to pearl. It didn't occur to me then to wonder what toll such an act of alchemy might extract.

"Very nice. *So* nice. You take," my grandmother said. All my life she had given me things—those mirrored shirts when I was a child, later ornate shawls and gold necklaces—a gift each visit. And always before, I'd accepted. But on that night, when I looked up at my grandmother, ready to say thank you and tuck the necklace into my pocket, I was met by her vacant mouth and startled again at the surprise of it. She looked decades older, and at the same time infant-like. And yet, there were her same high cheekbones, her still-taut skin, that unwavering gaze. Both stranger and grandmother, at once. A too-long moment passed, me staring dumbly, her waiting expectantly, until she gave a little shrug. "Only if you like. Take only if you like."

It didn't occur to me then that my grandmother might have noticed my pause and said this so as not to seem pushy. It's a word my mother had used at dinner earlier that night when my grandmother had offered me a second helping of food and before I could answer heaped a pile of okra and a folded flatbread onto my plate. "Mom! Don't be so *pushy*!" she'd said.

But with the necklace in my hand, I wasn't thinking of this exchange. My grandmother's words struck me instead as a kind of giver's remorse. Perhaps the sight of her pearls in my palm, callused and chalky from my farm work, or the fact that I didn't even know how to say their name in Punjabi, had reminded her that I might not be a worthy recipient. And she was right, wasn't she? I couldn't imagine any occasion I'd have to wear such a necklace. Even if an instance arose, I knew I'd never pull it off. The fraudulence would be obvious—no one would ever believe the pearls belonged to me.

"Take only if you like," my grandmother repeated.

"They're beautiful," I said. "But...I don't think..."

My grandmother's face shrank inward and I knew instantly I'd made a mistake. But already she was reaching for the pearls. "OK, I see, yes. You no like. It is OK. I see, yes." She folded her fingers again into a fist around the necklace, stood, and disappeared down the hall toward her room.

I remained on the couch, waiting to hear the shuffle and clip of her chappla coming back down the hall. Perhaps she'd bring something else, a bracelet, a shawl. The lamp buzzed. Minutes passed and eventually I switched it off and walked toward the guest room. At my grandmother's closed door I paused, put my ear to the wood: a hum of prayer.

⊷

In the guest room, my mother was reading in the twin bed next to the mat laid out for me on the floor. I told her what happened, how I wished I'd taken my grandmother's pearls. She shrugged. "I wouldn't worry about it. She'll forget and offer them to you again next time." I didn't say that it wasn't really the pearls I wanted, but to stay in that room beside my grandmother, to keep her hand resting on my knee. I wanted her to tell me more about the cockroaches in India and the people who come to her house, ready to be fed.

⊷

I tossed against the lumpy mat until I fell asleep and dreamt myself back into the sitting room. My grandmother is there beside me on the couch, again holding something in her hand. She opens her fingers and this time, in her palm, really are her teeth. Two dozen of them, tea-stained with long, tapered roots. "Very nice," my grandmother says. "You like? Very beautiful. You take, haanah?"

I stare at the teeth until she lifts them toward me and I cup my hand below hers. The teeth clink softly as she drops them into my palm. One by one, I lift each tooth and implant it into my own mouth, pressing the pointed roots down into my empty gums like seed garlic into soil. When they are all in place I tap my jaw up and down a few times, then look at my grandmother.

"Thank you," I say, and the words come out in Punjabi: *Thann Vaad.* "They are very nice," I say, and this too comes out in Punjabi.

"Naniji, I can speak! I can speak your language!" I shout. "You can tell me now. Please, tell me everything."

My grandmother nods, a slow, approving tilt of her head. She begins to smile but her lips, I notice, are not quite right. I lean in, peer closer to see they have shrunken, grown fingernail thin and brittle. She remains silent, watching me.

"Naniji," I say again, "we can talk now. Please, tell me."

Her smile spreads wider, her lips thinning further, and I see they are not lips at all, but shells. Oyster shells, dark blue and shimmering gray, the seam sealed tight.

"Naniji, please!" I repeat. "Talk to me."

At last her shell lips crack apart, open wide. But no words come forth. Instead, cradled inside her mouth rests a single pea-size pearl.

❧ 17 ❧

It was a clear afternoon not long after that visit to LA, my regret over those pearls still ringing in my ears, when my friend Fulton, a baker, walked up my driveway with his own offering tucked under one arm: a loaf of bread. As he approached I was sitting on my porch steps talking with his partner, Jean, my close friend from college. When he reached us he held out the loaf with both hands. "It's for you," he said with a grin. This time, I didn't hesitate.

The loaf was a football-size oval slashed lengthwise down the center. Where the bread had risen and split as it baked, a rust-colored cornice lifted off the surface to reveal a band of golden crust. "One hundred percent Sonora wheat," Fulton said after a moment. He'd just returned from spending the day with Dave Miller, a renowned baker who lived nearby, known for milling all his own flour and producing exceptional breads with local heirloom grains.

I lifted the loaf to my nose and took a breath, then eyed the underside—crisp and drum-like against the rap of a knuckle. Tiring of my tedious examination, Fulton snatched the loaf, tore it in two, then passed a half back. Inside, the crumb was butter-colored and flecked with auburn flakes of bran. Jean pulled a chunk off one end and I did the same.

"It's good," she said after a moment, and I nodded—the bread was remarkably tender, both subtly sweet and pleasantly sour.

"Of course it's good. It's *amazing*," Fulton said. Jean rolled her eyes, then got up and walked into the kitchen. When she returned with a block of cheese, Fulton was asking what I thought about growing some wheat on my farm.

I had never considered growing wheat, knew nothing about it. "Don't you need hundreds of acres?"

"You could start with a few," he said. Then, motioning to the open space surrounding us, he added, "and expand if it does well, right?"

I shrugged. "Maybe."

"I think Sonora would do pretty well here in the foothills," Fulton said. At the time he knew far more than I did about heirloom grains—who was growing them and what kind of demand existed among bakers. "People are wary of modern wheat," he told me. "Everyone's looking for something old, you know, something authentic, unadulterated. Bakers want to know the name of the variety, to be able to write it on the bread bag. And they want it to sound good, not just a number but something you can pronounce—*Red Fife, Brown Turkey, Sonora.*"

I looked past Fulton to the land spread out below us, our ten acres and the surrounding hills, and imagined fields of grain. Ryan and I could spare a few acres to plant a trial of wheat. And if the crop did well we had the option to lease additional land—fifty, even one hundred acres more.

I shook my head. "I don't know anything about growing wheat."

"Well," my friend said after a moment, "you could look into it."

❧

A week after Fulton's visit I'd done enough research to believe wheat might in fact be a good fit for our farm. An old variety like Sonora could be dry-farmed, which meant it could subsist solely on rainfall for irrigation. We'd simply sow the seeds in time for a late fall rain. They'd germinate and grow under the waning sunlight until the blades neared a foot in height. Then growth would pause through much of the winter. When the days began to lengthen again and the soil warmed, the stalks would shoot up rapidly until April or May, when they'd flower and form seed heads. After the last spring rains the wheat would begin to dry, turning from green to gold. It would be ready to harvest sometime in June.

Growing wheat this way could complement our vegetable production with scarce additional expense. The wheat crop wouldn't require any new irrigation infrastructure, not to mention the cost of the water itself. The plants would serve as a cover crop over winter—they'd prevent the soil from washing away and shade out the weeds that would otherwise quickly take hold. The wheat would grow unattended through the busy spring season, requiring no labor until harvest. Then, once the grain was cut, the straw could be mowed and incorporated into the soil, contributing valuable organic matter. The field would then be ready for fall vegetable plantings.

The idea of producing grains this way struck me as an exciting alternative to the dominant mono-crop, mega-farm model of wheat production. We had much to gain from incorporating wheat into our vegetable rotation, it seemed, and little to lose: even if we didn't manage to reap much of a harvest, the wheat would be beneficial to our fields. Ryan, too, was intrigued by the possibility. So I began to look into sourcing some Sonora seed.

I called seed companies around the nation, but few knew what I was talking about and those that did had no seed to sell. In the process I discovered several organizations dedicated to preserving landrace grains. At the time I'd only a vague notion of the meaning of the term *landrace*, but I noticed Sonora was commonly described as such. I found the organization closest to my farm, a nonprofit called Whole Grain Connection based in the Bay Area, and called the number.

A woman named Monica Spiller answered my call in a warm British accent, and, after a few pleasantries, I asked her if she knew where I might buy some Sonora seed. She didn't answer. Instead she asked if I had ever grown this variety before. I told her no, that this would be my first time growing wheat. She cleared her throat and let out a small half-sigh, half-laugh. Then she said she did have some seed, but she would not sell it to me.

Thus began the hour-long conversation in which Monica brought to light my nearly complete ignorance regarding grain production. *How do you plan to harvest the wheat, where will you store it, do you have a grain cleaner, a combine, a silo, a grain drill?* I could answer few of her questions.

Monica explained her unwillingness to sell large amounts of Sonora seed to farmers such as myself, who she was not confident would be successful in growing it out. Sonora wheat was among the first wheats grown on the American continent, she told me, and one of the oldest varieties still in existence. It was once grown widely across regions of northern Mexico, California, and the American Southwest. It is known for its drought tolerance, a trait that allowed it to thrive in these semi-arid landscapes, and for the light-colored and tender dough it produces. With a protein content around 9 percent, Sonora falls somewhere between a soft pastry wheat and a hard bread wheat. Dough made with Sonora is delicate, easy to stretch but not very elastic, making it difficult to use for leavened hearth loaves but ideal for flatbreads—staple foods in the regions where it was historically cultivated.

Sonora was once the predominant wheat variety grown in California, Monica told me. Over the course of the twentieth century, however, high-yielding modern wheat cultivars began to supplant traditional varieties. These modern varieties, grown under the right conditions—in conjunction with fertilizer, herbicides, and ample irrigation—could produce many times the yields of landrace varieties. By the 1970s, nearly all commercial cultivation of Sonora wheat had ceased. The grain could have disappeared entirely, the last handful of seeds forgotten in a graying barn.

Instead, a sample of Sonora seed had been preserved in the USDA seed bank, part of something called the National Plant Germplasm System. In the 1990s, Monica—a former chemistry teacher and whole grain enthusiast alarmed by the rising rates of dietary-related disease—embarked on an attempt to revive Sonora wheat and other landrace grains, and she requested a sample of seed from the USDA vault. She received just five grams of Sonora seed—a teaspoon of tawny kernels. Over the ensuing decade, Monica found farmers to grow out the grain, collect the multiplying seed, and replant until she'd propagated a substantial supply. In 2000 she founded Whole Grain Connection to provide seeds and resources to support to farmers in growing organic landrace grains.

I asked Monica if she thought, as my baker friend had assured me, that a market existed for heirloom wheat like Sonora. She told me she knew of many bakers seeking sources for heritage grains and a few specialty grocers around the Bay Area who were interested in buying Sonora flour. And then she mentioned a group of Indian American investors and grocers who had recently approached her in search of flour suitable for traditional Indian flatbreads. Sonora, Monica had learned from studying its origins, was once commonly cultivated in the Punjab region of northern India. She'd offered a sample of her stone-ground Sonora flour and they'd found it to be perfect for roti and paratha—its gold color and remarkable softness unlike the other flours they'd tried. Some declared it produced breads just like those they remembered from their childhoods in India. A few Indian markets around the Bay Area were interested in carrying the flour, and the owners were asking Monica where they could find it.

After hanging up the phone, I leaned back in my chair and looked at the mess of notes I'd scribbled across the back of a seed catalog. I was daunted by all that I didn't know about growing grains, and miffed by Monica's resistance to selling me any seed. It would be wise, I knew, to call it quits right there, to stick with vegetables and not bother with grains at all.

But the idea of this ancient wheat—its near erasure and now burgeoning revival—captivated me, and Monica's words left me abuzz with questions: What was the difference between the wheat I ate every day—flour purchased from the bulk bins at the co-op or paper sacks from the supermarket—and a landrace wheat like Sonora? What had been lost when these wheats vanished from the grain fields of the world? And could something of that loss be regained now?

These questions tugged at my thoughts, but welling up beneath them were the ones I didn't dare ask out loud, those I couldn't then articulate in words but felt pulling me in with a gravity that would prove irresistible: Might this obscure wheat contain within it a door to my own heritage? Could cultivating it offer me an opportunity to make up for all that had not passed down to me? If I could grow Sonora and produce flour from its berries, could I, in turn, reclaim a piece of the inheritance I'd lost?

↫ 18 ↬

In the sepia-toned pages of his 1921 monograph, *The Wheat Plant*, botanist John Percival traces the origins of some 2,000 forms of cultivated wheat obtained from nearly all the wheat-growing regions of the world. Not long after talking to Monica, I tracked down a used copy on eBay and fanned through the book in search of Sonora. I found a photograph of one isolated stalk, a length of kernels knit together like a braid: *Triticum vulgare,* variety Delfi. Percival describes the variety as comparatively rare, "confined to warm countries, being obtained only from India, Khorasan (Persia), Egypt, South Africa, and California." The sample in the photograph labeled Sonora was from California, and Percival offers detailed descriptions of two other forms closely resembling this, one found in parts of Southern Africa and the other found in parts of India, particularly Punjab.

There it was, confirmation that a landrace wheat akin to Sonora had once been grown in Punjab, just as Monica had said, where the harvest would've been ground into flour, mixed into dough, and rolled thin to produce the flatbreads fed each day to the children there—some who were now elders living in far-flung places and longing for the particular texture, that elusive flavor of their childhood breads. And among these children might have been my own grandparents.

I tried to imagine my grandmother as a child, sitting among the women in her village rolling out plum-size balls of dough. Perhaps her fingers, not yet accustomed to handling the sticky dough, move slowly, clumsy in contrast to the nimble motions of the women who hardly seem to be paying attention at all. But as I tried to picture this scene, I found I couldn't fill in any of the details: Who are the women alongside my grandmother? What does the room look like? What hills or rivers or plains surround them? I focused instead on an imagined bowl heaped with flour that is neither white nor brown, but a buttery shade of gold. When sunlight strikes the flour, it glows like a paper lantern.

I wondered if my grandmother would recognize Sonora flour, or if she had ever used it at all. Did she find her paratha, the ones she rolled out each morning on her linoleum countertop, different from those she remembered from India? Did she find them lacking and wonder what could be missing, had she forgotten something?

⟟

The morning I sat inspecting the grainy photo of the Sonora stalk in John Percival's book, I knew a scant two things about Punjab. The first I recalled from college classes: Punjab had been ground zero for the agricultural Green Revolution in India. The second I'd known all my life: Punjab was the place my mother was born. This fact existed for me like a dusty box kept in a cabinet of one's childhood home, its contents labeled clearly—*Photos* or *Extra Silverware*—something that had always just been there, requiring no further investigation. I'd never thought to look inside.

The only impression I could summon of my family's ancestral home in Punjab came from a brief conversation I'd once had with my grandmother. I was eighteen or nineteen. I don't remember what compelled her to share this fragment of memory with me, only that the two of us were sitting on the bench outside my grandparents' front door, the hot Los Angeles air whipped dry with Santa Ana winds. "In my village," she said, "there were peacock. *Big* birds, everywhere. You know peacock?" I nodded. She cast her gaze across the street, at the leaves of a neighbor's tree fluttering in the wind. As a child, she told me, she often walked in the farm fields around her village looking for the birds' dropped feathers, searching among the shadows of crops for an iridescent flicker. She collected handfuls of the feathers, then carried them to the temple where she poked each quill into the gold vases that adorned the shrine.

Now, with Percival's book in front of me, I thought of this story and tried to remember what crops my grandmother had mentioned. I'd been on the verge of adulthood when she'd told me this story, and hungry for any scrap of information about the place my family had come from. After she had finished talking and excused herself to her room to rest, I'd pulled out my journal and greedily scribbled down everything I could remember. Now I dug through my closet in search of the shoebox in which I kept old notebooks, flipped through each until I found what I was looking for. There, in hasty cursive, I had scrawled the words "Okra, Sugar, Corn, Wheat." *Wheat*.

I glanced from my journal to the Percival book and wondered if the fields my grandmother walked through as a girl might have been planted with Sonora. I traced my finger across the photo of the isolated stalk, read and reread the paragraph listing Sonora's particular morphological traits—*Young shoots*: erect. *Straw*: slender, of medium height. *Ear*: lax— eager to unearth some kind of insight. But the words, the measurements and descriptions of color, meant little to me then. I focused instead on those two place names—California, Punjab—brought together in rare proximity by the heading typed in bold: *Sonora*.

❧ 19 ❧

I called Monica again to beg for seed. "I'd rather not risk losing 500 pounds of Sonora seed," she told me. Then she suggested I talk to an experienced small-scale wheat farmer she knew who also lived in the Sierra foothills, just forty miles north of my farm. "Maybe he can be of help," she offered, more than hinting that I needed it. After hanging up with Monica I phoned the farmer and he invited Ryan and me to visit.

Reed Hamilton wore wool socks and no shoes when he answered the door and invited us inside his house. He slid a heap of papers and books to one end of the kitchen table, and Ryan and I sat at the other. On top of the pile lay a sun-bleached tractor manual, folded open, and I could see notes penciled into the margins.

As we talked about growing Sonora, the wheat farmer kept pausing and taking in long breaths before he spoke, as if afraid that we wouldn't want to hear the thing he was about to say: "You'll need a seed cleaner, a gravity table. That can set you back around $10,000 easy." "How do you plan to harvest the wheat?" "With an heirloom variety like Sonora, you can expect to get maybe a third of the yield you might get from a modern variety."

Reed led us outside, where several corrugated storage containers filled his yard. He used these steel boxes to store his grain and house his processing equipment. Ryan and I followed him inside one of them—a 30-foot-long, 8-foot-wide windowless rectangle tall enough for us to stand in. Plastic 55-gallon barrels lined the sides of the container, leaving a slim aisle down the middle. Reed tugged on a lid of one of the barrels, releasing a small burp like a cork pulled from a wine bottle. He replaced the lid and moved to the next barrel. Inside, I could see chestnut-colored wheat kernels, millions of them heaped on top of one another. After opening a few more barrels, he found the one he was looking for and scooped up a handful of its contents. This wheat was different from the others: tooth-colored and faintly lustrous, the kernels slipped through his fingers like cream. This was Sonora. "See, it's a little rounder and lighter than the hard red," Reed said, pouring some of it into my hand. I rolled the kernels around with my fingertips, a heap of tiny pearls. The wheat farmer emptied his hand back into the barrel and I did the same. A few of the wheat berries stuck to my palm and I drew my hand into my pocket, where the kernels fell into the folds of fabric.

Behind the storage containers, in a steel boneyard, combine harvesters and tractor implements sat among weeds. Ryan and I scanned the collection of machinery while Reed explained the complications of harvesting wheat on a small scale. Most wheat farms in the country are hundreds, if not thousands, of acres, he told me. He farmed just twenty-four. Harvesters suitable for small farms are hard to come by. Sometimes the best place to find small-scale grain equipment, he said, is on Craigslist— in the "antiques" section. *Beautiful yard art,* the ads read, *could make a great garden sculpture.*

Reed ran his hand over the red paint of his Allis-Chalmers All-Crop Harvester. The heap of steel looked to me like a contraption out of *Chitty-Chitty Bang-Bang.* I stared at it for a long time trying to decipher how it worked. The machine was the width of two cars and had a hitch mount on the front to attach to a tractor. To one side there was a spindly wheel, nearly four feet in diameter. Behind the wheel, a box that appeared to hold a series of screens spanned the width of the machine. Rubber belts and chains wove in all directions, and one long chimney-like pipe jutted out at an odd angle as if it had fallen over. "Seventy-five bearings in this thing," the farmer said, shaking his head. "Every time I get ready to use it I start a few weeks ahead of time—I know it's gonna need some work." Next to this machine, a nearly identical one sat in disrepair. Reed explained how he kept a spare combine of the same model to use for replacement parts because the parts for these machines were no longer manufactured.

We followed Reed past the storage containers back up to his house. I heard a phone ringing inside. The wheat farmer looked tired as I thanked him for showing us around. All this talk about the cost of growing wheat, the slim feasibility of a small-scale grain operation, seemed to have exhausted him. "To tell you the truth," he said, "I've been doing this now for five years. Last year, I made just under $4,000." He depended instead on a portable storage container business for his livelihood.

"Why do you do it?" I asked.

Reed kept walking. "Good question," he said with a chuckle. Then he added, speaking now, it seemed, to himself: "I grew up on a grain farm."

❧ 20 ❧

A round the time Reed had started growing grains in the Sierra foothills in the mid-2000s, a swell of interest in landrace and small-scale grains was growing in California and in many corners of the nation. Reed pointed Ryan and me toward a handful of other small wheat farmers in Northern California, connecting us with an internet forum of grain growers, processers, and researchers who discussed ideas, trouble-shot problems, and occasionally held gatherings. Soon enough, I found similar networks in other parts of the country, made up of farmers, millers, bakers, chefs, and general landrace grain enthusiasts. It was a subset of the alternative food movement I then knew little about, but it wasn't hard to understand how it had gained traction.

Conventional wheat production painted an unsettling picture of many of the more sensational ills of contemporary industrial agriculture: Miles of mono-crop fields, devoid of any life besides a single variety of genetically uniform wheat bred for yield and ease of processing with little regard for flavor or nutrition. Heavy doses of herbicides and pesticides, along with generous application of synthetic nitrogen fertilizer, doused over those thousands of acres. Crops machine-harvested by GPS-guided nearly self-driving combines with hardly a human in sight, then processed into refined white flour, a product that is all but tasteless, indefinitely shelf-stable, and devoid of almost all nutrition. And because wheat—more than vegetables or meat or dairy—carries especially primordial connotations, a biblical, elemental quality, this brutish adulteration seemed to strike a particularly tender nerve.

Within the lively world of alternative grains, I soon discovered, there were boutique millers and artisan bakers. There were gourmet chefs seeking heirloom grains of local provenance that could provide authentic culinary experiences to counter the bland homogeny of mass-produced commodity crops. There were educators and health enthusiasts like Monica Spiller, who started up orgs to promote the personal and environmental health benefits of whole-grain products made from organically grown landrace varieties. There were small organic farmers, too, who found these old wheat cultivars particularly well suited to low-input growing methods. Unlike modern wheat, landraces performed well without irrigation and didn't require high doses of nitrogen fertilizer or herbicides. And, with flour from such varieties commanding prices as high as $7 a pound, perhaps a small farmer with only a few acres available could find growing grains worthwhile.

The websites and promotional materials of these farmers, millers, and restaurants were filled with stunning photographs—fields of deep amber grain; rustic breads; freshly milled flour; plates heaped with colorful rice, blue corn, wheat berry salads—and language that evoked a set of recurring themes suggesting the far-reaching promises of the heirloom organic grain revival: a return to wholeness and authenticity. Agrarian revitalization. Purity and simplicity. The staff of life redeemed from its fall from grace.

❧ 21 ❧

After our visit with Reed, I called Monica a third time. At last, she agreed to sell me some Sonora seed. Not the 500 pounds I'd wanted, but 200—enough to plant two acres. I offered to pick up the seed the following week, but she told me she'd deliver the seed herself. "I've been meaning to take a drive up your way," she said, "you know, to see the fall colors."

Monica arrived on a clear October morning. I was working at the back of the farm, awaiting her visit while hefting long aluminum pipes across my shoulders and carrying them over beds of root vegetables to an adjacent field where I'd just seeded a new succession of salad greens. The sun had dried away any sign of dew and I'd stripped off my layers down to a T-shirt. Out on the road I noticed a pickup slow as it neared our sign post. A blinker flicked on. I set down the pipe, dusted off my palms, and jogged toward the parking lot.

Monica stepped out of her truck wearing a wide-brimmed sun hat and wool sweater. I shook her hand and glanced into the pickup bed. There they were: four fifty-pound paper bags marked "Sonora, 2011." I offered to show Monica around the farm, and Ryan climbed out from beneath the shovels and tines of a cultivating implement he was assembling to join us. There wasn't yet much to see, but we walked Monica out to our two newly built greenhouses and showed her the irrigation systems, the tidy half-acre blocks, one planted with fall vegetables and the others mowed and ready to be disked and sown with cover crop. She nodded and smiled as we walked—pleased, it seemed, and perhaps a bit relieved to see the place. Though it wasn't much to look at, all the essentials were there: tractor and implements, full sun, a stretch of flat ground. I got the sense she had offered to personally deliver the wheat not just because she felt like taking a drive.

At the southern edge of the farm we stopped at the freshly tilled two-acre triangle where we planned to plant the wheat. Monica eyed the acreage quietly for a moment, then nodded. "Yes, I think it might do well here." We turned to walk back to the truck and Monica told us again about the Indian American grocers seeking Sonora flour. She began to describe a roti, but I interrupted. "I know what a roti is," I said, explaining my Indian heritage. She asked what kind of flour my grandmother used. I didn't know. "Also, they say Sonora wheat is perfect for chakolya," she added. "Do you make chakolya?"

I'd never heard of chakolya, could only shake my head. "Sorry," I said digging my toe into the soil, wishing I hadn't mentioned my heritage at all.

"Oh, that's alright," she offered with a sigh that was also a gentle chuckle. She looked out at the thin line of clouds sketched across the horizon. "You grew up here, not India. The traditional ways...you don't know. How could you?"

I felt my face flush red at Monica's words and I opened my mouth to protest. But I'd nothing to say: she was right, wasn't she? I stared down at the tidy rows of carrots just beginning to emerge, bent to pluck a stray weed.

Back at Monica's truck, Ryan and I heaved the sacks of seed out of the bed and piled them in our driveway. I jogged over to the field where our fall crops were planted and collected a bundle of arugula, two lettuce heads, and a handful of radishes. I packed them into a box and handed it to Monica as she stepped into her cab. She thanked me for the produce, wished us good luck, and drove away.

Ryan returned to the cultivator and I carried the sacks of seed into the barn. Once all the bags were inside, I tugged one of them open. The Sonora seeds spilled over one other, just as creamy and lustrous as those I'd first seen inside Reed's barrel. I ran my fingers through the kernels, lifted a palmful up to the light. My face was still hot with shame, but with the Sonora seeds in my hand I felt my features rearranging into something else: excitement, perhaps, or resolve. All I needed now was a forecast of rain. Then I'd load these bags of seed into our broadcast seeder, strap it over my shoulders, and zigzag across the field, flinging grain until the two acres were confettied with the tooth-colored kernels. We would scratch them in with the old harrow we'd found half-buried in star-thistle behind the barn. Rain would drive the seed down into the soil and soon each kernel would crack open, unfurling a thread-thin root and one sharp shoot. The shoots would needle up through the soil and the field would flush green with new wheat. Come next summer, seven short months away, I'd hold in my hands fistfuls of flour. I'd bring it to my grandmother and she would roll it between her fingertips, lift it to her nose to smell that whisper of sweetness, and say, *Yes, this! This is what has been missing all these years. How did you find it?*

⊹ 22 ⊹

The afternoon I planted our Sonora seed, the first big storm of the season waited overhead. I marched a course across the two-acre triangle, just as I'd imagined, twirling the handle of the broadcast seeder that flung the seed like a sprinkler. Ryan followed behind with the tractor pulling the spring-tooth harrow—a grid of forty steel tines that traced shallow lines across the field, raking the seed into the soil. As we worked, the rain came gently at first, two drops on the back of my hand, a swirl of wind. Then it was pouring. In soaked jeans and mud-heavy boots, I plodded across the field until I'd distributed every seed.

The storm lingered overnight, then passed. Clear fall days resumed and, a few weeks later, my grandparents came up to visit. They stayed, as always, at my parents' house fifteen miles south, but on the first morning of their visit my mother drove them over to see my farm. Though there wasn't yet much to show, I led them around eagerly. Here, a quarter-acre field of garlic mulched with straw. Here, our propagation greenhouse, new plastic stretched taut over the aluminum arches. Here, our first crops of fall produce: radishes and carrots, arugula and collard greens. Here, the barn, the tractor and implements. I was too caught up in my own enthusiasm to notice my grandparents' faces, to wonder what they might have thought of it all—of me, their Californian granddaughter, born with all the privileges and opportunities of a middle-class American, choosing to become a vegetable farmer.

I'd saved the Sonora wheat field for last, and by the time I started to lead them toward it my grandfather had grown too tired to keep walking. He and my mother returned to the car to wait while I walked my grandmother out to the wheat. We stood together at the edge of the field and I swept my arm toward the acres of green sprouts. "It's not just any wheat," I said, not sure how to explain the significance of Sonora. "This wheat is an old type—people used to grow it in Punjab." My grandmother nodded, but I couldn't tell if she understood. "Some Indian shop owners near San Francisco say it makes the best flour for roti and paratha."

"Atta?" she asked. I nodded. Yes, flour.

"When will it be ready to eat?"

I explained that the berries would not be ready to harvest until summer, still many months away. "Oh, aahcha," she said, letting her gaze rest on the field for a long time. I didn't tell her that I had not yet found a way to harvest the wheat. I did not divulge all the steps the wheat would need to undergo—threshing, cleaning, milling—in order to become flour. Nor did I tell her that the infrastructure needed to achieve these things on this small scale no longer seemed to exist. The more I searched for the necessary equipment to harvest and process our wheat, the more dead ends I ran into. Still, I was certain I'd find a way.

My grandmother turned to face me, her eyes wide. "Please," she said, "when it is ready, can you save some atta for me?" I looked out at the wheat and tried to envision what it might look like in June or July, each bronze stalk fattened at the tip with a braid of berries. I promised I would. "Good!" she said. Then, lifting the hem of her silk salwar, she turned and walked out of the field.

Part 2

GOLD HILL

❧ 1 ❧

I f you stood in the center of our farm early on a summer morning, not long after the sun had crested the Sierras to the west, you might assume the region garnered its name—Gold Hill—from the appearance of the landscape: swells of grass-covered slopes gilded with early light. But the name comes instead from the precious metal found famously in 1848 in the dregs of a sawmill on the South Fork of the American River, just a scant two miles away. There the mill operator, James Marshall, stood watching the river flow through the tailrace when a shimmer in the water caught his eye. He reached in and plucked out a lustrous pebble, turned it in his fingers, then hammered it gently. It was not brittle like pyrite but malleable: gold.

In the days and years after that first shimmer, as tens of thousands of fortune seekers journeyed from every part of the world to these hills and the promise they held, Gold Hill emerged as a prime agricultural region. It was—and still is—a stretch of gentle terrain among a larger landscape of steep slopes and cold winters. Farms and ranches here provided food and spirits for the surrounding miner towns, then some of the largest settlements in the state: Coloma, El Dorado, Pilot Hill, and Placerville. These early farmers produced dairy products and cattle, hay and barley, apples and pears. Mainly they grew grapes destined for wine and brandy.

By the time Ryan and I arrived a century and a half later, agriculture was no longer a significant part of the local economy, and the once prominent Gold Rush–era settlements had receded into small towns and bedroom communities—the places my childhood friends and I had called "the sticks"—with names few people outside our region had ever heard of. The landscape lurched between rural and suburban: Cows grazed in enclaves of open space sandwiched between residential subdivisions. Families kept pet goats and small herds of sheep to keep the weeds down, watered tomatoes before changing into business-casual clothes and commuting an hour to offices in Sacramento. Homeowners planted olive trees (notoriously drought tolerant) to qualify for discounted "ag rate" water, meant to subsidize farm irrigation, then used it to fill swimming pools or maintain lawns. Hardly anyone made their living from farming. In fact, jobs in agriculture ranked among the least common occupations in El Dorado County, constituting less than 1 percent of all employees. Instead, most people here spent their working lives in cubicles or behind sales counters, the most common employment sectors being healthcare and retail.

Nevertheless, a proud rural identity persisted, manifesting in the glorification of all things hardscrabble and unpolished. Placerville flaunted its historic nickname, Hangtown, garnered by its Gold Rush–era reputation for vigilante justice. On Main Street, a life-size mannequin hung from a noose over a bar. Antique stores sold gold pans and vintage cowboy boots, old wagon wheels and horseshoes. A sign outside Placerville Hardware boasted the store's claim to be the oldest hardware store west of the Mississippi. Inside, the shelves were now stocked mostly with trinkets and gift items. A clothing shop called Redneck Bling sold Levi's and faux-leather belts with buckles the size of a person's palm.

Alongside this Gold Country hubris existed plenty of that particular Northern Californian brand of crystal-keeping, granola-eating, earth-mother hippy, often with one extreme overlaid right on top of the other: Cozmic Café, a downtown coffee shop located in a building with an old gold-mine shaft still snaking out behind the kitchen into the rocky hillside, drew crowds with Grateful Dead cover bands and environmental film screenings. A natural foods co-op managed to remain just barely afloat across the street from the feed store where "Don't Tread on Me" flags decorated pickups in the parking lot. A specialty tea shop offered dainty cups of green tea laced with jasmine flowers and a perfect view of the mannequin on Hangman's Tree across the street.

The primary agricultural sector remaining in El Dorado County was "Apple Hill," a string of apple orchards and vineyards located en route to Lake Tahoe. These farms-turned-tourist-destinations drew visitors from all over the state. Here, come autumn, a tourist could buy apples in every incarnation: apple donuts and apple pie, caramel dipped and dried. She could take photos alongside goofy scarecrows and picturesque barns and bundles of colorful corn, get her face painted, eat corndogs and fudge, taste wine. Nearby schools took students on field trips to these farms—as mine did—where a third grader could press cider, take home a pump-kin, witness the simple beauty and hard-won rewards of the farming life. No one mentioned, on those field trips, that many of the apples sold on Apple Hill were not actually grown on the local farms but were in-stead imported from the industrial orchards of Washington State. Nor did anyone stop to introduce the people harvesting grapes: crews of brown-skinned workers who looked nothing like the older white male proprietors in plaid shirts and overalls who were presented to us as The Farmers.

All the other class field trips I recall were to Gold Rush sites: Marshall Gold Discovery Park, Gold Bug Mine, Sutter's Fort. We toured the saw-mill where James Marshall found gold, watched volunteers in old-timey garb forge a horseshoe or pan for gold, learned of the stories of famed early frontiersmen Kit Carson and John Sutter. Once, in fourth grade, we all dressed up as notorious pioneers—Charlie Parkhurst or members of the Donner Party—and spent a day at our school principal's land where we reenacted everyday life on the frontier: churning butter, making sar-saparilla, branding pine stools with iron branding sticks. We learned, too, of the Indigenous tribes—the Nisenan, Miwok, and Maidu whose land this had once been—of the devastating losses they'd endured during and after the Gold Rush. But their story was depicted as a tragic foot-note, an unfortunate side effect of an otherwise noble quest to expand westward. We learned how it was this place, our foothills, that had held the wealth upon which our state's flashier locales—San Francisco, Sac-ramento—had been built, and how it was our county's early settlers and miners who pried all those riches loose.

Ryan and I named our business after the river where Marshall found that fateful flake of gold: South Fork Farm. I liked the subtle alliteration of those two F's, the way *fork* alluded to food, the tie to place. I wasn't thinking then about the history of that river. It's only now, years later, that I imagine that 1848 day—the shimmering in the water, the soft thud of a hammer against gold—and consider the ways in which the fate of my farm and its river namesake had been entangled all along.

❧ 2 ❧

What I did not learn during my elementary school field trips was this: By 1860, barely a decade after that first gold flake was found, the value of all the gold mined in California had been surpassed by another commodity: wheat.

In the years following the Gold Rush, land speculators and gold-rich businessmen accumulated giant swaths of California land into their few hands, monopolizing the majority of the state's arable acres before settlers could even attempt to stake claims. By 1870, Carey McWilliams notes in his classic book on California agriculture, *Factories in the Field*, more than half the available farmland in California had come under the ownership of just 0.2 percent of the state's population. Eager to wrest profit from these vast landholdings in the same way it had been mined from the nearby hills, these landowners searched for a crop that could perform just this kind of extracting. What they found was Sonora wheat.

Possibly the first variety of wheat ever cultivated in California, Sonora traveled across the ocean to North America aboard the ships of European explorers. Which explorers, and when exactly, remains something of a mystery. What we can say for certain is that by the time those early Californian land barons came upon it in the mid-1800s, Sonora had for centuries been cultivated with great success in northern Mexico and across parts of Southern California and what is now the American Southwest. In these semi-arid landscapes, the plant grew nearly by itself. The tall stalks thrived on nothing but decent soil and a handful of winter rains. Their height gave them a great advantage over most weeds and their deep roots reached buried water. Outside of the work of planting and harvesting, for almost the entire growing season there was nothing a farmer needed to do but wait. It was the perfect crop for an absentee landowner.

In the years after the Gold Rush, wheat was sown across millions of acres in California, and the state became the second biggest wheat producer in the Union, just behind Minnesota. Spanning as many as 50,000 acres, California's wheat farms at that time were the largest anywhere in the world. These mono-crop fields, which became known as the "bonanza wheat farms," resembled nothing of the small, homesteader-style family farm that holds such a prominent place in the American imagination and once occupied a good chunk of my own. Instead, as Henry George wrote in 1871, California has been from its beginning "not a country of farms but a country of plantations and estates."

For the most part, these early wheat farmers did absolutely nothing to maintain soil fertility—no crop rotations or fallow seasons or manure applications. They didn't attempt to control weeds, or preserve or improve the quality of their seed. Instead, they simply planted wheat across as much land as possible year after year, prying out the stored nutrients of the land with no intention of replacing what they took. Soon what had once been some of the richest farmland in the world could no longer yield a wheat crop worth harvesting. These gentleman farmers "worked their ranches as a quarter of a century before they had worked their mines," writes Frank Norris in *The Octopus*, his 1901 novel of California's bonanza wheat farms. "When, at last, the land worn out, would refuse to yield, they would invest their money in something else; by then, they would all have made fortunes."

The heyday of California wheat farming lasted only a few decades, passing just as quickly as the Gold Rush. By the turn of the twentieth century, growers were abandoning wheat in favor of high-value specialty crops: grapes, stone fruit, citrus. Still, those years of bonanza wheat farming would shape the character of California agriculture for centuries to come, through the spring morning nearly 150 years later, when I signed my lease and stepped into the story.

↜ 3 ↝

Before Ryan and I could legally use the word *organic* to describe our produce, we needed to undergo a certification process to ensure we met the official USDA organic standards. So that first fall I began filling out paperwork, paying the many fees, digging up county pesticide application records to prove no prohibited chemicals had been recently applied, and preparing for an inspection. We hoped to obtain official organic status by the time we opened the farm stand the following spring so that we could paint *organic* on our signs without violating the law.

From the dozens of certifying agencies out there, I chose the one I was most familiar with: California Certified Organic Farmers, more commonly called CCOF. I knew from my time living near its headquarters in Santa Cruz that this agency was the first of its kind, and since its inception in 1973 it has been a central force in the US organic movement.

Nearly all the other farms Ryan and I knew or had worked at used CCOF. Those that didn't chose not to certify at all. Some believed the process was corrupt, a moneymaking scam that had long been co-opted by Big Ag. Others found the fees and recordkeeping requirements too burdensome. Some simply didn't see the point: *Our customers know who we are, they see our fields, they trust us—they don't need an official stamp from a bunch of bureaucrats.*

The certification process was indeed laborious, especially for a diversified operation such as ours, and we considered forgoing the official designation. Our practices would be the same whether we were certified or not and we believed, like many of the other small farmers I knew, that our customers would choose to buy our produce because they knew who we were, not because of a fancy stamp on our packaging. But if we wanted to sell wholesale to grocery stores or restaurants, we wouldn't be able to get the price premium for organic unless we had the certification. I also felt that going through the process was a kind of initiation, a hurdle that, once cleared, would give our farm a measure of legitimacy. I was eager to prove that we weren't just some hobby farm—we were professional organic producers.

The application consisted of a thick stack of papers called an Organic Systems Plan. The OSP was divided into eight sections, each covering one aspect of the farming process—soil fertility, inputs, handling—and comprising a series of questions to determine how the farm aligned with the organic standards as defined by CCOF and the USDA's National Organic Program. There were pages of questions about how one planned to mitigate erosion or manage pests in storage areas. What about wildlife corridors and the post-harvest handling of crops? A whole lot of attention was given to the exact font sizes and color schemes of the organic insignia used on any product label (for example, "if both the USDA seal and the certifier seal are displayed, the USDA seal must be more prominent").

I listed the materials and brand names of all the possible soil amendments we might use, making sure they were on the list of approved organic inputs—compost, fish emulsion, blood meal. I drew detailed maps of the farm, assigning each half-acre section a number, delineating exactly where in the barn the yet-to-be-built washing and storage stations would be, printing out an example of our delivery label complete with all the required information in the right size fonts. Reading through my entries now, the eager assuredness of those early days oozes from the language. "South Fork Farm provides the community of El Dorado County with locally grown organic produce while maintaining and improving the health of the South Fork American River watershed and surrounding ecosystems," I'd written in response to question 1.1A (*Please help us understand your operation*). Our goals, I declared, were "to provide an alternative to conventionally grown produce for El Dorado County residents, to establish a sustainable diversified vegetable farm, to offer on-farm opportunities for community participation and education."

Despite the volume of paperwork, as I worked my way through the application and inspection it became clear that there were actually few ways to be denied organic status. These boiled down to breaking one of the hard-and-fast rules pertaining to inputs: No noncertified organic seeds (unless you can prove there is no organic alternative available), and no GMO seeds under any circumstance. No herbicides or pesticides not found on the National Organic Program's list of approved inputs. And, perhaps the most elemental component of organic agriculture: no synthetic fertilizers.

❧

The world's most generously applied fertilizer, used at a rate of more than 115 million tons per year, is synthetic nitrogen. An essential nutrient for plant growth, nitrogen is one of the earth's most abundant elements, comprising 78 percent of our atmosphere. But there's a catch: In its atmospheric form, nitrogen (N_2) is made up of two atoms bound so tightly together that the molecule is rendered nonreactive. In other words, this plentiful molecule filling the air is entirely useless to a plant. It's a water-water-everywhere-but-not-a-drop-to-drink kind of situation.

For a plant to access atmospheric nitrogen, the two atoms must first be broken apart, or "fixed." This feat requires tremendous energy. Lightning can do it, but more commonly it is achieved through the much more modest work of millions of nitrogen-fixing bacteria. These bacteria use an enzyme known as nitrogenase to break apart the bonds and transform atmospheric nitrogen into ammonia, which can then enter the soil where it is readily taken up by plants.

Long before people came to understand the chemistry of all this, farmers around the world implemented methods to replenish the nitrogen in their fields. Crop rotations with legumes (which have a symbiotic relationship with nitrogen-fixing bacteria) helped return nitrogen to the soil, as did the application of animal manure. Fallow periods allowed time for nitrogen to build up again. For much of human history, this was enough. But as agrarian societies began to shift into industrial ones and people left rural areas for cities, new off-farm markets for agricultural goods began to grow, providing an increasing impetus for farmers to seek higher yields, and, in turn, more nitrogen.

The few natural stores of fixed nitrogen found on the planet were quickly exploited: bat guano from the caves of Peru, sodium nitrate—known as "white gold"—mined from Chile. People began to turn the by-products of slaughterhouses and fishing industries—blood meal and fish emulsion—into commercial fertilizers. In the late 1800s it was discovered that fixed nitrogen emitted by coal furnaces used in the manufacturing of iron and steel could be captured for use as fertilizer. But none of these sources was cheap enough or accessible enough to allow for widespread application. It wouldn't be until the middle of the twentieth century that an industrial process for manufacturing synthetic fixed nitrogen was perfected, resulting in a cheap and near-limitless supply of fertilizer.

Today, more than twice as much fixed nitrogen is manufactured synthetically than is produced via all the world's biological processes combined. The production process of this synthetic nitrogen is now a major contributor to greenhouse gas emissions. Its overuse has resulted in dead zones in the world's oceans, increased air pollution, loss of biodiversity in places where ecological balance has been altered by excess nitrogen, and widespread contamination of groundwater and drinking water in industrial agricultural communities.

In organic agriculture, use of synthetic nitrogen fertilizer is prohibited. Instead, biological processes are actively managed to replenish nitrogen and create a fertile soil, which in turn provides the foundation for disease resistance, pest management, and yield increases. In the spaces on the CCOF packet asking the applicant to detail her "fertility plan," I described the organic methods for maintaining soil health that Ryan and I had learned over the years from the farmers we'd worked with and books we'd read, many of which had been first explained and popularized by Sir Albert Howard: planting leguminous cover crops, incorporating unharvested plant materials (like tomato vines or wheat straw) back into the field, and applying annual loads of compost.

At the time I completed the paperwork I had yet to actually begin implementing our plan, but I gamely filled in the blanks as if completing a test I'd long studied for. In response to question 1 of section 4.0 A, *Describe your "rotation" plan*, I wrote: "A well-designed crop rotation is our most important tool for managing pests and maintaining soil fertility. We plan to structure our rotation so that each crop is preceded in the field by a crop that is botanically unrelated, does not share the same nutrient requirements, and is not predisposed to the same diseases and/or pests. To facilitate this practice, we grow a diverse variety of crops and include grains, vegetables, and nitrogen-fixing cover crops in our rotation." I detailed the contents of our cover-crop mix, recorded the supplier of the compost we would apply by the transfer load each year.

If I'd crunched the numbers on all this, added up the cost of certified organic compost ($750); certified organic cover-crop seed ($700); and the fuel required to spread the compost, broadcast the seed, mow the cover crop in spring, and disk it under, I would have calculated the annual expense of all this (not counting the time and labor involved) to be upwards of $200 per acre per year. If I'd instead purchased synthetic nitrogen at around 30 cents per pound—a price that does not, of course, include the ecological and societal cost of producing this chemical—and applied it at the generous rate of 100 pounds per acre, my cost would have been somewhere around $30 per acre, or $300 for the whole farm.

↫ 4 ↬

One winter evening, after a day spent seeding in the greenhouse—flats of onions, spring brassicas, spinach—Ryan and I drove to my parents' house for dinner. We ate pasta and drank wine. After the meal I wiped down the kitchen counters while my mother loaded plates into the dishwasher. A Neil Young record streamed softly from the living room. Dishes clinked. I carried a pan to the sink, but when I handed it to my mother the handle wobbled. "My dad would hate to see that," she said, scrubbing it by hand and rinsing it clean. I lifted the pan from the drying rack, then dug around in a drawer for a tool and began tightening the screw. Without looking up, I asked my mother what happened after my grandfather, armed with his machete, had failed to find her and my dad in San Francisco all those years ago. "Did he just get over it?"

My mother didn't answer right away. "Well," she finally said, then paused as if the question had stumped her. She dried her hands and walked out of the kitchen, disappearing down the hall toward her bedroom. A moment later she returned carrying an envelope. She lifted the flap, peered inside, nodded, then began to talk.

After she and my father were certain my grandfather had gone home to LA, my mother explained, they left the friend's house where they'd been hiding and returned to my mother's apartment. There, wedged into the crack of the locked door, she found an envelope. She pulled out a note and read it quickly. Then she folded it back up and tucked it into a drawer before collecting some books and heading to her next pharmacy class.

The note survived the thirty-five years between that moment and the evening my mother slid it out of the envelope to show it to me. The note was handwritten on a ripped sheet of lined paper, the letters jagged, written decidedly in English. Though some of the words were misspelled, the message was clear. The note told my mother that she had shamed her family, destroyed their reputation and honor. She would no longer be considered a daughter. There was only one Punjabi word on the page, hovering above the signature. I pointed to the letters, asked my mother what they spelled. She thought for a minute, trying to find an English equivalent. "Doomed," she said at last. He'd signed the letter "your doomed father."

After she found the note, my mother called her sister to see how their parents were doing back home in LA. It was then she learned that while her father had been away, her mother had stopped eating. She'd gotten into bed and refused to get up. I imagined my grandparents' home during those days: my grandfather missing, my grandmother lying in bed beneath a wool shawl. A pot of dal goes cold on the stove, begins to ferment. A stack of buttered roti grows stale inside a towel-lined tin. Atop the counter a dusting of turmeric lingers like pollen dropped from a flower.

My grandmother remained in bed this way for several days, my mother told me. Soon she complained of voices in the room, of something like an evil spirit bewitching the house. Eventually, my grandfather took her to a hospital and she was diagnosed with having suffered a psychotic break.

But even the news of my grandmother's ill health did not sway my mother's resolve to marry my father. After a few days, my grandmother was prescribed antipsychotics and released from the hospital. Shortly thereafter, she informed my mother she was coming to visit and boarded a plane to San Francisco with a rolled-up mat beneath her arm. My mother, concerned for her mother's well-being and hopeful for a chance to begin to repair the frayed relationship, picked her up at the airport and brought her back to her home. In my mother's living room, my grandmother unfurled her mat across the floor, then sat cross-legged on it, pulled her scarf up around her head, and settled in. She pleaded with my mother, implored her to cancel the wedding, warned her of the ruin she would bring to herself and her family otherwise, and refused to move. Still, my mother declined to cancel and after two days managed to drag my grandmother off the mat, drive her back to the airport, and get her a return ticket home. By the time my grandmother's plane touched ground in LA, my mother had been disowned.

⟿ 5 ⟾

Spring arrived and the days stretched long. The winter had been dry, marking the second consecutive year of exceedingly low precipitation. Still, enough rain had fallen to keep our cover crop and wheat growing, and I was too caught up in the bustle of that first season to pay much notice to the worsening drought. Our greenhouse filled with seedlings. Tomatoes, eggplants, peppers. Ten thousand onions. Twenty flats of broccoli. Zinnias and sunflowers. Outside, the Sonora wheat, now awakened from its winter dormancy, resumed gaining height each day, surpassing the weeds that had begun to germinate with the warmer days; star-thistle and bindweed, Bermuda grass and amaranth. It was the tallest crop on the farm.

One afternoon, a truck with the official county seal on the door pulled into our driveway. A woman stepped out and introduced herself as an inspector for the department of agriculture. She cleared her throat, then informed me that my neighbor was planning to spray herbicides along her driveway bordering my southernmost field and had attained a permit from the county. "It's her right to do so," the inspector said, and if I didn't want to lose my organic certification I'd need to create a 75-foot-wide "buffer zone" along the perimeter of my land to prevent the chemicals from drifting onto my crops.

I looked across to the southern field where the Sonora wheat stood nearly three feet tall and imagined mowing a section of it down. I'd planted the wheat in a 200-foot-wide strip tracing the fence line. I would lose a third of the crop. Later, I looked through my organic handbook to verify the ag inspector's assertion that it was my responsibility to create a "buffer zone."

"Buffer zones," the CCOF handbook read, "must be sufficient to prevent contamination of organic land or crops by prohibited substances, including contact with products produced by genetic engineering (GMO). Producers must IMMEDIATELY notify CCOF of any known application or drift of a prohibited material to a field or product. Fields or farms where organic products are produced must have distinct, defined boundaries and buffer zones to prevent contact with the land or crop by prohibited substances applied to adjoining non-organic land."

I'd not yet met this neighbor when the ag inspector informed me of her plans to spray, but I'd been told she belonged to one of the most long-standing ranching families on Gold Hill, that her family had owned the land behind my farm, along with large chunks of the surrounding region, since the late 1800s. Though no one lived on that land now, she and her husband raised a small herd of cattle there and used a gravel road bordering our fence line to access it. I envied this woman's deeply rooted connection to her land. Most mornings that first summer I woke early, watched the dawn blush across the shallow bowl that held our ten acres, and wished that I, like my neighbor, could say this land had been in my family for generations, that it belonged to me and I to it. But I was the daughter of a pharmacist and a property manager. Neither had ever so much as worked on a farm, and both were transplants to the area—my mother from India, my father from Los Angeles.

My neighbor drove past our farm often. I would hear her white truck bumping slowly along the fence line before disappearing into the oaks. Then, the clanging of a gate, the low moans of cows. At first I hoped she might stop to say hello, or offer a nod in my direction. When months passed and this didn't happen, I worried that she resented us. Ryan and I were newcomers. We were young and organic. Worse still, we'd leased our ten acres from a land conservancy. When the land conservancy had first purchased the Veerkamp ranch, they'd terminated all existing grazing leases, furthering the tension between environmentalists and ranchers that had long festered in our county. "Now the environmentalists think they invented farming," I'd overheard the owner of the local farm supply store say not long after Ryan and I had arrived. Like my neighbor, this man belonged to a family with longstanding roots in agriculture in the region. Now he made his living selling supplies—mostly five-gallon buckets of Roundup herbicide to homeowners and hobby orchardists—instead of growing pears.

After the ag inspector's visit, I waited for my neighbor to drive past so that I could gather the courage to wave her down and introduce myself. Weeks passed and I didn't see her until one afternoon I looked up from my kitchen sink where I was rinsing lunch dishes, and there in our driveway a few hundred feet outside my window sat her white truck. My neighbor stepped out of the cab and began walking toward me, carrying something bundled in her arms. I met her in my front yard.

"Found this cat out on the road by your farm," she said. "Looks like it just got hit." The woman didn't introduce herself, and neither did I— we each knew who the other was. Ryan and I owned two cats, the one we'd brought with us to the farm and another we'd adopted in the hopes she might help mitigate the rat problem around our house. I looked closely at this cat, wrapped up in a flannel work shirt, bloodied but still alive, to determine if it was one of ours. It wasn't, but I'd seen this cat before. Yellow-eyed and ash gray, the stray had hung around my barn and hunted among my neighbor's pasture, heedless of the fences between our lands.

"That's not my cat," I said. The woman said nothing. Her eyes were not cold, as I'd come to imagine them, nor resentful. "No, not mine," I repeated. The woman stared gently at me as if my words were irrelevant until I realized they were. The cat belonged to neither of us, but it had been hit and abandoned in front of my farm on a road we shared. So here we were, standing together in my driveway with a dying cat swaddled in a work shirt. I looked down at my boots, embarrassed at what I'd said, as if I thought I could simply choose which parts of a place belonged to me and which did not.

"I'll take it," I said, and my neighbor held the bundle out to me like a casserole. I lifted the animal into my arms. It was clear the cat wouldn't survive much longer. Freed of the animal's small weight, the woman pushed her fingers into her pockets. "All right," she said softly. Then, "Thanks."

The cat died shortly after, and that evening I looked for somewhere to bury it. No place seemed right. At last I chose a ribbon of no-man's-land sandwiched between the neighbor's line of barbed wire and my deer fence—one strip of land, it seemed, we shared.

The next week my neighbor's truck appeared in my driveway again. Without stepping out of the cab, she told me she had an extra washing machine. "Could you use it?" she asked. "It's almost brand new." When I told her we didn't need one, but I appreciated the offer, she didn't drive away. She wiped a layer of dust from the car's clock with the pad of her thumb and told me why she planned to spray along her driveway: fire danger. "Come summer, one stray spark and those weeds would kindle a fire in no time." The woman put her truck in gear, then added, the truck already rolling forward, "If you want to go over to my side of the fence and mow the weeds down instead, you're welcome to." I watched her truck wind out of sight, not sure if the woman had been doing me a favor, or asking for one.

At dusk I held open the gate while Ryan drove our tractor up the road and onto the neighbor's driveway. In the pearly light he lowered the mower blade and drove along the fence line, leaving behind a wake of fallen weeds.

❧ 6 ❧

O n the last Friday in April, 2013, nearly a year after we'd arrived on the property, Ryan and I opened our farm stand for business. We woke before dawn and sat on our front porch steps with mugs of steaming coffee and toast spread thick with peanut butter. A full moon hung low in the still-black sky and the chill of the concrete seeped through my jeans. I shivered, though I knew in a few hours I'd be sweating under the midmorning sun. In the distance, our fields lay in darkness and I could make out only the glint of irrigation pipes, the curve of our hoophouses, a glimmer of moonlight on the wheat.

Before I'd even finished my coffee the jitters set in. Earlier in the week, we'd packed and dispensed the first of the CSA boxes for the year. For a few months we'd been making small wholesale deliveries of early-season produce—spring salad mix, radishes, baby arugula—to restaurants and the local natural foods co-op. But today would be the first time we'd stock the farm stand, open the gate to the newly graveled parking lot, and hope for customers to stream in.

Over the winter Ryan and I had created the retail space inside the barn. We framed walls around one corner to construct a small room and cut a doorway to the outside. Ryan built a garage-size wooden door that slid open on a steel track to let ample light flood in. I painted signs on slabs of cedar: *South Fork Farm Stand. Organic Produce.* We lined the space with tilted shelves, built wood display boxes to fit on top, bought a glass-doored fridge to keep tender vegetables cool.

The previous day, Ryan and I had harvested what produce could be picked ahead—new potatoes and spring onions, beets and carrots—and tucked it all into the walk-in cooler for the night. The bulk of the harvesting would be done that morning—collard greens and cut salad mix, arugula and radishes, Swiss chard and lacinato kale, cut flowers. I finished my coffee, pulled on my boots, and walked with Ryan down the hill as the black sky gave way to blue.

By nine o'clock, the shelves were heaped with produce, the fridge was filled with bagged salad mix, and a dozen mason jars held spring flower bouquets: blue bachelor's buttons and orange calendulas, coreopsis and lavender. I unlocked the gate and flipped the roadside sign from *closed* to *open*. Before I'd even made it back to the barn, a car pulled in.

At the end of the day, most everything had been sold. We put the remaining produce in the cooler and sat on camp chairs in the shade of the barn, then opened the cash box and counted the money. The total came to just shy of $600. Six hundred dollars! We didn't think to subtract anything—not the lease payment, the cost of seed, water, fuel, packaging, electricity, certification, soil amendments. Certainly not our own labor. We just zipped the stack of bills into a bank bag and felt the bulk of it inside.

❧ 7 ❧

In the seventeenth century, while Sonora wheat was thriving across regions of northern Mexico and in what was not yet the American West, British colonists landed on the continent's eastern shores and attempted to establish settlements and farms. Planting crops using seeds carried from England, they struggled to produce a single head of wheat. It wasn't only these early wheat crops that failed miserably, but nearly everything else the colonists tried to grow. They survived instead on the foods—squash, beans, corn—that were already being successfully cultivated by Native Americans.

Urgently in need of plant varieties better suited to their new environs, the colonists sought new seed anywhere they could find it. They implored sailor relatives and friends in faraway lands to collect and send planting stock, and they traded with neighboring colonists and Native Americans. Each new influx of settlers arrived with new seeds from their various homelands. Enslaved people and ship captains, too, carried seeds.

After independence, this widespread collecting and importing of new planting stock became a central duty of the new American government. "The greatest service which can be rendered any country is to add an useful plant to it's culture; especially a bread grain," Thomas Jefferson wrote in his 1800 summary of public service. Not long after, in 1819, US military and consul officers were ordered to collect seeds from their posts in foreign lands. A series of navy plant exploration expeditions obtained, sometimes by force, new planting stock from all over the world. These seeds were then distributed to American farmers who experimented widely, swapping seeds with one another, and sowing a diversity of varieties side by side. Much like their human cultivators, plant varieties from disparate regions of the world found themselves suddenly rubbing shoulders with one another on American farms. Natural crosses ensued, producing huge variability in their offspring. Farmers, enacting the age-old breeding process now called "simple mass selection," picked through this variability to save seeds from the plants that performed the best. In this way, over many decades, well-adapted varieties with far-reaching pedigrees emerged to form the foundations of American agriculture.

⤙⤚

Today, most wheat commercially produced in the United States can trace its ancestry back to one of two pivotal early varieties: Turkey and Marquis. Turkey was brought to Kansas in 1873 by Mennonite immigrants from Russia. Seeking religious freedom and lured by the Santa Fe Railroad's advertisements for the vast tracts of land it owned in the Great Plains, these immigrants came to America with the seed from their last wheat harvest. It thrived in the local climate, greatly expanding the wheat-producing capabilities of the United States.

Marquis's origin story begins sometime in 1842 when a ship arrived in Scotland, carrying among its cargo a barrel of wheat seed originating—depending on the source—in Ukraine or Poland. Here, as the story goes, a man passing by dipped his hat into the barrel to collect a bit of seed. He then sent this seed to a friend in Canada, a farmer named David Fife, who planted it in Ontario. Pleased with this new wheat's performance in his fields, Fife saved seed from the best stalks, sowing, selecting, and sowing year after year until he had a stable variety, which he named Red Fife.

Soon after, another ship, this one bound for Canada, held in its hold wheat seeds purchased at a market in Calcutta. The seeds were named after that city, though in fact they had originated a thousand miles north in the wheat fields of Punjab. In Canada, breeders crossed Calcutta and Red Fife to produce a new hard red spring wheat that proved exceptional. This new variety, Marquis, was acquired by the USDA in 1912 and quickly became the most extensively planted spring wheat in America, remaining so for nearly two decades.

Countless varieties contributed to the genetics of the modern wheat crop, and not all origin stories are as well documented as these. A glance through the 1939 edition of "Classification of Wheat Varieties Grown in the United States," a series of technical bulletins produced by the USDA, offers some insight into the uncertainties that persist. In regard to a wheat called Java—one of the first spring wheats to be grown in America and a variety that proved important in later breeding efforts due to its genetic resistance to Hessian fly—the bulletin includes many conflicting origin stories. One claims it came from Switzerland. The next attests that a New York merchant had found six or seven kernels in a chest of black tea and planted it out. And yet another source asserts this wheat was first introduced by a "woman who was roasting some Java coffee [and] found among it a grain of wheat, which she planted; saved the product and planted again, and so on for 3 years, when she distributed the seed among her friends, who all reported that it was an excellent variety."

"The introduction of plants into America has been much more than a great service; it has been an absolute imperative," writes the political scientist Jack Ralph Kloppenburg, "a biological *sine qua non* upon which rests the whole complex edifice of American industrial society." American farms are often heralded as emblems of self-reliance and independence. But a closer look at the seeds upon which they depend reveals instead a map of interconnection linking each field and farmer to a web of others, far flung and nearby.

❧ 8 ❧

Tucked into a cheap frame atop a side table at my grandparents'
house is an old photo of my mother and my grandmother from the
1970s. It is the only picture I've ever seen of my grandmother wearing
Western clothes. In it the two women stand shoulder to shoulder, both
squinting slightly as the sun illuminates their faces. They are dressed in
typical seventies outfits—my mother in high-waisted bell-bottom jeans
and a close-fitting sweater covered in mauve zigzags, my grandmother in
blue polyester slacks and a brightly striped tunic. Both wear sandals and
wide close-lipped smiles, their long black hair pulled back from their
faces. They look young, happy with themselves, as if they share a secret.
They look like sisters.

This was before my mother's marriage. Sometime in the years after,
my grandmother got rid of her Western clothes. I'm not sure if she tossed
them out altogether or tucked them into the back of a drawer, but I've
never seen any sign of them. She resumed wearing only traditional salwar kameez and, I've been told, brought a new vigor to practicing the
rest of her traditions. She cooked dal and subji in giant steel pots and
carried the food to the Sikh temple. She chopped hundreds of lemons to
make achar, packed them into gallon jars with ginger and cayenne, tablespoons of salt. She boiled milk for fresh yogurt each night, and ground
coriander and cloves, cinnamon and cardamom into garam masala. She
swiftly arranged marriages for two of her remaining children, and waited
for my mother—whose marriage she refused to acknowledge—to return
home with news that she had left her American man and was ready to
agree to an Indian husband.

During these years, my grandmother had her back porch enclosed
to make a room devoted to prayer, a home temple. She watched as the
walls were Sheetrocked, carpet was stretched over the floor, lights were
installed. When the room was finished she hung paintings of Sikh gurus
on the walls, decorated the ceiling with shiny garlands, and spread

intricately crocheted blankets and silk fabrics across a bed-like platform. When everything was in place, she informed the gurdwara that she and my grandfather had committed to observing strict Sikh practices and were ready to undertake the responsibility of performing the daily rituals required to become caretakers of the sacred text, the Guru Granth Sahib. The book was brought in and set in place on the bed. From then on, she and my grandfather carried out the required rituals each day. My grandmother prepared an offering of hot paratha and cha in the morning and they took turns reading the scriptures and carefully covering the book each evening.

Meanwhile, my disowned mother proceeded to disown her Punjabi heritage. I imagine her gathering up the remnants of the culture she'd come from—language, religion, food, attire—in the way she cleaned out our fridge when I was a kid: tossing all the spoiled food—rinds of moldy cheese and cilantro gone slimy—into the trash bin without a second glance, then returning with a rag to wipe the shelves clean. By the time I was old enough to look for traces of my mother's past, scarcely any of it remained.

⌁

It was the news of my mother's first pregnancy that convinced my grandparents to at last acknowledge their eldest daughter's marriage. Perhaps they were settled enough in their LA community now to believe they would survive whatever social ostracizing might ensue, or perhaps they simply had to choose the lesser of two disgraces: a daughter pregnant out of wedlock, or a daughter married to a white man. They invited her back into the fold, held a small Indian wedding (five years into her marriage), and over time amiable enough relations ensued between my grandparents and their daughter and son-in-law. My mother, however, seemed to have no intention of rescinding her own act of disowning.

By then, the early 1980s, my mother was officially an American, having obtained her citizenship in 1978. She possessed a doctorate in pharmacy from the University of California; the deed to a house and 4,000 square feet of American soil, owned with her white husband; and a driver's license with her smiling face adjacent to the seal of California: the Golden State, land of freedom and reinvention, where power resided not in remembering but in forgetting.

She raised her two daughters accordingly. My sister and I were to be capable and independent, unencumbered by tradition, by the expectations of others, by the weight of history. She never spoke of when she was fifteen and a new immigrant, rarely mentioned her childhood in Punjab and Nairobi. Outside of learning to count to ten and the few bad words we picked up from our cousins, my sister and I were taught none of our mother's native language. We weren't given Indian names—not even middle names—nor did we learn the name of the village in India where my mother was born, or why her family left and who they left behind, or what their lives were like there. Instead our gaze was directed toward the future, where we were free to pursue the lives we wanted. In turn, we were held accountable for whatever successes or failures we amassed.

"Boredom," my mother told me when I was a child and complained of having nothing to do, "is a state of mind." Other times, when I lazily feigned an inability to carry a stack of dishes to the table, or halfheartedly went through the motions of scrubbing the oily film from a pan—"*I'm trying*," I'd whine—she'd look at me squarely and say, "Don't try. Just do." My mother didn't accept the notion of an accident. She seemed to believe the term was simply a euphemism and that the thing should be called instead what it was: a mistake. If a waiter delivered an incorrect order or something about a garment struck her as unsatisfactory, she sent it back. If she sliced open an avocado and found the inside blotched brown and rotting, she put the halves together, slipped the fruit into a bag with the receipt, and returned it to the store. Once, when I was in middle school, she caught wind of the fact that my teacher had a certain ineptitude when it came to explaining the workings of algebra variables. After several afternoons spent walking me through my homework assignments, she appeared in my classroom to "volunteer" one morning. To my excruciating embarrassment, she returned week after week during math period, sitting with each work group of thirteen-year-olds until she'd made certain that every student in my class could solve for x.

For most of my life, I blamed the years following my mother's marriage—that time of dual disownment—for the rupture that left me severed from my heritage. I hadn't considered that the origins of this estrangement might stretch much further back than I could then imagine.

❧ 9 ❧

Spring, 1900. Here lies yet another starting place, another beginning for the story of wheat, and this one with all the right trappings for a fresh start: a new century, bright optimism, a feeling of having transcended the limits of an old era and stepping boldly into a new one.

In this year three European biologists, each working independently, publish papers describing their observations of the natural laws governing genetic inheritance in plants—discoveries, it turns out, that had been delineated nearly four decades earlier in a study previously ignored. This older study, published by the Austrian monk Gregor Mendel in 1865, focused on the hybridization of peas and explained how genetic traits are passed from one generation to the next—what we now know as Mendel's laws of inheritance. Mendel's concepts—things like dominance and recessiveness—are now so well established they seem almost self-evident, making it difficult to imagine a time when such ideas were not well understood. We know them even if we don't know what to call them: two blue-eyed parents are not likely to make a brown-eyed baby.

But until the early 1900s, the workings of heredity remained mysterious. Farmers and botanists around the world had successfully created new, improved varieties by saving seed from plants with desired qualities, but no one yet understood the principles guiding genetic inheritance—how and why certain traits passed from one generation to the next while others did not—and thus plant breeding efforts remained limited and largely up to chance.

The rediscovery of Mendel's work gave scientists the tools to more accurately predict the outcome of any cross. Thus, by purposefully crossing plants to produce offspring with favorable traits, breeders could systematically develop new varieties to serve their needs.

At the time of Mendel's studies, "plant breeding" was an activity relegated to the few individuals who took up an interest in what was then an esoteric field. Educational programs in the subject did not exist, nor did any major governmental institutions dedicated to this kind of work. The selection and propagation of plant varieties was simply part of the craft of farming, carried out by the cultivators themselves, who saved seeds from the plants that performed best in their fields and were most suitable to their unique needs as growers and eaters.

Today plant breeding is a major science and a formidable industry. Plant breeders have been awarded the Nobel Peace Prize. They are funded by the world's largest and most well-resourced governments and philanthropic organizations, and their work is the focus of some of the most powerful multinational corporations.

Whether or not anyone foresaw the place of prominence plant breeding would one day hold—of how it would slip from the hands of farmers into those of "breeders"—scientists at the dawn of the twentieth century recognized the gates of a frontier opening. At the 1902 International Conference of Plant Breeding and Hybridization, William Bateson, the English scientist who would soon coin the term *genetics*, spoke of the modern breeder newly furnished with the knowledge of Mendel's laws of inheritance: "[A breeder] will be able to do what he wants," Bateson said, "instead of merely what happens to turn up."

The rediscovery of Mendel's laws elevated the value of seeds: these held the raw materials—genes—from which new, improved varieties could be created. Where a pivotal gene—one containing a rare disease resistance or unique growth habit—might be found was anyone's guess. In the years between 1900 and 1930 the USDA upped its seed-collecting efforts, sponsoring more than fifty expeditions to amass plant genetic material from all over the world.

In a biography of one of the more famous of these American "plant hunters," a man named Frank Meyer, I find a 1908 photo taken in Wu Tai Shan, China. Meyer stands on a rocky mountainside, Davy Crockett-esque with a walking stick and knee-high lace-up boots, a proud furrow on his brow and sacks of plant material at his side. A conqueror's stance. Below the photo, a quote from his accompanying letter reads: "Returning from a successful raid in the high mountains, tired but satisfied."

The seeds these plant hunters brought back to America were distributed to farmers and breeders, and the USDA cataloged and stored them in a network of seed banks. This network would eventually become the National Plant Germplasm System, the institution from which, nearly a century later, Monica Spiller would request a sample of Sonora wheat seed.

⊷ 10 ⊷

My mother was planning another drive down to LA that spring to visit her family for a few nights. By then, our Sonora stalks reached higher than my hips. Soon they would start to flower, and then set seed. I wanted to ask my grandmother what she remembered about the wheat of her own childhood: Had it been pale yellow or reddish brown in color? Did it produce flour different from the flour she now bought in California? A distinct flavor, texture, aroma? So, nearly a year after the last visit when I'd failed to accept my grandmother's pearls, I joined my mother for another trip to LA.

The day after we arrived, I returned from a walk around my grandparents' neighborhood and found my mother in the kitchen filling a tea ball she'd brought from home with green tea leaves, also from home. Meanwhile a pot of cha—black tea, a pinch of fennel seeds, two cracked cardamom pods, and milk—simmered on the stovetop for my grandparents. I asked if she could help facilitate a conversation between my grandmother and me.

"I just want to ask Naniji some things about the wheat she remembers from her village, back in India. You know, the flour her family used." I felt childish asking my mother to help me talk with my own grandmother, but without her translation I was afraid I wouldn't get far.

My mother shrugged. "Sure," she said, and switched off the stove. She poured two dainty mugs of steaming cha. There was some left in the pot and she lifted it toward me. I nodded and she filled another cup. Then she stirred a teaspoon of sugar into each, and together we carried the tea into the sitting room where we expected to find my grandparents together.

Instead my grandfather sat alone on a couch facing the TV. An Indian movie played on the screen, the dialogue barely audible. He took his cha from my mother, then motioned for me to set the other cup on the coffee table. "Your Naniji will be back soon, she is on the phone."

We sat sipping quietly for a moment, then my mother looked to her father.

"Dad," my mother said. "Jackie has some questions about India, about your village."

"Aahcha?" my grandfather said, looking into his cha. He lifted the cup to his mouth, took a sip, and turned to face the TV. On the screen two women with silky hair and kohl-lined eyes stood on a balcony overlooking a busy marketplace. After a moment he muttered something quietly in Punjabi.

"Oh, I don't know," my mother said, "she wants to know about the wheat, if you can remember it. Just tell her anything you want. And in English, so she can understand."

"Aahcha. OK," he said, glancing from my mother to me, then back to the TV. I tried to catch my mother's gaze, to shake my head, mouth, *It's OK, nevermind*. But she was still looking at her father, waiting for him to speak, and when he didn't, she said, "What was it like where you grew up? Do you remember the wheat?"

He stared into his cup and spoke in soft, swift English. "Where I am from, the village is called Mohem. In the north, close to Pakistan." He glanced up at me and I nodded. "When I was a boy, it was all the same— Pakistan, India, everything was British." He looked uncomfortable, as if he wanted to stop talking but now that he'd begun was bound by some unseen force to finish. "Then, 1947. I am fifteen years old, the British leave and make the partition." My grandfather lifted his free hand and held it out in front of him. His fingers were slender and long, knobbed with burls of knuckles, bare except for one thick gold band. They looked, it occurred to me, just like my mother's. He moved his hand slowly forward as if driving a wedge through soil. "Here is the line. India, one side," he said, "Pakistan, other side."

Just then, my grandmother's shadow fell across the coffee table. I turned to see her standing behind me in the doorway. Her eyes shifted from husband to daughter to granddaughter. She parted her lips as if she might say something, then pursed them tight and stepped into the room. She settled herself on the couch next to me, lifted her teacup, and faced the TV.

For another long moment no one spoke. A murmur of voices chortled from the screen, followed by cheery high-pitched singing. Everyone on the TV was smiling, but at such a low volume the song seemed almost melancholic.

My grandfather looked from the TV to me, cleared his throat. "I was fifteen years old," he said again, each word in slow, deliberate English. "It was a very bad time. So much fighting." He turned to face his lap, as if peering deep into the cup of tea held there.

"Whole villages set on fire. Nobody was safe. In my village, every night, someone must stay awake to keep watch." My grandfather's voice, always quiet, grew quieter as he spoke, as if he were moving slowly away from us. He began to describe a rooftop where he sat up one night to keep watch. From there he could see far out into the distance, across miles of flat fields. There was a bell tower on the roof, from which hung a rope. If he spotted any sign of danger he was to ring the bell in warning. At some point in the night, my grandfather saw a group approaching in the distance. He pulled the rope and the bell clanged. But the men were not deterred. From the rooftop he watched the men set fire to his village. Even as he clanged the bell he could hear screaming.

As he spoke my grandfather had grown deathly still, so when his voice caught in his throat and his shoulders jerked forward the movement was so sudden that my first thought was of the heart attack my mother often worried about. My mother reached for her father's hand. "Dad," she said. "Are you OK?"

Only my grandmother recognized her husband's motions. "He is crying," she said flatly, a told-you-so frown curling the corners of her mouth as if to say, *And what did you expect?*

My grandfather withdrew his hand from my mother's grasp and released three audible sobs—the only unrestrained sounds I'd ever heard him utter. No one moved. A minute passed. Then my grandfather lifted his hand to wipe his face and my mother tentatively laid her arms around his shoulders. He did not return the embrace, not quite, but simply patted my mother's arm.

Soon my grandfather regained his composure. He was no longer crying, but his head remained low. My mother slid back across the couch and wiped her own eyes. When my grandfather spoke again he did so in Punjabi, his gaze fixed on his lap, his tone once again a controlled murmur. He told my mother a few details she would relay to me later—how entire families, old people, men, women, and children, were dragged out of hiding and killed, babies were put into fires—and soon the conversation ceased. Everyone's eyes returned to the TV, where the same two women sipped lassi from straws and whispered conspiratorially to one another. A moment later everyone except me chuckled at the screen. There were no subtitles. I'd missed the joke.

I left my family in the sitting room and began putting away the last of our lunch dishes. My aunt came in to join everyone on the couch and I could hear the breezy chirp of the three women chatting in a mix of Punjabi and English. The conversation had returned to food—whether or not the dal at lunch had needed more spice, which achar was the best. My grandfather remained silent, then stood and, addressing no one in particular, said, "I am going now to rest." A quiet shred of English slipped into the chatter. He disappeared down the hall and I listened for the click of his door pulling against the frame.

∾

The next day my grandmother told me her own story of Partition. She'd been an eight-year-old girl in the summer of 1947, living in a village in the Lyallpur district of western Punjab. And so, when the line was drawn dividing the region into two separate nations, she found herself suddenly in Pakistan—the wrong side for a Sikh family such as hers. She and her family joined a caravan of migrants traveling eastward by foot to the Indian side. They left everything behind and walked together for several weeks before reaching a small village outside the city of Jalandhar.

"And why did you end up there, in that village?" I asked.

My grandmother looked confused, repeated my phrase. "End up?"

"I mean why did your family stop to settle there—did you know someone?"

"Ah!" my grandmother said, and shook her head. "No, no. We did not *end up* there. No, there is where we start. This village, it is our home."

With my mother translating, my grandmother explained that the journey east after partition was not the first migration her family had undergone. In the 1920s, more than a decade before my grandmother was born, her parents had left their ancestral village in eastern Punjab, migrating west to Lyallpur in pursuit of better work for her father, a laborer who made and mended farm tools. When Partition came two decades later, the family traced the same 180-mile route in reverse. After walking for more than a month, my eight-year-old grandmother and her family—her mother and father, four siblings—reached their ancestral village and the shelter of a relative's house. They had nothing to unpack, all their possessions abandoned in Lyallpur. The first thing they came to own in their new country was a gift from my grandmother's grandmother: a sack of wheat berries.

I didn't ask if the kernels were white or red. Instead I asked what it had been like to walk all that way after Partition. My grandmother looked at me, then down at the table. "Terrible," she said at last. "It was . . ." She paused, took her glasses off to rub the back of her hand over her eye, then put them back on. "It was very long time ago, I don't remember much. I was only eight years old, so, you see, I don't remember." She glanced from my mother to me, then stood, said something in Punjabi, and walked out of the room. When I passed by the sitting room later, she was on the couch with her chunni pulled up over her head. I could see nothing of her face, only a curtain of silk and the book of prayer in her hands.

⬧

Back home, I sat at my desk and googled "Partition." I was familiar only with the most basic facts about Partition and British colonialism in India, remembered from some brushed-over summary in a college history class. Now I read article after article, peered into black-and-white photographs of refugee camps and trains packed with people, attempted to inhale the stories whole. But it was as if I'd had the wind knocked out of me, and despite my efforts I couldn't quite catch my breath. All I could think was: How had I never considered any of this, never realized this history was my own? I'd never considered that the mention of Partition could, nearly seventy years later, bring my own grandfather to tears, that all this time it had been just right there, hardly beneath the surface. I lifted my gaze over the screen to peer out into the night. But the lamplight rendered the window into a mirror, and all I could see was my own reflection.

↤ 11 ↦

One morning not long after returning from LA I typed "Sonora" into the searchable online database of the National Plant Germplasm System, wondering what the entry might tell me about the variety's provenance. It didn't take long to find it among the 500,000 accessions in the system. I clicked the link open and read that the original seed for this cultivar had been acquired in Mexico and added to the USDA's collection in 1907. After some searching, I also located the Punjabi counterpart variety, known by the name Delfi. This accession, the database states, was donated to the USDA in 1915 by the Lyallpur Department of Agriculture, where it had been collected by A.L.C. and G.L.C. Howard. When I first read through this entry, it didn't occur to me to pause at the name of the collectors—Howard. What caught my eye instead was that other name: Lyallpur. The name of the place, I'd just learned, where my grandmother was born.

In the early decades of the twentieth century, I would later learn, Lyallpur—now the Pakistani city of Faisalabad—lay at the heart of Indian wheat production in a region known as the Canal Colonies. Here, in 1885, the British had embarked on a massive endeavor to transform the uncultivated and arid plains of western Punjab into a hub of agricultural productivity that could fuel England's industrial development and growing empire. The region, as the British saw it, was ripe for agricultural development—vast and flat and scarcely populated. There was only one problem: It was a desert. Receiving barely four inches of rain annually, settlements existed only in the slim ribbons of soil directly adjacent to one of the five rivers that wound through the parched landscape. The vast stretches of land in between these waterways, called "bars," were far too dry to support agriculture or permanent settlement, and were instead inhabited by semi-nomadic cattle grazing communities.

"Every tree and bush in the Bar with its stunted growth and gnarled, knotted limbs showed the fight which any living thing had to wage in that desert with a merciless sky. Small wonder that to the inhabitants of the rest of Punjab, the Bar with its pathless, waterless expanse was a *terra incognita*, of which everyone stood in dread," wrote Geoffrey F. de Montmorency, the deputy commissioner of the district of Lyallpur, in a 1908 volume of *The Agriculture Journal of India*. But after a rare rainstorm, the region was "transferred [*sic*] into a rolling plain of grasses...a paradise."

Declaring the region a wasteland and ignoring nomadic occupants, the British constructed what would become one of the most extensive canal systems in the world, one that would carry water from the region's five rivers to the drylands in between. Millions of acres of parched desert were transformed into grids of irrigated fields capable of supporting permanent settlement and vast agriculture, "a country," de Montmorency wrote, "laid out like a chess board."

One important component was still needed in order to fulfill the vision of an agricultural powerhouse: people to work the land. And so in the ensuing decades, farmers and laborers from the neighboring regions of east Punjab were recruited to leave their home villages and migrate to the Canal Colonies, where they could cultivate the abundance of irrigated farmland. And what did those farmers plant? Wheat, of course. "It is the great Colony crop," states an official assessment report from 1909. "Everyone tries to sow and mature as large a wheat area as he can."

Word of the plentiful newly irrigated land and booming agriculture didn't take long to reach the tiny village in east Punjab where my grandmother's father worked as a toolmaker. One morning in the mid-1920s, my great-grandfather and his new wife prepared to join the masses of migrants heading west on foot to Chenab Colony, the largest of the Canal Colonies. When the couple arrived, however, they found that laborers like my great-grandfather were not offered allotments. Instead, land was strategically doled out to influential social classes—wealthy land-owning farmers from other parts of northern India, professional elites, and retired military and government servants—in order to ensure their cooperation with imperial rule. Many land grant agreements included loyalty clauses that required recipients to give "active support of the Government and its officers in any time of trouble or disorder."

Meanwhile, landless workers like my grandmother's father—the carpenters, field workers, cleaners, and toolmakers whose labor fueled the region's new wealth—were denied access to ownership and found their political power further weakened. In the Canal Colonies, writes Imran Ali, it was "more rather than less difficult for the underprivileged to change economy and society so as to fulfill their need for social justice."

Still, my great-grandparents remained in the Canal Colonies. I don't know if they believed they might one day yet receive a land allotment, or if the work was better or perhaps paid more than it paid at home, or if they simply couldn't bear the thought of turning around and making the journey all over again in reverse. They settled in a village outside of Lyallpur where my great-grandmother bore five children and my great-grandfather spent his days carting tools from farm to farm, mending sickles and plows. Beneath that merciless desert sky my family lived for more than a decade, and never received so much as a stitch of land. Over those years, they did come to own other things: steel cooking pots and stacks of salwar kameez, sleeping mats, a buffalo for milk. But even this would not be theirs for long. In 1947, the line of Partition was drawn and they left everything behind to trace their steps back after all.

One afternoon, years after we'd left the farm, I paged through a musty library copy of M.S. Randhawa's *A History of Agriculture in India, Volume 3*, part of a four-volume history published by the Indian Council of Agricultural Research in 1983. Reading through the chapters on the Canal Colonies, I came across a description of wheat cultivation that noted how this same crop was grown year after year without manure and yet, perplexingly, the fertility of the soils seemed undiminished. "The question arose," writes Randhawa, "whence do the large wheat crops derive their nitrogenous manure? According to Sir Albert Howard the answer was to be found in the leguminous weeds which thrive so luxuriantly as a bottom growth in the wheat fields of Punjab." These low-growing, clover-like weeds fixed nitrogen without disrupting the harvest or growth of the wheat plants.

There was that name again—Howard. Encountering it this time I was struck with a vague sense of familiarity, like running into an acquaintance from home in a foreign airport and being momentarily unable to place the face out of context. Why did I recognize this name?

I flipped to the index and traced a finger down the line until it landed on *Howard, Sir Albert*. I was directed to chapter 37 where, at the top of the page, I found the words *Wheat Improvement*. "At the beginning of [the twentieth] century, when research on wheat on modern lines was first taken up at the Imperial Agricultural Research Institute at Pusa," the page read, "the outstanding personality in charge of the investigations was Sir Albert Howard, who laid the foundations of the genetic improvement not only of wheat but also of a range of other crops."

I said the name out loud, repeated it until at last a flicker of memory emerged: a coffee table in someone's college living room, Paulo Coelho's *The Alchemist*, half-drunk cups of kombucha, and a paperback copy of *An Agricultural Testament* by Sir Albert Howard. Of course—the father of organic farming. But why was I finding him here, in a chapter about wheat improvement in colonial India?

If I'd had any more than a cursory knowledge of this man's life I wouldn't have been surprised, but since I didn't, I read on to learn that early in his career—long before he gained notoriety as the crusading founder of modern organic agriculture—Albert Howard, alongside his wife and fellow agricultural scientist, Gabrielle, had spent nearly two decades working on the improvement of Indian wheat production as Imperial Economic Botanist.

The Howards had arrived in India in 1905, hired to head up the newly minted Imperial Agricultural Research Institute (IARI). This institute was the brainchild of Lord Curzon, then British viceroy to India. At the time, India was suffering a scourge of maladies—severe famine, bubonic plague outbreaks, economic depression—and Curzon feared the British were in danger of losing their dominion over the subcontinent. As part of his effort to quell simmering Indian resentment and the growing movement for self-rule, Curzon sought to improve Indian agriculture via a system of institutions devoted to research and education, modeled in part on the United States Department of Agriculture. The central organization in Curzon's scheme was IARI, funded significantly by a friend of his wife's family, an American millionaire named Henry Phipps. The site of the institute, a government estate in Bihar near the Ganges River, was given the name Pusa—*P* for Phipps, and *usa* for USA.

At the IARI, the Howards began a sweeping effort to survey and classify the vast diversity of wheat varieties already under cultivation across the wide-ranging climates of the subcontinent. In 1909 they published a monograph, *Wheat in India: Its Production, Varieties and Improvement*, and over the course of the ensuing fifteen years the Howards and their assistants isolated, bred, and distributed over fifty distinct varieties of Indian wheat. These improved varieties—the first modern Indian wheats created using Mendelian genetics—resulted, in many cases, in a significant increase in yield. They were widely adopted across India, and some spread across the globe to places as far as Argentina.

Many of the Howards' modern varieties, and subsequent cultivars bred by plant scientists they'd trained and worked with, made their way to the fields of the Canal Colonies. Here wheat was produced not just for subsistence and local markets but also for export. Modern varieties that met the needs of importing countries like Britain—wheats well suited for leavened sandwich breads rather than the flatbreads of Punjabi cuisine—began to supplant local landraces.

The success of the Howards' wheat-breeding efforts at IARI demonstrated the role that science and modern plant breeding could play in transforming Indian agriculture. Thus, the Howards' work for the British Raj during these years set into motion the ideological and institutional groundwork that would, half a century later, enable the unfurling of the Green Revolution.

When reading about Albert and Gabrielle Howard's work at the IARI, Sir Albert Howard bears little resemblance to the hero of organic farming's origin story, that trailblazing outsider committed to ecological health and the preservation of traditional farming practices. Instead he appears to be a well-regarded member of the British scientific community, a skilled botanist working to improve Indian crop yields in accordance with imperial interests of maintaining political stability while extracting profit from a colonized land.

After reading about the Howards' start in India, I pulled up the National Plant Germplasm Systems database and found, once again, the listing for the Sonora-type wheat acquired from Punjab. I reread the entry and this time recognized the collectors' names: A.L.C. and G.L.C Howard. It occurred to me that it was quite possible the Howards crossed paths with my family members there among the wheat fields of Punjab sometime in the 1920s.

I imagined Sir Albert Howard walking the plains around Lyallpur, that former desert turned verdant checkerboard, stooping to study the undergrowth at the edge of a wheat field, pulling up a yellow-flowered senji weed and noting the clusters of nitrogen-fixing nodules along the root system. Behind him I imagined another man pushing a bicycle up a dusty road, handlebars strung with tools, on his way from one farm to the next to mend broken implements: my great-grandfather.

I've no way of knowing, of course, if such a moment occurred. I know Howard remained in India until 1931, and that my great-grandparents lived in the Canal Colonies for more than a decade, long enough to have had four other children by the time by grandmother, the fifth, was born there in 1939. So they were in the same places, working around the same crop, during overlapping years.

What I can say for certain, however, is that the products of each man's lifework converged there in the wheat fields of west Punjab, where the scythes formed and sharpened by my great-grandfather's hands surely found their blades up against the stalks of Sir Albert Howard's improved wheat varieties. And while my great-grandfather was a poor Indian tool-maker with no formal education and Sir Albert Howard was a wealthy British scientist with a master's from Cambridge, both men found themselves driven by the forces of Empire to the arid plains of west Punjab, where they each worked in service of the same endeavor: to pry, from the clenched fist of a parched desert, a harvest of wheat.

From this point of collision, however, the trajectories of these men's lives diverged.

← 12 →

The first week of May, when our farm stand had been open for nearly a month, Ryan and I drove four hours north to Ukiah to visit a small-scale grain expert named Doug Mosel. Doug ran an organization called the Mendocino Grain Project, through which he grew wheat, rye, oats, and barley and supported other grain farmers by providing harvesting, cleaning, and milling services. The grains produced by the MGP were sold directly to customers through a grain-share program, sought after by a handful of bakeries, and were available at a few local grocery stores. Everyone I'd met in the grain world thus far knew of Doug.

Ryan and I arrived a few minutes early at the address Doug had given us, a warehouse in an industrial strip just outside of town. From the outside the building looked like any other warehouse—garage door, rectangle building, flat roof. At the far end of the parking lot sat two combines, one about the size of a passenger van, the other much larger. I walked around the machines while we waited for Doug, noticing how clean and well-kept they were, absent of rust or caked mud.

Doug pulled up in a pickup with a fat yellow lab in the passenger seat. The dog leapt out of the cab first and Doug stepped out after him. He wore gray Carhartt pants cinched to his narrow waist with a leather belt. He shook our hands warmly, pulled a key from his pocket, and jostled the warehouse door handle until it clicked open. Inside, my eyes adjusted slowly to the dim light and for a moment I could make out only the shadowy shapes of giant machines spaced out across the building like dinosaur skeletons in a museum. Doug slid open the garage door and a flood of midday sun poured in. Now I could see that the warehouse was packed with tools and equipment, storage bins and buckets. In spite of the clutter, an atmosphere of order prevailed. Doug swiftly navigated the narrow aisles between the jutting limbs of machines and stacks of grain bins, moving about the space like a seasoned builder moves across the rafters of an unfinished roof. I stepped with caution, afraid that even a nudge of a bucket might throw off the balance of order.

I recognized a few of the machines. The Clipper seed cleaner, a red apparatus with its name written in playful type across the side like a carnival ride, was similar to a machine I'd seen at Reed's. It was made up of a series of screens that shook back and forth, allowing grain to pass through while removing larger seeds and bits of chaff and straw.

Next to the Clipper, another type of sorter made of twin metal spirals towered over my head. This machine could be used to separate certain kinds of weed seed from a grain crop, Doug explained. Harvested grain was poured into a hopper at the top of the spiral slides. Round-shaped seeds spun fastest down the slides, creating enough centrifugal force to pull them outward into a separated channel. Seeds with edges to slow their fall remained in the inner track. Doug spoke fast—he had only half an hour to talk before other obligations drew him away, and I could tell he wanted to get in as much as he could. There was also a stone flour mill, a gravity table—a vibrating surface tilted slightly downward to separate seeds by mass, allowing a grower to extract the plumpest, densest grains from the smaller, lighter ones—and an elaborate exhaust system to deal with all the dust involved in sifting and milling. When he'd showed us everything, I stood back and looked over the room. Though I knew little about grain-cleaning equipment, I knew enough to understand that a lot of money sat in this warehouse—far more, I'd have guessed, than Doug was making growing and selling wheat.

So, attempting to pick my words carefully, I asked him how the finances of it all panned out. Doug chuckled and told me he believed the market for locally grown organic grains was growing and he hoped his granary would continue to serve more and more farmers as the acreage in small-scale grain production increased. "Right now," Doug said, "there's a lot of personal investment and debt in this room." But someday, he believed, the granary would start paying itself off and the income he made harvesting, cleaning, and milling grains for the local farming community would pay the rent for the warehouse, maintain the machines, and keep the power turned on. He didn't include sustaining his own livelihood or paying himself a salary. "I cut hay to keep up my grain habit," Doug said with a laugh.

On the way out we paused at the two combines parked outside and

Doug explained how the smaller one, called a Hege, was designed for small research plots. It could be loaded onto a trailer and easily transported along the narrow and windy roads of Mendocino County to reach the fields of small farmers tucked into the hills. The Hege also enabled a collaboration he'd recently begun with wine grape growers in which grains were sown in between rows of vines, a mutually beneficial arrangement that provided cover crop for the vineyards and extra acreage for Doug. The Hege was perfect for harvesting in the tight spaces between vines.

Our time ran out, and I thanked Doug for showing us around. He wished us good luck with our harvest and told us to call him if we needed help with anything. Then Ryan and I climbed into our truck and Doug into his. We followed him out of the parking lot and then turned in separate directions, Doug heading north to check on a nearby field, Ryan and I heading south to the highway.

❧ 13 ❧

After stumbling upon those passages about Sir Albert Howard's work as a wheat breeder in colonial India, in the years after I'd left our farm, I'd begun to wonder about the rest of his story. Howard's work on wheat improvement as Imperial Economic Botanist for the British Empire had never been mentioned in the tale of the father of organic farming as I'd heard it. How, I wanted to know, had this man gone from being the highest-ranking officer of an imperial agricultural institution to a humble devotee of traditional farming methods and crusader for Mother Nature?

In his introduction to *The Soil and Health*, the 1947 book that is one of Howard's most well-known works, he describes his years in India as formative to his ideas about organic farming. "Indian agriculture can point to a history of many centuries," he declares. "What could be more sensible than to watch and learn from the experience which had passed so prolonged a test of time?" In India, Howard asserts, he eschewed his Western scientific training and instead regarded the traditional peasant farmers, along with the local crop pests, as his instructors. After "five years tuition under my new professors," he writes, "I had learnt how to grow healthy crops, practically free from disease, without the slightest help from mycologists, entomologists, bacteriologists, agricultural chemists, spraying machines, insecticides...and all other expensive paraphernalia of the modern experiment station."

Though I'd never read these pages before and hadn't known the particular details of Howard's story—that his fabled awakening had taken place in India while he was at work on wheat improvement—I was well acquainted with the basic outline: traditional peasants teach renegade Western agricultural scientist a better way to farm. It's a compelling enough story, and I'd never before really thought to question it. But reading it now, knowing what I now knew of Howard's imperial career and my own family's history, it struck me as flimsy. The story left little room for the details I'd thus far pieced together of my great-grandparents' lives, of my grandmother's birthplace in the Canal Colonies. How could I square Howard's depiction of an ancient Indian agriculture rooted in tradition with the image of west Punjab divided up "like a chessboard" by imperial powers who, after claiming the land as their own and dispossessing the nomadic inhabitants, constructed an elaborate system of irrigation canals and then recruited masses of workers to grow vast fields of wheat for export markets?

It was these misgivings that led me to the work of historian Gregory Barton, who, in his 2018 book *The Global History of Organic Farming*, stakes out a different version of the story. Barton combed through previously unavailable archives of Sir Albert Howard and his first and second wives, the sisters Gabrielle and Louise Matthaei. He scoured letters Howard wrote to friends and family during his years in India, and the long-forgotten articles and reports he published over the course of these decades of fabled organic revelation. Among these primary documents Barton found hardly a kind word about Indian peasants and scarce evidence that Howard's inquiry into organic growing methods stemmed from a respect for their traditions. Barton's findings stood in such contrast to the popular mythology of Howard that I went searching for some of the primary sources for myself. Sure enough, in his 1927 book *The Development of Indian Agriculture*, Howard declares the Indian peasantry "enslaved to superstition" and "backward." He laments their "indifference and illiteracy" and writes that "it is the human factor that stands in the way of progress... till the inhabitants of the villages of India can be awakened and a general desire for rural uplift can be implanted in the people themselves, it must take centuries to effect any real and lasting development of rural India." A starker contrast to his 1947 descriptions of his "peasant professors" is hard to imagine.

Even more surprisingly, perhaps, is the fact that Barton found none of the ecological criticisms of chemical agriculture one would expect from the "father" of organic farming. Instead, Howard's writings over his years in India reveal a different set of concerns that drove his search for organic farming techniques.

During his tenure in India, from 1905 until 1931, synthetic nitrogen fertilizer remained scarce and expensive—it wouldn't become cheap and readily available until after World War II—rendering it inaccessible for most Indian farmers. Animal manure, often the primary natural source of fertilizer on small diversified farms that incorporated livestock, was also scarce in India due to its use as heating and cooking fuel and the lack of livestock on colonial plantations and mono-crop farms. Given these parameters, Sir Albert Howard was faced with the challenge of finding a way to sustain the productivity of India's farmland—the wheat fields as well as the tea, cotton, and sugarcane plantations upon which the British Empire depended for food supplies and revenue—that was within reach of the Indian peasantry. Put another way, the question set before Sir Albert Howard was this: How could the British continue to ward off famine and social unrest while extracting wealth from land that lost fertility with every harvest?

Howard's answer was a combination of techniques that would form the foundations of modern organic farming. At the center lay his "Indore method," a process that harnesses the power of microorganisms to quickly produce compost fertilizer as potent as animal manure from the much more abundant resource of vegetative waste. The method involves building heaps of plant material in such a way that creates an ideal environment for microorganisms to thrive. These organisms then rapidly break down the pile into highly fertile compost. Today, farmers, gardeners, public waste treatment agencies, and private companies use variations of Howard's method to produce the compost we buy in bags at garden centers, or make in our backyards, or—as Ryan and I did at our farm—get delivered by the transfer load to spread over our fields. Whether made on site or purchased, compost is the primary fertility amendment for many organic farmers today.

Barton argues that organic farming protocols, particularly Howard's composting technique, should be credited to British imperial science— to the work of Howard himself and his many forgotten colleagues—and not to "ancient peasant wisdom." He cites a study published by researchers at England's Rothamsted Experimental Station in 1921, several years before Howard developed his Indore method, that described the scientific foundations for producing compost from vegetable matter. But whether Howard derived his methods from observing Indian farmers, stole it from earlier research by British scientists he would later deem "laboratory hermits," or invented it himself, it is not so much who should be credited that strikes me as important, but rather what drove Howard's initial pursuit of an organic farming system in the first place. It was not, as the mythology suggests, a prescient ecologically minded aversion to chemical agriculture or a noble reverence for "Mother Earth," nor a respect for traditional knowledge or a bold nonconformist streak. Instead, Howard's search for nonchemical farming methods was fueled by the far less romantic force of economic and political parameters: the high cost of synthetic fertilizer, the scarcity of manure, and the imperial objective of wresting wealth from colonized lands.

⊷ 14 ⊷

May 2013 drew to a close and our Sonora wheat began to dry. The tall stalks crisped into a glossy blond, while each plump head of berries turned deep amber and a coppery patina spread over the field. The frenzy of our first spring in full operation devoured each day. Wednesdays we harvested and packed boxes for CSA customers. Twice a week we fulfilled and delivered wholesale orders from the local food co-op and a few restaurants. On weekends we stocked the farm stand. Along with our vegetables we'd begun selling bread made in a wood-fired oven we had built on the farm the prior winter. The profit margin on a value-added product like bread was far higher than that of raw produce. Like nearly all the other small farms in our area—which sold pies and coffee, hotdogs and fudge, or offered tourist attractions like corn mazes or wine tastings—Ryan and I found we, too, could use a supplemental source of income. Under the tutelage of Fulton, my baker friend who'd first turned me on to Sonora, I learned to make naturally leavened bread using a sourdough starter. Word of our farm's bread spread quickly, and the sixty loaves I baked each Saturday sold fast. Spurred on by the thrill of that first season, Ryan and I worked the long days and hardly noticed that spring was quickly turning to summer.

When June arrived we'd yet to find a feasible way to harvest our wheat. I knew we needed to get the grain out of the field in the next few weeks in order to preserve the moisture and protein content. If left out too long, the stalks would grow brittle and difficult to harvest, weevils would infest the field, and birds and squirrels, too, would make quick work of the berries.

So far I'd been able to think of three methods to harvest the wheat, none of which seemed viable. The first was to do the job by hand. This would involve me and Ryan walking up and down the two-acre field swinging scythes. These tools—curved blades affixed to long handles— would slice through the stalks, dropping the wheat to the ground. Then, we'd have to gather the wheat into bundles and find a place to store it out of the reach of rodents and birds until the winter, when we might be able to find the time to thresh the kernels from their ears. This method of harvest, requiring an enormous amount of human labor, was the primary means through which wheat was harvested up until the end of the eighteenth century. A skilled farmer might be able to harvest two acres in a day this way. Then, in the late 1700s, a new tool called a cradle rose to prominence. The cradle was simply a scythe modified with an attached frame to catch the cut stalks, therefore combining what had been a two-step process into one, doubling the rate at which a farmer could harvest. Hand cutting with a cradle was the most common way to harvest wheat through the nineteenth century.

The idea of hand harvesting our Sonora was daunting, but not entirely ludicrous. While the process would be labor intensive, the wheat had so far cost us no labor outside of the minimal time it had taken to prep the soil and broadcast the seed. So if I averaged out the labor of harvest over the course of the entire growing cycle, it would not turn out to be especially high. Still, it was our first season in full operation and we were already stretching the days as far as we could. Ryan and I had seven acres of vegetables to tend, CSA boxes to fill each week, regular wholesale orders to keep up with, and the farm stand to run. We had fall crops to seed, certification records to maintain, ceaseless irrigations leaks to fix, and weeds to hoe. The wheat, we'd agreed when we planted it, could not take priority, and I couldn't imagine where we'd find the extra hours needed for a hand harvest. Plus, we didn't have space to store two acres worth of bundled grain. Even if we could fit it inside the barn, rodents would surely devour it.

The second option was to use a combine. Named for their ability to cut and thresh the wheat in a single pass through a field, the first combine harvesters were developed in the 1830s and '40s. They were horse-drawn and could harvest twenty-five acres of grain in a day. But they were expensive, and few farmers had the capital to invest in such a new and pricey technology. In California, however, where the wheat fields were the largest in the world and those mine-owners-turned-farm-owners had money to gamble with, these first combines were eagerly put to use.

Over the ensuing decades, mechanical advances led to more effective tractors and combines, and more farmers began to adopt these labor-saving machines. A farmer who could afford a combine had the capacity to grow as much wheat as they had space for, no longer limited by the amount of labor available to cut and thresh. By the turn of the twentieth century, much of the world's land had been put into wheat, and farmers everywhere scrambled to produce their harvests as cheaply as possible in order to compete on the bloated market. Smaller farmers who did not have the capital to purchase expensive machinery or enough land to make the investment worth it were driven out of business by increasingly lower prices. During these years, the structure of farming across America began to resemble the model pioneered in California: the number of farms declined drastically as the average size of a farm increased. More and more farmland in fewer and fewer hands. By 1950 nearly all wheat grown in the United States was harvested via combine, and wheat production had reached a state of chronic surplus.

Today, a modern combine harvester can cut 200 acres in a day and can cost upwards of half a million dollars. The fastest combine on the market holds a record for harvesting 1,759,000 pounds of wheat in a single eight-hour workday. These machines are equipped with GPS, have air-conditioned cabs, and include advanced computers capable of measuring yield and moisture content while harvesting. YouTube offers a bounty of videos of such machines at work, their monstrous capacity somehow mesmerizing. It seems likely, in a not-so-distant future, these combines will be entirely self-driven, requiring no human operator at all.

In big grain-producing regions, where several growers operate in close vicinity and equipment sharing can greatly reduce costs, it's not uncommon for a farmer to hire a combine operator to come harvest the crop. At one point, in a rash moment, I wondered if we might be able to arrange this and looked into it. The only combines for hire, of course, were colossal machines designed to harvest hundreds of acres each day. These were grossly too large for our fields—the idea of hauling one up the narrow and winding roads into the foothills to harvest our two measly acres of specialty wheat was laughable.

The third option was Doug Mosel. Our farm was a twisty four-hour drive south from Ukiah and our request would be last minute, but I wondered if Doug might be willing to bring his tiny combine, the Hege, to our farm in time to harvest our Sonora. Ryan, more fluent in the language of machinery and transport, called Doug. I sat nearby, straining to hear Doug's voice through the phone. Ryan explained our situation, and I listened with the uncomfortable realization of just how ridiculous it was: here we were, at the start of June, our two acres of Sonora shoulder-high and ready to cut, with no plan for harvest.

But Doug didn't point out our poor planning, our clear desperation. He listened kindly, talked fast, but not impatiently. His schedule was full, he said. He'd be busy harvesting grain and cutting hay for the next month or two, but he might be able to squeeze us in if something went faster than expected and he wound up with a free day. He promised to call the following week, when he might have a better idea of his availability. I tried not to think about how I couldn't remember the last time anything went faster than expected.

A week passed and Doug still hadn't found time to harvest our Sonora. I waited for him to call with news that he would be heading our way soon. Another week passed. When I could wait no longer, I called to check in and Doug told me the same thing: he'd let me know as soon as he found time, he hadn't forgotten about us.

I hung up and walked out to the wheat field. I could hear the stalks brushing against one another in the breeze as I approached. The sun neared the western horizon, and the ground radiated the day's heat. I looked out across the field, stalks as tall as my chest, each proudly holding a spike of kernels as thick as my thumb. How many pounds of grain waited in this field? How much longer could it stand here unharvested?

The next morning when I got up, I found Ryan sitting behind his computer at the kitchen table. I stepped past toward the kettle on the stove, but he reached for my arm. "Look," he said. On the screen was a photo of a combine no larger than a pickup truck, red and shiny in front of a field of knee-high grain. I stared at the machine, trying to decipher its many parts: here a seat and steering wheel, here the cutting blade, the threshing drum.

"It's a Hege, just like the one Doug has," Ryan said. "For sale by Montana State University."

"Montana?"

Ryan shrugged. "At least it's not on the East Coast." The ad was posted on the university surplus auction site and we read through the details together. There was a phone number listed, but it was barely dawn, too early to call, so I left Ryan at the computer and made coffee. I walked down to the fields to harvest wholesale orders before the coming heat drove off the last of the cool night air and settled in over our basin.

By nine, I'd finished the harvest and worked up a nervous excitement imagining the combine at our farm, cutting neat lines through our wheat field. I imagined the pearls of grain spilling from the machine's chute, filling barrel after barrel. I packed the orders in delivery boxes, then put them in our walk-in cooler and jogged up the hill to the house.

Ryan was on the phone with the university when I walked in the door. I sat nearby, trying to infer the content of the conversation. But he was already thanking the person on the other end and saying goodbye. He hung up and pushed a piece of paper scribbled with notes across the table to me. *Great condition. Routinely serviced. $2,600. Can ship tomorrow.* We had enough saved from prepaid CSA subscriptions to cover this expense, and within hours we'd sent the money and arranged a transport company to pick up the harvester. It would arrive in a week.

❧ 15 ❧

The combine reached our farm in the late afternoon and Ryan climbed into the seat to drive it off the trailer. He sat silent for a moment on the square cushion of open space surrounded by pulleys and gear shafts, levers and knobs. Though Ryan had never before driven a combine, he didn't seem daunted. The machine had come with a manual, but he only flipped through it before tossing it aside for later. Then he moved his hand from one shaft to another, hovering above each knob for a moment. I imagined him working it all out in his head: *this one does this, and this one that.* After a few minutes he'd figured it out, dipping into a reservoir of mechanical instinct stemming from his childhood days spent on his grandfather's lap atop the same Ford tractor we now used on our farm.

Ryan turned the key and the machine belched into motion. Two four-foot-wide toothy blades scissored back and forth in front of the vehicle. Behind the blades a conveyor belt led into the gut of the combine. Through a tiny window I could see the thresher spinning inside. At the back of the machine three metal screens shimmied over one another. Ryan moved a lever to lift the conveyer belt, another to stop the blades from scissoring. He put the combine in gear and the machine lurched forward, paused, and then slowly rolled off the trailer onto the ground, its four tiny wheels, no larger than those of a golf cart, carrying everything.

Over the next few days Ryan and I attempted to harvest our Sonora. The combine was supposed to cut the straw below the ear and, with a wheel of comb-like tines, pull it onto a conveyer belt. The belt would deposit the wheat into a spinning drum where the grain would be threshed loose. Then, a series of shuffling screens would separate the threshed kernels from the straw and a fan would blow away the chaff. The isolated grain would then pour from a spout into a collection barrel attached to the side of the machine. After a first pass through the field, however, I looked into the barrel and found not a heap of glossy grains but a mess of chopped-up straw, fully intact ears, and tangles of weeds.

From the ground, I watched the many moving parts of the combine closely as Ryan drove, then examined the diagrams in the manual. There were endless combinations of possible adjustments—the cutting blade could be raised or lowered, the space between the threshing drum and the concave narrowed or widened, the speed of spinning quickened or slowed. We called the manufacturer with questions. Then Doug, who patiently walked us through the intricacies of the machine. Then Reed, who listened to our descriptions of what was ending up in the harvest barrel and suggested tweaks. With each adjustment and each pass through the field, the output changed slightly until the machine produced workable grain. Some fully intact heads still made it into the harvest barrel, and plenty of chaff and weed seed. But this could be resolved later, through the cleaning process, Reed had assured us, and he offered to let us use his equipment—sifters and seed cleaners—to remove what the combine couldn't. The full heads would have to be sifted out, and our yield would be smaller because of this loss, but at least we would have a harvest.

On our final pass through the field I walked beside the combine as Ryan maneuvered it slowly through the last stand of wheat. The kernels dropped steadily into the barrel, pinging and rattling against the steel like coins spewing from a slot machine. It sounded like we'd hit the jackpot.

↢ 16 ↣

In what strikes me as an uncanny alignment in the laws of physics and biology, it turns out that the two activities humans have been most preoccupied with for much of history—food production and war—consume the same limited resource: fixed nitrogen. This essential requirement for plant growth also happens to be the main component of gunpowder and bombs.

It is unsurprising, then, that as the twentieth century unfolded and war broke out, the ongoing search for more fixed nitrogen ratcheted up. In 1909, a German scientist named Fritz Haber invented a process to break apart the nitrogen molecule using fossil fuels, thus converting the abundant but useless atmospheric nitrogen into its coveted fixed form. While this method was groundbreaking it was also, at its inception, tremendously costly and inefficient. In the ensuing years another German chemist, Carl Bosch, worked to scale up Haber's method. After years of refinements spurred forward by the two world wars, The Haber-Bosch process eventually yielded synthetic fixed nitrogen that was both cheap and essentially limitless.

Both Haber and Bosch were awarded Nobel prizes in chemistry for their work, and, after the end of World War II, cheap synthetic nitrogen was heralded as the solution to impending food scarcity in many a war-torn countryside. Factories once dedicated to war chemicals pivoted to agricultural chemicals, and the newly created International Food and Agricultural Organization (motto: "Let There Be Bread") launched campaigns to promote the use of synthetic nitrogen across the globe.

↢

All this added up to an unlucky turn of events for Sir Albert Howard, a man who'd spent his career developing methods for sustaining fertility that did not require what were then expensive chemicals. With the advent of cheap and widely available synthetic nitrogen, the economic motivation to implement Howard's more labor-intensive processes began to evaporate, and his organic methods drifted toward obscurity.

In a dreary pamphlet he published in 1940 after leaving India and re-settling in England, Howard lamented the lack of interest in his methods. "There is obviously little or nothing to be hoped now from the farming community taken as a whole," he wrote. Largely ignored by governing bodies and the mainstream agricultural science community, in this last decade of his life Howard began to appeal instead to anxious consumers and nonfarming urbanites who, uneasy about the rapidly industrializing world and nostalgic for a more wholesome existence, might be drawn to his nonchemical organic methods. In their private gardens, or their children's schoolyards, perhaps these individuals could keep alive some semblance of his life's work.

In his writing and lectures from this point on—the period in which all of his better-known works were written—Howard's rhetoric shifted to cater to this new audience. He moved, as Barton writes, "from scientist to scientific skeptic; from bureaucrat to prophet," simplifying his ideas into something closer to a creed, elevating the link between soil health and personal health, leaning on romantic notions of ancient Eastern wisdom and the pure guide of nature. In the final years of his life these ideas became the backbone of Howard's writing, and the economic and political motivations that had driven his early inquiries into nonchemical growing methods were expunged from the story. While this shift didn't help his case with policymakers or the mainstream scientific community, it did drum up enthusiasm among his growing base of followers, who found these sentiments alluring in a postwar era thick with new anxieties about modern life.

Here was the Howard I recognized: Not the imperial wheat breeder but the eschewer of establishment science and praiser of peasants. The espouser of phrases such as "Nature's farming" and "Earth's green carpet." The writer of bumper sticker–ready dictums I'd come across in Wendell Berry books or in the email signatures of organic enthusiasts: "Artificial manures lead inevitably to artificial nutrition, artificial food, artificial animals, and finally to artificial men and women."

Among the growing cadre of followers drawn to Howard's writings during these years was the notorious American publisher J.I. Rodale. A health-food evangelist who was deeply distrustful of establishment science, Rodale denounced doctors and promoted his own brand of disease-prevention measures such as taking extensive regimens of vitamins or eating copious sunflower seeds. He was an early anti-vaxxer, encouraging his followers to reject the polio vaccine and opt instead for his dietary cure.

When Rodale encountered Howard's writings on organic farming and its connection to personal health and wholeness, he was immediately enthralled and struck up a correspondence with him. Soon Rodale was inspired to buy a farm in Pennsylvania to trial Howard's methods and, in 1942, he launched *Organic Farming and Gardening* magazine— later renamed *Organic Gardening*—making Howard associate editor. Via this publication, Rodale spread Howard's ideas to an American audience, sparking the beginnings of the organic movement in the United States.

In an early issue of *Organic Farming and Gardening*, published in 1942, Rodale writes: "One of these fine days the public is going to wake up and will pay for eggs, meats, vegetables, etc., according to how they were produced. A substantial premium will be paid for high quality products such as those raised by organic methods.... The better earning class of the public will pay a high price if they can be shown its value, and that they will save on doctor bills."

ᘓ 17 ᘔ

The second week of September 2013 brought the first cold front of the season. It crisped the morning air, sweetening the collard greens and sending the maple trees outside our farm stand into a fit of color. Ryan and I loaded our four barrels of Sonora seed into the truck bed and headed down Highway 49 to see Reed, the wheat farmer to whom Monica Spiller had first sent us for counsel. He had agreed to let us use his equipment to clean our harvest, separating the wheat kernels from everything else that had made it through the combine—weed seed, chaff, straw. We planned to then set aside some of the cleaned wheat seed to plant later that fall, and would save the rest to sell or have milled into flour.

Reed greeted us in his driveway, hands in his front pockets, and he smiled at our load, shaking his head slightly as if he couldn't believe we'd gone ahead and grown Sonora after all. We unloaded the barrels onto the ground near the cleaning equipment and Reed popped off a lid to peer inside. I turned away as he pulled out a handful to examine the harvest, embarrassed at the mess of our wheat, cluttered up as it was with wads of straw and star-thistle heads. But the farmer didn't appear concerned. "Not too bad," he said, "the cleaner should take care of most of this. You'll probably need to put it through twice."

Reed flipped a switch and a series of screens rattled into motion. The screens shook back and forth to separate the wheat kernels (or anything the same size as a wheat kernel) from everything else. The larger "trash"—weeds and straw, chaff and whole heads—vibrated out to a bin on one side while the kernels dropped down into an opposite bin. Reed handed Ryan and me each a dust mask, something we hadn't thought to bring, then he retreated into his house to let us work.

After several hours spent pouring bucket after bucket of wheat through the machine, we'd cleaned it all. Reed came out to examine our work. With all the trash removed, we wound up with close to 700 pounds of cleaned wheat. It was less than half of what we might have gotten had we not lost so much to our delayed harvest and user error with the combine, and a fraction of the average yield for modern wheat in California that year—5,000 pounds per acre. But I didn't care—I was just thrilled to have it. Reed, too, was grinning. "Not too bad for your first year," he said, "I've had worse." Despite the low yield, lost heads, and late harvest, there we were with two barrels of wheat berries gleaming in the evening light.

↩ 18 ↪

The cheap and limitless synthetic nitrogen produced via the Haber-Bosch process immediately led to soaring yield increases in many crops. Corn, for example, which had been producing yields consistently around 20 bushels per acre in the United States up until 1935, jumped to 34.4 in 1945. Potatoes soared from 66.3 hundred pounds per acre to 97.7 over those same years. Wheat yields, however, showed only limited improvement. This was due to a particular problem with the morphology of the plant.

Most traditional wheat varieties are tall, like our Sonora. They have long, slender stems that reach four, five, or sometimes even six feet in height. In addition to the edible grain held in the ears, these tall stalks were once considered a valuable part of the wheat crop—useful for animal feed, bedding, and building material, or to replenish the soil. The height also provides a critical advantage over low-growing weeds, which are quickly shaded out by the towering plants.

These lanky stalks, however, pose a problem for the farmer seeking greater grain yields: If the ears grow too heavy with seed, a tall stalk will fall over (or "lodge") under the extra weight, rendering the wheat impossible to harvest. Extra nitrogen, then, could fatten up the grain heads but ultimately result in a lost crop. It was useless on a wheat field.

At the end of World War II, a USDA wheat specialist named Samuel Salmon was sent to Japan to assist the devastated country in mitigating an impending food shortage. There, in the Japanese countryside, he encountered a distinctly short-strawed wheat variety being cultivated by local farmers. These unusual wheat plants, some only as tall as one and a half feet, were far less susceptible to lodging. They must have caught his eye immediately.

Salmon arranged for samples of this wheat, particularly one variety known as Norin 10, to be sent to the United States. The samples made their way into research stations around the country, where breeders eagerly crossed the new seed with local varieties in an attempt to produce a short-strawed wheat suitable to local growing conditions. If successful, that particularly vexing characteristic of wheat—its limited ability to respond favorably to increased fertilization—might finally be overcome.

❧ 19 ❧

At the time those first samples of semi-dwarf seed were sent from Japan to the United States, a giant American philanthropic organization, the Rockefeller Foundation, was knee-deep in an experimental effort to "develop" Mexican agriculture. Via a program known as MAP—Mexican Agriculture Program—the foundation set out to work with the Mexican government to modernize and increase the country's domestic wheat production. The approach would use plant breeding to create improved varieties and replicate America's high-input, large-scale, mono-crop model. According to the foundation, the program was part of their broader mission to promote the "well-being of mankind throughout the world" by bettering the lives of poor farmers. Historians, however, suggest MAP grew from a much more complicated set of motivations.

By the time Mexico gained independence from Spain in 1821, nearly all the country's land had been appropriated from Indigenous occupants via European conquest. An elite 1 percent of the population controlled 90 percent of the land, while 90 percent of Mexicans were landless. Over the next century, efforts to redistribute land moved forward in fits and starts, culminating in the Mexican Revolution and the 1934 presidency of Lázaro Cárdenas. An economic nationalist committed to the ideals of the revolution, Cárdenas enacted sweeping land reforms, breaking up large estates and redistributing them to communally owned peasant co-operatives. In 1938, Cárdenas nationalized the assets of foreign oil companies operating within his nation's borders, seizing oil properties and declaring that all petroleum reserves on Mexican land belonged to the Mexican people. This included the refineries of Standard Oil, the American company upon which the Rockefeller fortune had been made.

At the end of the 1930s Mexican agriculture production fell due to a mix of pest infestations, poor weather, and distribution challenges. Cárdenas's political opponents blamed his radical agrarian policies for this turmoil, and a more conservative presidential successor, Ávila Camacho, was elected in 1940. The Rockefeller Foundation and the United States, eager to help this new government steer Mexico away from Cárdenas's socialist agrarian vision and toward a modern industrial state friendly to liberal capitalism, offered to provide technical assistance in developing Mexican agriculture. Mexico's new leaders accepted the offer, and in 1943 the foundation sent a team of scientists to establish research stations in Mexico.

MAP focused on wheat improvement, not because it was particularly important to the traditional Mexican diet based around maize and beans, but because of its value as an export crop that could generate funds to help fuel the growth of industry in Mexico. Both the Rockefeller Foundation and the Mexican leaders involved in MAP, writes historian John Perkins, "had no particular wish to improve the lives of peasant farmers *in their capacities as peasant farmers*" (emphasis his). Instead, both understood that agricultural modernization was needed to shift Mexico's development away from Cárdenas's socialist agrarian ideal toward an industrialized capitalist democracy, changes that "in their eyes, were for the better."

Leading the foundation's MAP was a young plant pathologist named Norman Borlaug, who was charged with breeding disease-resistant wheat varieties for Mexico. Borlaug had set up two research stations, one in the northwest region of Sonora, the other in the central region of El Bajio. The two regions, separated by more the 1,200 miles, differed greatly in climate, so that their growing seasons were at different times of the year. This allowed Borlaug to enact an unconventional process known as "shuttle breeding." Because of the alternating growing seasons across the two climates, Borlaug could plant two generations of wheat in a single year: he could first plant in Sonora in November for an April harvest, then cart those seeds south to El Bajio where they were planted in May and harvested in October, in time to be sent back north for the November sowing. This allowed him to create new varieties (a process that often required ten years) in half the time, but it was a side effect of this method that would ultimately prove to have far greater consequences.

Conventional wisdom of the time advised breeders to create new varieties by growing out crosses in the places where the varieties were intended to be used. This would ensure the new seed would be well adapted to the local conditions. Borlaug's system of moving his varieties back and forth between two diverse regions resulted in seeds able to tolerate a broad range of soil and climatic conditions. Seed, in other words, that wasn't picky.

Over his first seven years in Mexico, Borlaug's work led to modest but steady increases in the disease resistance and yield of Mexican wheat, and by the start of the 1950s the breeding program seemed to have achieved its full potential. Borlaug then shifted his focus away from breeding and toward getting the new seeds to farmers and advising them on how to best grow them.

⊷

By this time the Cold War was in full swing, and the potential to weaponize agricultural development—to use it to exert political influence on the countries that had yet to choose a side, then known as the Third World—was no longer a tacit matter. "In this struggle for the minds of men the side that best helps satisfy man's primary needs for food, clothing, and shelter is likely to win," states a 1951 Rockefeller Foundation report titled *The World Food Problem, Agriculture and the Rockefeller Foundation.* "Communism makes attractive promises to underfed peoples; democracy must not only promise as much, but must deliver more."

President Truman focused his 1949 inaugural speech around this theme, describing a new vision for American foreign policy centered on deploying technical assistance to developing nations in order to defeat communism. "Greater production is the key to prosperity and peace," he declared. "And the key to greater production is a wider and more vigorous application of modern scientific and technical knowledge."

Even Sir Albert Howard echoed this sentiment. "The real Arsenal of Democracy is a fertile soil, the fresh produce of which is the birthright of nations," reads the introduction to his final book, published in 1947, *The Soil and Health.*

☙ 20 ☙

After watching my grandfather break down when confronted with my questions about his past, I didn't dare ask any more during that visit. And so, many months later, with my first Sonora harvest snug in barrels in a corner of our barn, I joined my mother on another trip to LA.

The morning after we'd arrived, when my mother was out for a walk, I slipped into a chair next to my grandmother at the kitchen table, where she was peeling ginger. Lifting a root toward me she said, "Udthruck. You know udthruck? For the dal, you need a lot of udthruck." I nodded and watched her scrape the back of a knife along the contours of the lumpy root. "I use the dull side, you see?" she said, and explained how the sharp edge cuts past the skin into the tender flesh but the back of a knife scraps away only the outermost layer, so nothing is wasted.

"That's a good trick," I said.

My grandmother paused, then laughed. "Haanah! Yes, very good trick, I know many good trick!"

Encouraged by this moment of easy rapport, I ventured a question. "Naniji," I said, "in Punjab, when you were young, do you remember the wheat grown there?"

"Wheat? Yes! Yes, very much wheat. And also corn, and sugar. Cotton too. And vegetable—eggplant, mustard green, peas. Like you, haanah? You grow peas, eggplant?"

I nodded, and she turned back to the ginger. The front door swung open and my mother stepped in, said hello, then walked past us into the living room. I was about to ask my grandmother whether the wheat, and the flour it produced, had been reddish-brown in color like most wheat flour found in American stores, or more yellowish like Sonora, but before I could ask she began to talk again.

"When I was a girl, I walk by many farm to go to school," she told me without looking up. "In my village, you see, school only for boys. No school for girls. So every day, I walk long time, all the way to next village.

There, they have school for girls. For a few years, I walk. Then, you know, I am to be married, and after that, no more school. After that..." My grandmother stopped peeling and looked up at me. "I don't know the right words in English. Maybe your mum, she can help?"

In the living room, my mother had the phone in hand and an array of paperwork spread out on the coffee table, ready to make phone calls to various doctors to straighten out billing issues for my grandparents. She agreed to translate and followed me back to the table, taking a seat on the other side of my grandmother. But when my grandmother resumed talking her words remained in English. "I never want to marry, you know? But..." Her voice fell to a murmur I couldn't decipher. She looked down at her hands, then started again to work her knife over another chunk of ginger. This time, when she spoke she used Punjabi. And so it was through my mother's translation that we both learned the details of my grandmother's marriage.

The marriage was arranged in 1948, not quite a year after Partition, when she and her family were living with relatives in her parents' village. My grandmother was just nine years old at the time. She knew nothing of the arrangement until, as a young teenager, she was informed of her engagement to a man from a nearby village seven years her senior whom she would marry once she turned sixteen. The news—both of the identity of her future husband and the nearness of the wedding date—put her in a state of despair.

I was very scared then, I begged not to marry him. I wanted to marry someone else, I don't know who, a pilot maybe, my mother translated. *I thought of running away, anything to escape this fate.*

By the time the wedding date arrived in 1955, her soon-to-be-husband was no longer living in Punjab. He'd left India for Kenya, then still a British colony, where he had an opportunity to apprentice as a machinist in the city of Nairobi. There he would earn far better wages than he could earn as a laborer mending farm tools in the agrarian villages of Punjab. He returned to India for the wedding, and stayed just three months. By the time he left again for Nairobi, my grandmother was pregnant. She stayed with her family in Punjab to endure her pregnancy with her sisters and mother close by.

As if suddenly remembering something, my grandmother turned from the cutting board to look up at me, switched back to English. "You know, I wanted to be a singer? When I was a girl, sometimes I sing at the gurdwara. My father, he play music. Tabla, you know tabla? When I sing, everybody they say, you have very nice voice! Very beautiful voice!" A grin spread across my grandmother's face and her eyes shone behind her glasses. "Before I marry, sometimes I write song in a book. Many, many song I write down." She turned again to the ginger. "In those days, I have so much…I don't know how to say it." She paused, scraped the knife over the nearly bare ginger, and watched the last curl of skin fall to the table. "Life," she said at last. "So much *life*. But then I get married. Then I don't go to school no more. Your Nanaji he was very, how do you say? Strict? And slowly, slowly it all went away." With the knife clenched in her fist, she swept her hands out from her chest as if fanning away a puff of smoke. "Jackie…," she said, looking up at me, her grin gone. I tried to hold her gaze, waiting for her to say more, but after a moment she shook her head and returned to Punjabi.

The winter following her wedding, my grandmother gave birth to my mother. She'd just turned seventeen. *I didn't want a baby, I didn't know what to do with a child, a girl child.* My mother translated each sentence without emotion, attending dutifully to her task as if she were simply a hired interpreter, as if she was relaying a story that had nothing to do with her. *I hated it all, I wanted only to get rid of the baby girl.*

My grandmother stopped talking. The naked ginger rested in her cupped hand, and she began to rub her thumb over the surface of the root. I thought she might say more, but a patch of hairy fibers on the edge of the ginger caught her attention. Beneath her hands, flesh-colored peelings littered a cutting board. With the sharp point of the knife, she deftly carved out the fibrous bit, then brushed it and the peelings aside. She placed the ginger on the cleared board and with one swift slice, split the root in two. The pieces fell flat side up, each a perfect mirror of the other, and we all stared at them for a moment before my mother stood, pushed back her chair, and walked away.

The next morning I found my grandmother in the kitchen preparing to make gobi paratha for breakfast. "Naniji," I said, knowing my accent mangled the word, one of the few Punjabi words I used. "Can I watch you?" She nodded but did not look up from the bloom of cauliflower on her cutting board, the knife in her hand, deftly trimming flowers from the stem. I took a step closer. "Will you teach me?"

My grandmother's hands went still. She turned to face me. "Jackie," she said, her voice hushed, "I don't go to school like your mommy, you know. I don't go to college like you. But look. I know how to do many things. I know how to cook everything. I can make paratha, roti. Any dal, any subji, I can make. I can make all of it." My grandmother lifted her hands toward the stove, spread open her palms as if in offering. "Look."

On that day and the days that followed, my grandmother invited me into the kitchen before each meal, showing me how to mix the roti dough, how to press the water out of shredded daikon before folding it into a flatbread, how to brown the onions to their deepest shade for chole without burning them. One afternoon, in the middle of making dal, she slid her chappla sandals onto her feet and motioned for me to follow her outside. We walked to the edge of her lot where a strip of soil just a few feet wide separated her driveway from the neighbor's. Here, a line of small trees grew. I'd never taken notice of these before, had assumed them to be random shrubs some long-ago landscaper had planted to fill the gap. But my grandmother reached up into the tree branches and plucked a fistful of slender leaves. She folded one between her fingers to tear it, then held it to my nose. "Limbri," she said—curry leaf. I took a breath, inhaled that distinct scent I'd long tasted in my grandmother's dal: both peppery and citrus-sweet. I glanced from the limbri tree to the bushy plant beside it. My grandmother followed my gaze. "Guava," she said, "very nice fruit!" I looked closer and sure enough, hidden among the leaves were plum-size green fruits. Across from the guava, tracing the side of the house, a bitter melon vine.

My grandmother handed me the crushed limbri leaf, and I lifted it again to my nose. "You like?" she said, and before I could answer she began breaking off sprigs with her fingers until she had gathered a whole bundle. Back in her kitchen she wrapped the leaves in waxed paper, sealed them into a ziplock bag, and directed me to take them home and keep them in the freezer. In the coming years I'd ration these leaves and refill my stash each time I visited my grandparents. I'd slip a handful into the water when steaming rice, drop the leaves into hot oil and brown them with minced onion and turmeric and half a tomato before adding cauliflower cut just the way my grandmother had taught me. Sometimes, when opening the freezer for something else I'd see them there and pull one out, crush it in my fingers, take a breath.

↤

The morning before we left LA, I sat next to my grandmother again at her kitchen table. My mother sat at the other end, flipping through more stacks of medical paperwork, listening quietly as my grandmother and I talked. I drank a cup of cha and watched my grandmother prepare a squash to cook into a subji for us to take on the long drive home. It was opo squash, she told me—a variety of summer squash I didn't recognize. "Very good squash. I make for you, and roti too, so you can have good lunch on your drive, haanah?"

After removing the peel with a paring knife, my grandmother looked up at me with a kind of glimmer in her eyes, then smiled with her lips closed. It was a look that might pass across the face of someone about to reveal a juicy bit of gossip or some good news. "You know," she said, her eyes still shining, "I believe in love marriage, even then, when I was a girl. *No one* believe then, but I do. I always believe."

At this my mother set down the papers and let out a little "Ha!"

"Mom," she said after a moment, her voice breezy despite the charge I could tell she was about to lay upon my grandmother. "Then why did you..." She switched to Punjabi, but it was clear enough what she was asking: Why had my grandmother done so much to try to stop my mother's own love marriage?

My grandmother didn't answer. She did not say the things that, looking back on this afternoon, I imagine she could have said: That she was in charge of the survival of four children in a foreign land where she did not speak the language. Or that her only relations were a handful of other Indian immigrants and that if she severed these ties, she'd be left entirely alone. Or that finding a good marriage for her daughters was the only way she knew to ensure them a prosperous future.

Instead, my grandmother kept her gaze on the squash, on the perfectly even dice that fell into the bowl with each swift slice of her knife. She didn't look up but offered a sheepish smile, attempting, it seemed, to match my mother's half-teasing tone. But when she spoke her voice was somber.

"It was different then," my grandmother said. She shook her head, lifted her palm toward my mother as if to say *stop*. "Back then, I couldn't...no." She slid the knife through the last of the squash, lifted the bowl into her hands and carried it to the stove. From the kitchen, she turned to face my mother and me. "I always believed," she said, and in one fluid motion flung the tail of her scarf over her shoulder and flicked on the stove, setting loose a whoosh of blue flame

I don't know if my mother believed my grandmother that day, or if I did myself. I watched her pluck a chunk of roti dough from the batch waiting in a bowl beside the stove. She kneaded it between her palms, then spun it flat and slapped it onto the hot tuva. Who can know the woman my grandmother might have been had her life unfurled under a different set of circumstances?

ᴤ 21 ᴥ

The year my grandmother's marriage was arranged, 1948, the newly independent India found itself up against the threat of a looming food crisis. By this time the Canal Colonies of west Punjab where she had been born had long since achieved the purpose envisioned by their imperial designers: the former desert had become the region's bread-basket—one that, up until Partition, had produced most of the wheat that fed the subcontinent. When the British drew the line dividing Punjab between two separate nations, however, the majority of the irrigated farmland fell to the west of the division, suddenly belonging to the new nation of Pakistan. Meanwhile, India retained 80 percent of the population.

And so, on top of the dislocation of millions of people and the ensuing violence and destruction, Partition meant that India was immediately faced with the problem of an upended agriculture system and the threat of food scarcity. The new government, led by Jawaharlal Nehru, struggled to agree upon and enact land reform policies and economic development programs to uplift the Indian economy from the ruins of colonial rule. Their goals oscillated between creating the egalitarian society of self-sufficient rural villages that Gandhi's followers envisioned and the more urban, capitalist country that others wanted. In the meantime, Indian leaders, eager to avoid the risk of another mass famine like the one that had killed 3 million of their people just five years prior, sought to import millions of tons of wheat—preferably not from their new adversary, Pakistan.

At the same time, the United States was struggling to address a different problem. Since the 1870s, when the land giveaways used to encourage western expansion had resulted in more wheat planted than could be consumed, America had on and off suffered from a problem of oversupply. The technological developments of the 1930s and '40s—powerful tractors and combine harvesters, chemical fertilizers and pesticides—further increased production, pushing that persistent problem of oversupply into chronic status: each year, American farmers dependably produced far more grain than could be sold. The end of World War II threatened to worsen this problem as war-generated demand evaporated. To prevent prices from plummeting to devastating lows, the US government began buying farmers' surplus wheat. While this policy worked to keep the excess grain from flooding the market, it led to another problem: What was the government to do with this ever-growing mountain of wheat?

These sets of circumstances aligned into a kind of equation: One country with a large population of impoverished people and a sudden disruption in their own domestic wheat production. Another with a massive amount of excess grain in need of disposal. The former newly independent, rippling with unrest, and in search of a new political order that might better the lives of its rural majority. The latter deeply committed to the promotion of capitalist political economies and engaged in a battle to gain political influence over the Third World.

A piece of legislation forming a tidy solution to this equation was passed in 1954. Public Law 480—later known by its euphemistic nickname, "Food for Peace"—allowed the US government to unload its surplus grain onto foreign countries by giving it as aid at little or no cost to the recipient, therefore keeping US grain prices from plunging while simultaneously furthering American geopolitical interests. During these years, millions of tons of this surplus American wheat were sold to India—the largest recipient of PL 480 grains—at prices far below the cost of production. This flood of cheap American wheat pushed domestic prices so low that Indian farmers could not compete, and local production dipped further still, increasing dependence on American imports in a vicious cycle.

After a bit of matching dates, it occurred to me that though I had for years now imagined my grandmother in her Punjabi village making her daily roti and paratha from landrace wheat like my Sonora, and feeding my mother her first meals with such wheat, it's just as likely that the wheat my family ate then was not a traditional Punjabi landrace or even one of Howard's improved local varieties, but rather surplus wheat imported from the United States—some modern commercial variety grown on the plains of eastern Washington or Kansas.

I couldn't help but feel a sting of disappointment at this realization, along with a wash of embarrassment at my own ignorance, the romantic naïveté that had led me to believe otherwise. Many months later another thought surfaced:

If one were to look closely into the origins of this surplus American wheat, one would likely find in its genetic lineage the variety Marquis— one of the two ancestors shared by the majority of commercial US wheat. And Marquis, I recalled, had come to the United States from Canada, where it had been born from a cross between two varieties: Red Fife, with roots in Ukraine or Poland, and Calcutta, a landrace originating in the plains of Punjab.

⊷ 22 ⊷

One fall morning I drove a few hours north to visit the renowned baker who had made the loaf of Sonora bread my friend had brought me that first summer on the farm. For more than twenty years, Dave Miller, who was something of a legend among artisan bakers, had been making exceptional bread using traditional methods: he ground all his flour on a stone mill on site, leavened his dough with a sourdough starter, and sourced heirloom wheat—including Sonora—from local organic farmers.

When I arrived at Dave's bakery, located in a converted garage at his home, he swung open the door and invited me in before dipping his hands into a bin of dough partway through the fermentation process. Squares of pink linoleum checkered the floor. Racks of empty baskets lined the walls, bins of dough were stacked atop rolling carts, and a mixer plunged two steel arms up and down into a spinning bowl, mimicking the motions of human hands. A wood-fired deck oven stretched across the back wall.

Dave moved around the space swiftly and calmly, making only the necessary movements. He knew the exact distance from mixer to dough bin, rack to sink, the way a gymnast knows the length of her beam. While he worked, Dave explained his process, showing me the bins of rising dough—rye, seeded, Kamut—that would later be shaped into the 400 or so loaves he would sell the following morning at his city's farmers market. Then he motioned to a room next to the bakery, separated by a large glass window. Here he housed his flour mill, a machine made of three-foot-wide granite stones stacked horizontally atop one another. The bottom stone remained stationary while the top stone spun slowly, crushing the whole wheat berries into flour.

This mill, Dave explained, is central to his baking philosophy. It allows him to buy grain directly from farmers, so he knows where and how it was produced. Each batch of wheat, he told me, expresses certain flavors determined by the variety, as well as the landscape and climate in which it was grown. A whole wheat kernel—the plant's seed—contains all the vitamins, antioxidants, proteins, and enzymes that enable it to sprout into a living plant when combined with moisture and warmth. Undisturbed, a grain of wheat can remain viable as a seed for many years, and these nutrients remain intact. Once the seed is crushed, however, oxidation occurs and nutrition and flavor begin to degrade quickly. By milling his grain only minutes before mixing it into dough, all the nutrition, flavor, and aroma are preserved and transferred directly into the bread.

Most flour found on grocery shelves is ground on industrial steel roller mills. Unlike a stone mill, which grinds the grain in its entirety, a roller mill first shears the bran (the seed's skin-like coating) and the germ (the embryo) from the wheat kernel. These parts are then separated out, and the isolated endosperm is ground to produce refined, or "white" flour. To make what's called "whole wheat" flour via a roller mill, some of the separated bran is reconstituted with the white flour. Because roller-milled white flour doesn't contain the oils present in the germ and bran, it has a virtually endless shelf life—it can be transported long distances and stored indefinitely without going rancid. But it is also bereft of much of the nutritional value (not to mention flavor) found in wheat. In the 1940s, as roller-milled white flour replaced whole grain flour in the American diet, producers began to fortify it with iron and B vitamins in order to avoid a national health crisis. Prior to the adoption of roller mills, flour was commonly milled locally via a stone mill—in 1840, some 23,000 stone flour mills served communities across America. Today, just 200 industrial roller mills process the majority of the country's flour.

Dave slipped into his milling room, and I watched through the glass as he poured Sonora berries into the hopper, then turned on the machine. The hum of the motor and the roar of the runner stone thrummed through the glass. Dave reached down into the bin filling with flour, cupped some in his palm, and inspected the grind. When all the grain had been milled, he flipped a switch and the stone ground to a halt. He loaded a cart with the freshly milled wheat, rolled it into the bakery, then scooped up a palmful and held it out for me to smell. I took a breath and there it was—that buttery sweet-corn aroma I remembered from the loaf Fulton had brought me last year.

I watched Dave weigh out the water and mix it into the freshly milled Sonora flour. Sonora's low protein content—the same quality that makes it ideal for flatbreads—meant it was a challenging flour to use for the kind of hearth loaves this baker produced. The dough required a carefully monitored fermentation period that stretched over more than twelve hours, and then skilled shaping. But the result was well worth it—a uniquely flavored loaf with a tender, airy crumb and a golden crust.

After I returned home that evening, I called Fulton to talk with him about my visit. Fulton, too, milled his own flour using a stone mill and had recently told me he was thinking about embarking on a new business building stone flour mills. He'd offered to build one for our farm. At the time I wasn't sure we needed one, but after visiting Dave, I was convinced. Since this would be Fulton's first attempt at constructing a mill, we would split the risk—I'd pay for all the materials, and he would do the work at his own expense. I'd get a stone mill, and he would get to try out his design. That night my dreams were full of flour mills.

❧ 23 ❧

Our Sonora seed waited in the back corner of our barn, cleaned and ready to be planted once the fall rains began. Occasionally I lifted the lids off the three steel drums to make sure no rats or bugs had managed to find a way into the containers, or simply to admire the heaps of lustrous berries. After my visit with Dave I dug my fingers into the barrel, lifted a handful of berries, and thought of something I'd read on his website: "It's easy to forget that bread, in its simplest form, is nothing but seeds—nutrient-dense, flavorful, life-giving seeds (14,000 or so per loaf—I counted!)."

The barrels felt like a triumph, evidence that this foray into grain growing might be worthwhile, and they bolstered my motivation for the project. Ryan and I began talking with the land trust about the possibility of leasing additional acreage to grow more grains. It seemed a near perfect use for the adjacent land. Dry-farming grains would require none of the additional infrastructure that most other locally suited crops demanded and that the conservancy could not afford to build—deer fencing and irrigation systems for vineyards or berries, trellising for hops. I'd found a no-till grain drill—a heavy implement designed to cut furrows into uncultivated ground and deposit seed into them—available for rent from the local Natural Resources Conservation Service. Using this implement to sow the grain, we'd conserve soil health and a great deal of labor. I drafted a proposal to lease an additional fifty acres, and prepared to send it to the conservancy for consideration.

But before I got around to emailing off the proposal, my enthusiasm deflated. Was this meager harvest really enough to warrant expansion? And how would we clean and process more than 50,000 pounds of grain? Surely we couldn't cart it all down to Reed's facility. And though we'd spoken to two Bay Area bakers who'd expressed interest in sourcing Sonora from us, we'd yet to actually sell a grain of wheat. We could use our harvest from last year to plant seven acres, but we would still need somewhere around $4,300 to buy the seed needed to plant the other forty-three acres. That money, plus the additional lease payment, might be better put toward paying off a chunk of our loans. And then there was the possibility of a third year of drought. Dry-farmed fields would be entirely dependent on rain. Though I knew Sonora had been successfully dry farmed in this region for more than two centuries—possibly a lot longer—this testament of time no longer seemed assuring in the face of a potential third year of a drought climatologists were calling unprecedented.

So instead, Ryan and I decided to plant only what we had space for in rotation with vegetables, three acres or so. I saved the drafted proposal to my desktop; next year we could reconsider leasing more land. Later I measured out a portion of our Sonora harvest, roughly half, to use for seed. The rest of the grain would remain sealed up in the barn until our stone mill was up and running and I could grind it into flour.

⟿

The fall equinox brought a deluge of rain, the first storm of the year. I put on a jacket and mud boots and walked out into the fields to watch the nonirrigated sections, hard as rock, transform into spongy mud. A season's worth of dust washed away from the greenhouse roof, running down the plastic sides in little snakes of coffee-colored liquid. A rain like this in September seemed promising—perhaps the coming winter would be a wet one after all.

The storm didn't last long, and by late afternoon the sun glinted off the rain-washed gateposts and fence wire. Everything took on a fresh sheen—the barn siding, our old flatbed truck, the tractor. Even the plants—each green leaf, crimson pepper, and purple eggplant—revealed a forgotten depth of color. The soil soaked up the water greedily and by evening hardly a trace of the storm remained. I dug my boot toe into the dirt. Half an inch below the surface, the soil was still dry enough to release a puff of dust.

The next month passed rainless. Ryan and I prepared the farm for winter: We rolled up lines of drip tape and took down tomato trellising. We disked under the residue of summer crops, spread compost. By mid-November the fields were ready to be seeded, some in wheat and the rest in a cover crop mix of oats and legumes. But with no rain in sight, we couldn't plant. I checked the ten-day forecast each morning, crossing my fingers for a cloud icon among the line of little yellow suns.

One morning, our flour mill arrived unassembled inside a wooden crate. Ryan and I dragged it into the barn and unpacked the many pieces. Fulton was planning to fly out later that winter to put the mill together, but in the meantime we were eager to see the parts. There were two stones cut from pink granite, each twenty inches in diameter and six inches thick. From the center of each stone a series of shallow grooves led outward, cutting a pattern of lines across the surface. I ran my fingers over them and examined the array of other parts that lay across the barn floor, trying to imagined how they would all fit together to match the 3D sketch Fulton had sent of his design: two motors, a trapezoid-shaped hopper, a hefty rubber belt, a metal wheel, a steel rod.

⌐⊃

The last week of November the forecast predicted a storm. Under a sky dappled gray, but not yet dropping rain, I walked zigzag patterns across the fields with a broadcast seeder strapped over my shoulders, just as I had the year before. But this year the Sonora seed had come from my own fields. I wanted passersby to be able to see the wheat as it grew, to watch the stalks flush green, then copper, then gold, to see the way the field moved like liquid in a breeze. So I planted the Sonora in the field closest to the roadside. When I'd broadcast all the seed, the field glinted with blond specks as if strewn with confetti. Then Ryan drove the tractor attached to the harrow over the field and the seed slipped out of sight into the soil.

On the back section of the farm I planted two acres of another land-race wheat, Red Fife. Reed had had extra seed and suggested I grow some along with the Sonora. "Better not to have all your eggs in the same basket," he'd said. Red Fife was a "harder" grain than Sonora. It contained higher protein content, making it well suited for leavened breads and popular with bakers. The stalks were also shorter than Sonora and therefore had less of a tendency to fall over under the weight of the berries, though they could be less tolerant of drought. After all the wheat was sowed Ryan and I planted the remaining land, except for the half-acre block of winter vegetables—beets and carrots and greens—with cover crop.

That night I awoke to rain sheeting against my bedroom window, and by morning humid warmth thickened the air as if the last of the summer heat had been exhaled from beneath the earth. I walked out to the fields, pushed my finger into the soil to see how far the rain had penetrated. The moisture had seeped an inch or so down—not much but enough to soak the seeds.

Early December brought a few brief rains and one snow, but by the middle of the month all signs of precipitation had evaporated from the forecast. As rainless days stacked atop one another, climatologists started to talk about a formidable atmospheric presence they'd deemed the "ridiculously resilient ridge." The ridge, made by a region of high pressure sitting over the northeastern Pacific Ocean, was suppressing storm activity along the West Coast, resulting in exceptionally dry and warm conditions.

I spent the first few weeks of the new year in a T-shirt pruning rows of perennial herbs and flowers. The warm weather and lack of rain pulled me out to the farm each day, though I knew I needed to spend time indoors catching up on paperwork, doing taxes, laying out our crop plan for the coming year. I needed freezing mornings, dark skies, and hammering rain to fill up a reservoir of winter in myself that I knew I'd depend on to get through another scorching summer.

↤ 24 ↦

As postwar America began dispensing its extra wheat to India and other Third World countries in the form of food aid, the political power such surplus grain supplies could grant a country became clear. "I have heard . . . that people may become dependent on us for food. I know that was not supposed to be good news. To me that was good news, because before people can do anything they have got to eat," Senator Hubert H. Humphrey bluntly told a 1957 Senate committee. "And if you are looking for a way to get people to lean on you and to be dependent on you, in terms of their cooperation with you, it seems to me that food dependence would be terrific." And so, the search for ever-greater wheat yields gained new impetus.

It was during these same years that breeders at Washington State College of Agriculture created the first viable crosses between local wheat varieties and the semi-dwarf Norin 10 seeds received from Japan, resulting in a semi-dwarf wheat suitable for local growing conditions. Field trials of these semi-dwarfs had just begun when Norman Borlaug, the shuttle-breeding MAP plant pathologist in Mexico, learned of their existence and requested samples. He crossed them with his Mexican varieties and, after several attempts, succeeded in producing a cross that displayed both short stature and suitable resistance to local diseases. When coupled with increased fertilization and irrigation, Borlaug's semi-dwarfs could produce as much as 50 percent greater yields than even the best of his taller improved varieties. Similar results were achieved in the United States, where in 1959 breeders at Washington State released the first semi-dwarf wheat variety for commercial production. Three years later, in 1962, Borlaug did the same in Mexico. With the arrival of these short-strawed wheats, the problem of wheat lodging under heavy yields quite suddenly vanished. By 1963, a year after Mexico adopted the new semi-dwarf varieties in tandem with irrigation and fertilizer, the country had swung from importing wheat (upwards of 200,000 tons per year in the 1940s) to *exporting* 72,000 tons.

This shift provided Mexico with the means to fund the development of an urban industrial economy and transformed the agricultural landscape into one dominated by large commercial farms. In the process, small and subsistence farmers were eliminated. Many moved to cities, where they became low-wage factory workers; others journeyed north to California, where they became laborers in the state's strawberry fields and lettuce farms.

↞

Sir Albert Howard did not live to see the rise of semi-dwarf wheat. He died in October of 1947, two months after India gained independence from the Empire he had long served. So, what Howard might have thought of these new varieties is only speculation. As a wheat breeder perhaps he would have been thrilled, would have found this development groundbreaking.

Or perhaps he would have recognized immediately where these new wheat varieties would lead. Perhaps he'd have understood how they would push global agriculture—not just the growing of wheat, but of most crops—toward increasingly chemical-dependent systems. By the later years of his life, Howard had become critical of private industry co-opting agricultural research, so maybe he'd have been wary of the Rockefeller Foundation—which was heavily tied to the petrochemicals—becoming so involved in wheat production. Perhaps he could have guessed, too, that the power of these new wheat seeds would be substantiated for the world in the vast plains of Punjab. "The Western democracies are handicapped because Asiatic and other underprivileged people attribute their present plight to the domination of the capitalist colonial system, and resent the political and racial discrimination under which they have lived," the Rockefeller Foundation's 1951 report, *The World Food Problem*, declares. "These are handicaps which only effective action can overcome."

❦ 25 ❧

By the early 1960s, the news of the wildly increased harvests that US and Mexican farms were reaping from the new semi-dwarf wheat seeds—now called "High Yielding Varieties" (HYVs)—had spread to breeders around the world. So, too, had the narrative that nations' ongoing population growth, particularly in the Third World, would lead inevitably to food scarcity and social unrest if not met by a drastic increase in crop yields.

By this time the Rockefeller Foundation had entered into an agreement with India to help establish a cereals improvement program there similar to MAP. The Ford Foundation, another leading American philanthropic organization, had also committed funds to an agricultural community development program in India. In the spring of 1963, following the success of the semi-dwarf wheat varieties in Mexico, Indian agricultural leaders and the Rockefeller Foundation invited Borlaug to visit India. Later that year, a small shipment of Borlaug's high-yielding wheat varieties—enough for trials—arrived in India in time for fall plantings.

It might have taken many years of crossing Borlaug's seeds with Indian wheats to produce a stable semi-dwarf variety resistant to local diseases and suitable to the region's climate. But because of the effects of Borlaug's "shuttle breeding," his varieties were already adapted to a wide range of conditions and performed well in their brand-new environment: the results of the first Indian trials suggested the new varieties could, if grown with generous nitrogen fertilizer and increased irrigation, produce up to eight times the average yield then being obtained by Indian farmers.

Although such yield increases were hard to refuse, Indian leaders held mixed views on the prospect of widely adopting these HYVs and their high-input growing requirements. Some believed further trials were necessary to confirm that the new seeds wouldn't be wiped out by local diseases or pests. Others objected to the switch to capital-intensive agriculture, noting the disproportionate advantage such a shift would have for wealthy farmers who owned large farms and could afford the expensive inputs—tractors, combines, seeds, fertilizer, irrigation—while small, less resourced farmers would surely be left behind.

Such concerns were not unfounded. In fact, all one needed to do was look closely at rural America to see these worries realized. Despite the enthusiasm from government and philanthropic leaders, the widespread adoption of capital-intensive agriculture had not worked out well for the majority of American farmers or their communities. Instead, hundreds of thousands of farmers were forced off their land as the number of farms in the United States was cut in half over the course of the decades spanning 1944–69. By the end of the 1960s, the situation in rural America had grown so dire that President Johnson issued an executive order establishing a commission to evaluate and report on the status of rural poverty in the United States.

The report, poignantly titled *The People Left Behind*, delivered a devastating picture. The commission counted 14 million people living in acute rural poverty—a number that would be far higher, the authors said, if it included those who had already left their homes to migrate to urban areas in search of work, only to find that they'd "exchanged life in a rural slum for life in an urban slum."

"Today's rural poor have been left behind in the wake of basic changes in the fabric of rural life. Many are refugees from an agricultural revolution."

This agricultural revolution, however, had led to tremendous leaps in national production, bolstering America's surplus grain supply. And this surplus food had gained new value in the eyes of government leaders—it was a bargaining chip in foreign relations, something no longer belonging in a pantry but in an arsenal.

In 1965, as India debated the prospect of widely adopting HYV, communist and Marxist parties gained momentum in many states across the country. In response, the United States changed its food aid policy. In order to continue receiving aid, India would be required to adopt policies that industrialized agricultural development, allowed US private investment in India's fertilizer industry, and promoted capital-intensive technologies.

In short order the Indian government approved two of the Mexican HYV for commercial cultivation, and 18,000 tons of seed of the variety Lerma Rojo 64 were loaded onto a ship in Sonora, Mexico. Two months later the ship docked in Gujarat, India, marking the single largest seed transaction in the history of the world.

⇔

By the time this colossal shipment of semi-dwarf wheat seed reached the shores of India, my grandmother was no longer in the country. She'd boarded her own ship, this one heading west, away from the subcontinent. With my infant mother in her arms she'd crossed the Indian Ocean, leaving behind the wheat fields of Punjab to join her husband in Nairobi.

I asked my grandmother one afternoon if she had been happy to leave her village or if she had wanted to stay in Punjab with her family. She didn't respond at first and, after a moment, I assumed she hadn't understood me. I started to repeat my question, but before I could finish she lifted her palm and shook her head. "No," she said. "What I wanted? It did not matter what I wanted."

Some months later, an aunt gave me a stack of old black-and-white photos taken in the days and years after my grandmother arrived in Kenya. In one, she stands alongside my grandfather with a toddler—my mother—in her arms. In the background is a latched door, a coat hanging from a hook on the wall, a chunni draped over another. She is eighteen years old.

I stared at the photo for a long time before tucking it away, then took it out again a few hours later, and again the next day. No matter how many times I looked at it the photo remained enthralling, almost taunting. I peered at the faces, my grandfather's deep-set eyes, thick brows, bearded jaw; my mother's chubby cheeks and plump lips. Mostly I looked at my grandmother: high cheekbones, searing eyes, lips pressed into a line that is neither a smile nor a frown. I searched her face for a clue of what she might have felt in that moment: fear? pride? anger? relief? sorrow? But I couldn't penetrate her gaze.

Instead I looked for the face of the woman I knew, the grandmother who cooked paratha each morning in a house in the San Fernando

Valley. I looked, too, for a hint of myself, for a similar bone structure, a familiar feature, evidence of the link connecting me to her.

In the years when these photos were taken, I know, my grandmother would still have had all her own teeth. I flipped through the stack searching for a glimpse of them. But in every shot she offers only a close-lipped smile, or no smile at all. Her teeth are nowhere to be found.

✦ 26 ✦

One afternoon that winter, Reed stopped by for a visit. We walked through my fields, compared our planting dates and soil amendments. He knelt next to our field of Sonora, just six inches tall, and dug two fingers into the soil. I watched closely, eager for his thoughts. Reed had been growing grains in this region for many years—surely he'd experienced worse conditions. I wanted him to say something reassuring, to tell me that he'd seen Sonora persist in ground dry as chalk, that this drought was nothing to be worried about. But he only nodded. "Yep," he said. "Your ground's just as dry as mine."

Before he left, he told me this might be his last season growing wheat. "Hardly makes enough to cover costs as it is—if I have to start irrigating I'll take a loss. Looks like we've got some dry years ahead." I turned toward the hills in the distance, still bronzed with dried summer grass when they should have been flushed green with new growth.

The next morning I awoke to fast-moving clouds and scanned their felty grays for a promise of rain. The forecast predicted a 70 percent chance of precipitation, more than I'd seen in months. I checked the tarps over our woodpiles to make sure they were tight, scanned the farm for any tools left uncovered. But all the rain preparations had been finished months ago. There was nothing left to do but wait.

Midday, the first few drops fell, a clinking on the barn's tin roof. I ran outside, watched the rain hit the ground, each drop releasing a tiny breath of dust from the soil. For several hours the drizzle continued, but I wanted it to pour, to pummel my fields and stream down the hillsides.

By evening, the rain had stopped. The clouds grew threadbare like an old T-shirt, then pulled apart completely and drifted away. Behind them that same blue sky lay waiting. I guessed we'd gotten a tenth of an inch at most. Still, it was something, enough to keep the wheat going for a while longer, and for that I was thankful. In the sunset light, cider-colored raindrops clung to the bellies of the mulberry branches outside our kitchen window.

⥀

Because our farm lay across the curve of a dip in the landscape, cool air often rolled down from the surrounding slopes and gathered in our fields. Some mornings I could see a puddle of fog pooled over the farm. Perhaps this was why our wheat survived that dry winter of 2013–14, why the soil managed to cling to enough moisture to sustain the slim stalks. Or maybe the few showers of rain fell at just the right intervals to keep the wheat alive. By April, the Sonora stood over four feet tall and I could see the tips swelling as the heads of berries began to form. The Red Fife remained shorter—a little under three feet—and though more weeds grew up between those shorter stalks, this field, too, looked healthy.

Spring arrived early and I was once again swept up in the flurry of the season, seeding summer crops, harvesting spring greens and sugar snap peas, baking bread. By May, the earliest tomatoes were already blushing red, and each Sonora stalk carried a rattle of berries. I squeezed my fingers around one of them, pulled it apart to examine the wheat inside. The kernels were rounder and larger than the prior year's. The stalks, too, were taller.

The wheat was not the only crop that looked better as we neared our third summer on the farm. Benefiting from two years of compost applications and cover crops, careful tillage and weed management, the soil was visibly enriched. Everything grew better. I couldn't help but imagine how productive our land would be in five, ten, fifteen years of such stewardship. I said this aloud to Ryan one afternoon as we prepared beds for a new carrot planting. As soon as the words left my mouth, though, I felt a flutter of unease. After all, it wasn't actually *our* land.

Ryan drove the tractor down each row, pulling the disk. I watched the soil spill from the steel plates in dark brown ribbons, feeling suddenly possessive of that soil, resentful that it was not truly mine. I turned away and focused instead on pouring a bag of sweet-smelling carrot seed into our seeder. I pushed the machine down row after row until the landscape was ridged like corduroy, until the burn of covetousness I felt had receded.

But with each passing month, my unease grew. The fact that the land

I farmed would never belong to me festered like a toothache. I tried to convince myself that it didn't matter—what difference did it make if I owned or leased the land? Ryan and I had a five-year lease, with the option to renew after each period. It was possible, hypothetically, that we could remain on this land until the end of our days.

I wanted to support the idea that farmland was not a commodity to be privately owned, not an investment, but was instead a collective resource. And wasn't that just what I was doing by leasing farmland from a land trust? It meant I would have to live with a degree of uncertainty, but was that really so bad? I tried to convince myself it wasn't, but I couldn't seem to silence the growing murmurs of doubt.

There was an economic component, of course. In America, property ownership is among the most effective strategies to build wealth. If Ryan and I owned the land we worked, we would be paying off a mortgage instead of paying rent. This investment would likely, with the ever-climbing land values in California, provide a significant return by the time we reached retirement. Scraping by for decades as a vegetable farmer was one thing if I knew that by the end of thirty years I'd own a chunk of verdant and productive California land upon which I could live out the rest of my life, leave to my children if I had any, or sell to a new farmer. It was another thing if I knew I'd only be nearing the end of yet another renewal period of a lease agreement, with nothing to show for the last three decades but whatever meager savings I'd managed to store away. This was disquieting, but my unease with being a tenant was rooted in something beyond the financial implications.

In the preface of his book *The Unsettling of America*, Wendell Berry writes about an exchange he witnessed between an agricultural economist and a farmer. While giving a talk, the economist posited that no essential difference existed between owning and renting a farm. "A farmer stood up in the audience," Berry writes, "and replied: 'Professor, I don't think our ancestors came to America in order to rent a farm.'"

When I stumbled across this passage that third summer on the farm, I read it again and again, finding it both discomfiting and affirming. I felt uneasy that I recognized this sentiment in myself—it seemed greedy, stemming from a crude sense of entitlement. Yet when I thought of my grandparents, of my mother, I knew that these forbears of mine had indeed not come to America so that their children and grandchildren could become tenant farmers, just as landless as their families had been in Punjab. At the same time, I also understood that mine were not the "ancestors" the farmer had been speaking of. They were not the early white colonists upon which the prevailing image of the classic yeoman American farmer is based. Nor were they the frontier-pushing homesteaders who were promised free land in exchange for cultivating it (and, in turn, assisting in the country's project of westward expansion).

And yet, these mythologies of America's imagined agrarian past loomed large. If a homesteader earned land through audacity and industriousness, then the inverse, too, seemed true: lack of ownership could only mean an insufficiency of such qualities. I didn't then know that homesteading never actually occurred on a significant scale in California. By the time settlers seeking their promised 160-acre plots reached the state, most found all the arable land already privately owned—not by other homesteaders who'd beat them to it, but by gold-rich businessmen and land speculators who held estates thousands of acres in size. Even if I had understood this, I'm not sure it would have quelled my growing, gut-level desire to own my land.

Land ownership was thoroughly entangled with the agrarian ideal as I saw it then. It was essential to the DIY ethic of small farming, to its culture of self-reliance. Who could imagine our country's most iconic small organic farms—Scott and Helen Nearing's New England homesteads of stacked stone walls, Eliot Coleman's lauded organic farm in Maine, Wendell Berry's famous Lanes Landing Farm in Kentucky—on rented land?

"They don't even own the land they farm," I overheard an older man say to another at a grange hall farmer's potluck one evening that summer. "Let's see how long they last." I knew this man was eager to write us off—we were young, new, and on his turf—and I tried to ignore his comment. But it had struck a nerve, a weak point I hadn't before known was there.

Not long after that potluck, Ryan and I began to search for a way to purchase the land we farmed. The conservancy—which had a big loan out on the property and was now questioning the decision to acquire it in the first place—had agreed to discuss a sale of the portion we'd leased if we could find a way around all the legal barriers and come up with a fair price. There were several obstacles: The land was under a conservation easement, which meant we could not build another residence on the property. Because our house was located on a different parcel than our fields, this was problematic. The zoning requirements didn't allow for small parcels—we'd have to purchase more than the ten acres we farmed. The market price for the land was high. After a year of failed attempts to work around all these constraints, the truth emerged, no longer contestable: We were—and, as long as we stayed, would always be—tenants. To continue farming here meant the land I farmed and the house I lived in would never be, in the legal sense, mine.

❧ 27 ❧

May 2014 was halfway over and fast clouds moved over the farm, their underbellies rippled and bruised. I watched them from my kitchen window while frying a pan of potatoes. It looked—though I didn't want to jinx it—like rain. I was eager for any last bit of precipitation before the wet season ended and the summer's dry heat set in for good. A swirl of wind tumbled the mulberry branches and I waited for the sounds of raindrops pattering on the tree's broad leaves. None came. After dinner I walked out with the bucket from beneath our kitchen sink in hand, dumped the dishwater on the honeysuckle vine and felt a drop on the back of my neck. Then another. Soon the rain was falling steadily and Ryan and I sat under the cover of the porch, listening until the sky grew black. A pleasant breeze blew grassy and cool through the house that night, and I fell into a contented sleep. It did not occur to me to consider what a late-season storm like this might do to the Sonora field—those chest-high stalks now top-heavy with plump ears. I thought only about how badly we needed the water.

The next morning, I walked down to the farm to harvest wholesale orders. The ground was already mostly dry, but the scent of rain-wet earth lingered. I strode out into the beet field feeling renewed, and began pulling up the roots one after the next. The beets slid easily from the damp soil, and it took only a few minutes to fill two bins—fifty pounds' worth. With the bins stacked between my arms, I made my way back to the barn to wash and pack. Then I caught sight of the wheat.

The field looked as if someone had spread a giant picnic blanket across the center, flattening the stalks, pressing the heavy ears into the dirt. I set the beets down and ran over. A few swaths of wheat remained upright, mostly along the edges of the field, but the majority had fallen under the weight of the rain and the push of the wind. Lodged. For all I'd heard about this infamous problem, I'd not yet seen what a lodged field of wheat looked like. But there it was, a perfect vision of quashed hopes.

At the west edge of the farm, I inspected the Red Fife. With stalks a foot or two shorter than those of the Sonora, this wheat had weathered the storm just fine and now stood upright and greener than ever. With Reed's words ringing in my mind—*better not to put all your eggs in the same basket*—I returned to the Sonora field and walked the perimeter, not sure what I was looking for. Lodged wheat, I'd heard, could sometimes spring back up, and I hoped for some kind of indication that this would be the case. Perhaps the Sonora only needed to dry out.

A week passed. Two. By the end of May, the stalks had turned golden but remained toppled over one another, a tangled mat. The berries would be ready to harvest in the next few weeks. But if it remained lodged, the wheat would be impossible to cut.

☙ 28 ☙

The Sonora remained splattered across the field several weeks later when my grandparents, who'd driven up from LA for a visit, came to see the farm. The stalks, brittle and bleached blond, fell this way and that like a thousand bowling pins knocked over. Each carried a head of berries, the kernels promising—plump and golden. But these kernels, I'd finally admitted, would go to the birds. There was no feasible way to harvest the lodged field.

I refrained from pointing out the Sonora as I toured my grandparents and aunt around the farm. I hardly looked at it myself anymore. The mess of it made me cringe, and I regretted planting it right along the roadside, the toppled stalks splayed across the landscape for all to see. Instead, I led my visitors to the field nearest the parking lot, where half an acre of winter squash and pumpkin plants stood proud. Hundreds of young fruits, fist-size and green, were scattered among the vines. In the next field, zucchinis and crooknecks proliferated alongside rows of trellised tomato vines. It was my grandparents' first visit to the farm since we'd been in full operation, and I wanted them to see the abundance. My grandmother touched my arm and pointed to a deep pink tomato. "This one, it is ready, haanah? Can I pick it?" I handed her a bucket to fill. She moved down the row and plucked one fruit after the next, not greedily but with a kind of urgent diligence, until the bucket was full.

Late that afternoon, after finishing up my farm tasks for the day, I drove over to my parents' house for dinner and found everyone on the back deck, where two pots popped and sizzled atop propane burners. My grandmother sat at the patio table, a lemon in one hand and a paring knife in the other, making a batch of achar. My mother and aunt stood at the propane burners, sipping margaritas from coffee mugs so their parents didn't have to look directly at the evidence of their daughters' departure from Sikh customs.

I'd brought a box of potatoes, six eggplants, and a basket of jalapeños.

I set the produce on the patio table near my grandmother, and she smiled. "Nice," she said, lifting an eggplant from the pile and turning it in her hands. "Very nice." She set the eggplant back on the pile and returned her attention to the lemons. She sliced one in half, made a cut down the center of each half, and then cut twice across each width. Twelve pieces, seven cuts. She brushed the pieces to the side and repeated with a new fruit until the cutting board was filled with chopped lemons. Then she dumped them into a bowl, clearing the board to start again.

I offered to help and gathered a cutting board and knife, trying to slice the fruits exactly like she did. When the bowl was half filled, my grandmother ran her fingers through the fleshy chunks. She picked out three, frowned and sliced them in half. "These ones are too big, haanah?" She gave a sly grin, as if she found my mistake humorous. With the next fruit I focused more closely on the placement of each cut, tried to make sure no piece got away larger than any other. But this took time, and I wondered if my grandmother noticed my slowness. Did she think to herself, *My god, my own granddaughter, a grown woman and she can hardly even use a knife!* For every lemon I chopped, she chopped two.

My mother pulled up a chair beside us with her coffee-mug margarita and a stack of papers in hand. "OK, a few more questions," she said to my grandmother, who didn't bother to look up from the lemons. My mother switched to Punjabi, said something I couldn't understand, then waited. My grandmother pulled another lemon from the bag and muttered something hardly audible before plunging her knife into the fruit and swiftly dissecting it.

I glanced at the papers in my mother's hand. *Advanced Directives,* the top form read. There were several questions about preferences regarding medical treatment should my grandmother not be able to communicate, followed by lines to fill in. In some of the spaces my mother had jotted answers while others remained blank. My mother took a sip from her mug, then asked another question in Punjabi. My grandmother let out a long sigh, muttered a response, then looked away. My mother wrote something down and read off the next question, translating it into Punjabi. My grandmother didn't answer this time, just returned her gaze to the lemons and resumed chopping. When my mother repeated the question, my grandmother set down her knife, pushed back her chair, and spoke back curtly.

My aunt turned from a pot of simmering dal and lifted the papers from my mother's hand, shooting her sister a look that said *enough.* "Mom," my aunt said, then asked a question that wasn't on the form. "What kind of food do you want served at your funeral?"

My grandmother looked up for the first time since these questions had begun, pushed her glasses up the bridge of her nose. "Bhindia," she said without pause. Okra. Here was one she knew exactly how to answer. After a moment, she smiled and added, "Roti de nal." With flatbread. Turning back to the lemons, she sliced the last one, then stood and carried the bowl of shining fruit into the kitchen.

☙

When my grandmother returned to the porch with a bowl of dough, she ignored her daughters and turned to me. "Jackie," she said, "come sit." I sat and she looked up at me. "I want to ask you, how long you going to farm?"

"I'm not sure," I said.

My grandmother turned to the dough and began to work it between her fingers. "Vegetables—they don't make much money, haanah? You can get a nice job, you have good education, very good education! You can get a good job, buy nice house?" She looked at me expectantly and I tried to think of something to say. I didn't know how to explain that while she was right—vegetables don't make much money, and I could probably get a job with a decent salary, save enough to put a down payment on a "nice" house somewhere—I was looking for something else. How could I tell her that I'd found the privileges of middle-class American life, hard won by my grandparents, to be unfulfilling?

How could I explain how it felt to spend a cold March day crouching in rain gear, thinning row after row of beet seedlings and then, two months later under a warm May sun, to pull hundreds of purple globes from the soil and feel the weight of each one in my palm? How could I describe the way, in my fields, the outcome of my work was tangible, my agency evidenced? I could sow cover crop, spread compost, and *see* the soil grow darker. I could fill bin after bin with those beets, deliver them to the food co-op, to restaurants, and then dice up a few for myself, roast them with spring onions and new potatoes, fill my belly with their mass. And at night I could lay my body—callused and wind-chafed and work-strong—between two line-dried sheets that smelled of sun and cut grass and drop into the heavy sleep of earned rest.

Amid the ceaseless news of the ecological wreckage produced by our food system, I could walk my ten acres and see something different: A killdeer nest tucked between broccoli rows. Swallowtails on the butterfly bush and bees swarming the calendulas and tulsi basil. Eighty different plant varieties—native flowers, heirloom watermelons, landrace wheat. And on the roots of a bell bean pulled from the soil, nitrogen-fixing rhizobium nodules lined up like strings of pearls.

Even when things went wrong—the night a howling storm shredded the plastic from one of our greenhouses and twisted its metal frame, or the time an early heat wave made our spring broccoli bolt with pale yellow flowers before any of it had had a chance to form a single head—there was a sense of connection, of being threaded to the environment, and with this came a kind of antidote to loneliness, to meaninglessness.

A burst of laughter behind us broke the quiet, and my grandmother and I turned to see my mother and dad and aunt gathered by the edge of the pool, bowls of chips and salsa between them and mugs of drinks in hand. My mother's cheeks were rosy from laughing.

When I turned back to my grandmother, she was still waiting for me to answer her. Even in the shade, the gold thread of her turquoise kameez shimmered. I wondered what my grandmother might have pictured when she imagined a future in California. I couldn't help but feel that my own pursuit of a kind of California dream had begun to unravel something of my grandmother's.

"Yes," I said. "You're right."

"Haanji, yes!" She smiled, then shrugged, and added softly, "When you are ready, yes? When you are ready, then you can do something else." She turned to the propane burners, poured a puddle of oil into a pan. As the oil hissed against the hot steel, she lifted a bowl filled with cubed okra and turned it into the pan.

I picked up the pen my mother had been using, then reached in my pocket for a True Value receipt I'd tucked away earlier. I wanted to write down the recipe as my grandmother cooked, to be able to remember how to make bhindia just like she did. With the okra sizzling in the pan, my grandmother cut an onion in half in her palm. Then she held the onion over the pan and sliced each half into quarter-inch strips, letting

the pieces fall atop the okra. She stirred in a pinch of turmeric, a teaspoon of dried green mango powder, and two chopped jalapeños. I
looked down at the recipe I'd scratched out on the back the receipt. It
appeared so simple, just a list of ingredients, and I knew this list did not
contain the thing I wanted to preserve. I shoved the receipt back into my
pocket and tried instead to study my grandmother's motions—the way
she rested one hand on her hip, the other on her wooden spoon, how the
corners of her mouth were turned down in concentration, her bottom
lip jutting out as she turned the okra to evaluate the shade of browning.

↫ 29 ↬

The next afternoon, I could hear my aunt laughing from the back-yard when I pulled into my parents' driveway to have lunch with my family. She and my grandmother were sitting around a bowl of fermented dal, chopping potatoes, their faces still lit with humor.

"We were just remembering one time in Nairobi," my aunt explained, "how your mother and I got caught sneaking the green mangoes from the roof—they were drying up there, you know, for umb achar?—anyway, we were just eating them as fast as we could!" Laughter overtook her again.

My grandmother pointed to the bowl of creamy dal and explained how she had learned to cook dosa—a crepe made from dough of fermented lentils—from her neighbors in Nairobi, families from Gujarat who became her closest friends there. "From them, I learn, too, to use limbri leaves, you know limbri? Also, sometimes, you call curry patha?" I nodded, reminding her of the leaves she'd given me from her tree. "Ah, yes, those!" she said and returned her attention to the potatoes. She and my aunt worked quietly for a moment, the slide of their knife blades through waxy flesh a kind of rhythm.

"What was it like in Nairobi?" I ventured.

No one said anything for a moment, then my grandmother picked up another potato and spoke. "It was very clean. We had good neighbors, all from India. And the Kenyans too, very nice people," she said.

"Ha, nice to you!" my aunt put in, laughing again. She told me how my grandmother gained a reputation for her generosity toward the Kenyan vendors who would come through their neighborhood each morning with baskets of fruit on their heads. "They always gave Mom the first pick because she was so nice to them. She would save our old clothes to give them, you know, that kind of thing."

My grandmother listened then turned to me and said softly, "They were treated so bad. Very bad, it was not nice."

My aunt, who had been just a child during her years in Kenya, widened her eyes, then looked to me. "Yeah, well that's because they would just get a machete and walk into a house and kill people!"

At this, my grandmother only shook her head. "We were in their country."

Later, I would think of this exchange and wonder which country, of the five she'd lived in before coming here, my grandmother claimed as her own. Born in British India, at Partition she found herself suddenly in Pakistan. Then, after crossing the new border on foot, she entered the Republic of India. Less than a decade later, she left to live in the British colony of Kenya. In 1963, after Kenya won freedom from the British, she found herself once again suddenly in a new country—independent Kenya—without ever having moved. In the following years, tensions rose between Kenyans keen to shake off the vestiges of subjugation and foreigners residing in the country. And so, caught again in the fallout of decolonization and eager to avoid more violence, my grandparents sought the means to leave. This time, now a family of six, they faced three options: return to Punjab, try their luck in London via the British passports they could apply for as citizens of a former colony, or somehow get to America.

There was no debate, my grandmother would tell me years later. They chose to try for America. By then, my grandfather had become a skilled machinist and had been working for East African Airways for many years. He applied for a work visa to the United States, where he'd heard workers with his skills might be granted entry. When I asked why they choose America, my grandmother didn't mention Punjab. She only told me that in London, she knew, there were many Indians—too many cousins and aunties already living there. "But California?" she said with a shake of her head. "Very few Indians here then. We know only one family when we move. One!" Her eyes widened, and she leaned closer. "In California," she nearly whispered, "maybe things can be different. *New.* You know what I'm saying?"

☙

Back at the farm that evening, I watered the greenhouse seedlings—flats of Swiss chard and curly kale, a last succession of melons—then turned off the drip irrigation and walked the fields in the cool night air. At the edge of the Sonora field, I paused. Even matted down as they were, the stalks still rustled pleasantly in the breeze. I knelt to pluck a spikelet of seed from one bowed head, then turned it in my hand. In botany there is a term for a plant's dispersal unit such as this spikelet: a diaspore. A diaspore, which shares a root, of course, with the word *diaspora*, consists of both the seed itself and additional material designed to aid in dispersal—a tail to catch the wind, a sticker to cling to an animal's fur. Within this unit exist two distinct yet essential functions of survival: the capacity for movement and the ability to root. I rubbed the spikelet between my fingertips, blowing the crumbled chaff into the breeze, until I held only the naked berry in my palm.

⊷ 30 ⊷

In 1971, after he and his family had lived in Nairobi for more than a decade, my grandfather was granted a work visa allowing him to come to America as a trained machinist. This came as a great relief, but the price of the six plane tickets he needed to get him and his family there remained out of reach. When he'd saved enough money for the second leg of the journey—London to California—East Africa Airways, the company he'd loyally served for fifteen years, promised him free standby seats from Bombay to London. So the family began making their travel plans. First they would return to India to say farewell to their families. Then they'd fly to London and stay with my grandfather's sister for a few weeks. From there they'd fly to California, where they'd made arrangements to stay with friends from Nairobi—the only people they knew in America—until my grandfather found work and they could move into their own apartment. So, on a February afternoon in 1971, they left Kenya and headed back to the arid plains of Punjab.

A few months before they arrived in Punjab, Norman Borlaug won the Nobel Peace Prize for his role in what had, by then, been named the Green Revolution. The term was coined by William Gaud, an administrator for the Agency for International Development who praised US philanthropical support of fertilizer, irrigation, and high-yielding seeds in the Third World. These agricultural developments, he said, "contain the makings of a new revolution. It is not a violent Red Revolution like that of the Soviets, nor is it a White Revolution like that of the Shah of Iran. I call it the Green Revolution." By now, the new high-yielding seeds—just five years after their introduction—occupied 35 percent of India's wheat fields, and the country's wheat production had nearly doubled. In turn, the nation's nitrogen fertilizer use had undergone a twenty-fold increase, and 70,000 new wells had been dug to provide irrigation to formerly rain-fed fields. "Never before in the history of agriculture," Borlaug proclaimed in his Nobel lecture, "has a transplantation of high-yielding varieties coupled with an entirely new technology and strategy been achieved on such a massive scale, in so short a period of time, and with such great success."

I wonder, now, if my grandmother noticed the changes that had come to her village when she returned from Kenya. Did she wonder why the wheat stalks flanking the paths did not brush her ribs as they had before, but reached only to her knees? Did she wonder if she'd misremembered their height, their varying colors, or if the stalks had in fact been this short all along, the hue of tan so uniform? Had it been only her child eyes that looked out at these ordinary fields and perceived them to be towering, dappled with shades of amber and gold? Did she notice, upon her return, the stacks of fertilizer bags, the new wells? Did she sense a feeling of optimism among the villagers, of amazement at the new seeds that promised to double—triple!—a farmer's yield? Maybe the new technologies had yet to reach her particular village, or maybe she already knew better than to believe in such things as miracle seeds.

When I asked my grandmother about this time, she said that she remembered mostly the agony of waiting. She'd hoped her stay in India would be brief, a week or two, enough time to say goodbye to her parents and siblings before boarding the plane to England. But India's air travel industry had been disrupted: the workers had gone on strike and most flights had been canceled. The remaining flights were full, and standby tickets were nowhere to be found.

My grandfather had already bought the tickets for the second half of the journey, London to LA. He'd chosen a date far enough out to allow a few weeks for the family to visit with his sister in London, and so the situation was not yet dire, but day after day passed with no standby seats available. The date of the flight to LA neared. It began to seem possible that they'd miss it, that they'd never leave India at all.

Two weeks passed, then three. One morning, a single seat opened up. My grandfather took it, hoping he could bring his family over more easily once he was already there himself. But it made no difference. Now, my grandmother and her children stayed with friends in Bombay so she could go to the airport each morning, sometimes dragging her children, other times leaving them under my fifteen-year-old mother's watch, to beg for seats. Each day, the men behind the counters only shook their heads. *No seats,* they told her, always with the same smug leer. Then, one afternoon, she thought she saw them laugh. The longer she stayed in India, the more the idea of going to America began to seem to my grandmother like a dream, like something she had imagined.

When only a few days remained before the date of their flight to America, my grandfather called to say they no longer needed to wait for standby seats—with his employee discount and money borrowed from his sister's family, he'd managed to pay for the remaining five seats. The tickets, he'd said, would be ready to pick up at the airport.

But when my grandmother returned the next morning, the men behind the counter gave her the familiar smirk, the same shake of their heads. *No tickets*, they told her. She stared for a moment, then another customer stepped up and she was waved aside. With nothing left to do but leave, she nearly walked away when she heard, in the familiar rhythm of Gujarati, one of the countermen say to the other, *That woman, who comes every day to beg for a seat? Sometimes with so many children? I have her tickets, you know, they came yesterday. Let's see how long before she gives up.* The other man laughed.

My grandmother had always spoken with the men in Punjabi. They assumed she would not understand this other language. They couldn't have known that my grandmother was quick with languages, that her closest friends in Kenya were from Gujarat.

My grandmother spun around, stepped in front of the line, and said in crisp Gujarati, *Give them to me*. The man, perhaps too surprised or embarrassed to do anything else, handed them over.

When I asked my grandmother why these men had been so cruel, why they'd tried to keep the tickets from her, she shook her head. "I don't know," she said. "Maybe, the man, he is jealous, I think. To see a woman and four children get on a plane and go to America, and he stay there, behind a ticket counter in Bombay."

Once she had the tickets in hand, there was only the hurried packing, a last scramble of goodbyes. The next morning she was boarding a plane, already the former resident of five countries and the bearer of five children, one stillborn, the other four standing beside her—three girls with their hair in braids, one boy with a bun atop his head. Tucked in the pocket of her bag was the address of an apartment in California.

My grandfather met his family at Heathrow. There was no time left for any more visiting—they simply climbed onto the next plane.

❧

I imagine my thirty-two-year-old grandmother on that plane to California. Her narrow shoulders would have fit easily into the seat, her children
surrounding her—on her lap, at her sides. I imagine she carried a set of
aluminum dishes stacked one on top of another and secured with a wire
clasp ratcheted tight. She might have waited until the plane was dark and
the travelers in the rows around her were asleep before pulling the containers out of her bag. One by one she would have unstacked the dishes
and removed each lid. In the first tin, rice with peas and cumin and fried
okra. In the second black dal. In the third a stack of buttered roti.

⇜ 31 ⇝

By the time the plane carrying my grandmother and her family hit the tarmac at LAX, nearly three decades had passed since J.I. Rodale first struck up a correspondence with Sir Albert Howard. Over most of those years, Rodale's attempts to kindle public enthusiasm for Howard's organic philosophy had failed to yield much. But now, as the sixties gave way to the seventies, his efforts were beginning to bear fruit in parts of America.

In California, Joni Mitchell's "Big Yellow Taxi" drifted on the radio waves, urging farmers to say no to DDT. "Give me spots on my apples, but leave me the birds and the bees," she sang. In Berkeley, counterculture activists took over a vacant lot, declared it "The People's Park," and built a vegetable garden there. In San Francisco, a group called the Diggers served up brown bread baked in coffee cans at their Free Bakery, while young people pored over the pages of the *Whole Earth Catalog* and Ram Dass's *Be Here Now*. Across the Golden State, back-to-the-land hippie counterculture converged with a newfound interest in Eastern religions and a burgeoning environmental movement, providing fertile ground for Howard's organic ideas to take root. Many people were drawn to organic foods and farming for the personal health-related benefits Rodale so ardently espoused, while others found allure in Howard's rhetoric of wholeness and the wisdom of ancient traditions. Some in the counterculture saw organic farming as a component of the radical social transformation they envisioned. For these activists, organic farming offered tools to move toward an anticapitalist, egalitarian society. They started food co-ops and communal gardens, learned how to make sourdough bread and forage mushrooms.

Small farmers, most of them new to agriculture, carved out fields from the marginal spaces not already occupied by California's colossal conventional agriculture industry to try their hands at growing organic vegetables and fruits. They used methods described in the many books published by Rodale Press (*Compost Science, How to Grow Vegetables and Fruits by the Organic Method, The Encyclopedia of Organic Gardening*). Santa Cruz, with its favorable climate, semi-rural landscape, and close proximity to the urban counterculture hubs of Berkeley and San Francisco, became an epicenter for the organic farming movement. Here, in 1967, an eccentric British gardener named Alan Chadwick was invited to design a garden at the University of California's newly established Santa Cruz campus. With a cohort of eager apprentices, he built a whimsical and productive organic garden, intensively planted with fruit trees and annual vegetables, flowering perennials and herbs.

Meanwhile, mainstream media, politicians, and academics dismissed organic food as a hoax. News stories portrayed organic as a "food fad." Earl Butz, then US secretary of agriculture famous for his words "get big or get out," mocked the growing enthusiasm for organic production and aggressively rejected concerns about high pesticide and fertilizer use on industrial farms, claiming instead that these chemicals were essential to meet the nutritional needs of growing populations. "Before we go back to organic agriculture," he said in a *New York Times* interview, "somebody is going to have to decide what 50 million people we are going to let starve." (A few years later, at the World Food Conference, Butz would brashly declare, "Food is a weapon.") The head of Harvard University's nutrition program, Frederick Stare, vehemently denounced organic food and coauthored a book called *Panic in the Pantry,* which asserted the US industrial food system produced the safest and most nutritious food available. Not surprisingly, Butz and Stare, as well as many other outspoken critics of early organic farming, had close ties to the conventional food industry.

Despite this mainstream dismissal and hostility, the movement continued to gather interest. By 1971 readership of Rodale's *Organic Farming and Gardening* magazine surpassed 700,000, a 40 percent leap from the prior year. *Prevention* magazine (its health-focused counterpart) topped a million copies sold. That year the *New York Times Magazine* ran a cover story on J.I. Rodale, calling him "The Guru of the Organic Food Cult."

⊷

Reading about the beginning of the organic movement in California, I asked my mother what she remembered about her own experience arriving in the state during these same years. She began with the story I'd already heard: her first glimpse of the city from the airplane window, how there were more lights than she'd imagined possible, how the plane descended into the center of that twinkling maze.

Her family of six settled into the already crammed apartment of some family friends, and she started high school as a sophomore.

"And what was that like?" I asked.

"What? High school?" My mother shrugged, "It was fine, I played badminton, I studied."

"Yeah, but I mean, were there other Indians? Was it hard to be, you know, new to the country, a foreigner?"

My mother shook her head. "No, I never thought of myself as a foreigner. I mean, I'd already learned English in Nairobi." She looked to her hands and began pressing back on her cuticles. "I do remember one time, in Spanish class. It must have been the first time an American teacher ever called on me. I was so embarrassed, I peed." She glanced up at me, then back to her fingers. "Not enough that anyone knew. But still."

I kept my eyes on my mother's hands, watched her slide her thumbnail against the tender rind of one cuticle after the next, and tried to reconcile this new information with the mother I'd always known—headstrong, heedless of other people's opinions. When she'd finished all her fingers, she fanned them out to inspect her work, picked a fleck of dirt from under one nail, then folded them into her lap and began to speak again.

While she and her three younger siblings learned to navigate school, and while my grandmother memorized the American names of vegetables, my grandfather began to look for work. Week after week passed, with no job offers. Then a month went by, and another. One evening he returned to the crowded apartment after another day's fruitless search and walked into the bathroom. Maybe he locked the door. He stayed in the bathroom for a long time. When he finally emerged, his hair—which, when he unwound it from its tidy knot to comb it each day, had reached the middle of his back—was shorn to a few inches. His beard, too, gone. And on top of his head, where his turban had always been, rested the smooth curve of a baseball cap. Not long after, he found a job.

A few weeks into school, my mother met a teacher who coordinated a group for foreign exchange students. He invited her to join even though she was not, of course, actually an exchange student. There she got help with classwork and began to make friends. When graduation approached a few years later, this same teacher would help her apply for—and win—a scholarship to UCLA.

↭

One of those summer evenings in 1971, a few hundred miles up the coast from the crowded San Fernando Valley apartment where my grandfather had shorn his hair, the chef Alice Waters opened the doors to her soon-to-be world-famous Berkeley café, Chez Panisse. Here at this boutique, French-style restaurant, the word *organic* appeared on an American menu for the first time.

Though Chez Panisse began as a casual place for Waters to serve her bohemian friends wholesome meals, it would soon become an acclaimed—and expensive—gourmet restaurant. It cemented the term *organic* into the American culinary vocabulary and inspired a slew of similar cafés around the country, inadvertently fusing the term *organic* with upscale fine dining.

The success of Chez Panisse was a testament to J.I. Rodale's prediction from that 1942 issue of *Organic Farming and Gardening*: "One of these fine days...a substantial premium will be paid for high quality products such as those raised by organic methods." But J.I. himself didn't live to see it. Two months earlier, at the height of his organic-guru celebrity, he was interviewed on a taping of the Dick Cavett Show. "I've decided to live to be a hundred," he told Cavett. "I've never felt better in my life." The episode was never aired. Moments later he suffered a heart attack onstage, and before the end of the night, he was dead at the age of seventy-two.

After J.I. Rodale's death, his son Robert took over the work of running his many publications. Meanwhile, as a growing number of consumers sought organic foods, and upscale restaurants like Chez Panisse touted such ingredients on their menus, goods labeled "organic" began to command higher prices. In turn, fraudulently labeled products started to circulate. The mainstream press printed sensational news stories about these cases of fraud, stirring up skepticism and confusion among the public.

Robert Rodale, determined not to let "this important industry [be] ruined by a few charlatans," began to pursue the then-novel idea of creating an organic certification agency. The agency would define what could count as "organic" and then verify whether or not a producer met the requirements. Those that did would receive a stamp of approval. Thus, certification would prevent fraudulent claims while codifying the distinction between organically and conventionally grown foods into legible, marketable value.

But nailing down what exactly constituted an "organic" farm proved complicated. Up until this point, the term had embodied a range of meanings and values for different farmers and consumers: Some felt organic farms needed to be small and family run, others prioritized the building of soil, and still others valued crop diversity or minimal use of machinery. There were many questions to be considered: Should organic farmers be required to produce or use compost on their farms (one of Howard's most central tenets)? Must one incorporate specific rotations or tillage practices, use green manures or cover crops? And what about inputs? While some groups of chemicals fell clearly into the prohibited category (such as organophosphates and synthetic nitrogen), a plethora of others resided in a murky gray area between natural and synthetic, toxic and safe (such as copper sulphate). And should social concerns be included? Should organic standards require farmworkers to be paid a living wage or receive maternity leave? Should direct-to-consumer sales be mandated? Should there be size limits? Perhaps wary of wading too deeply into this maze, Rodale chose a simple, easily measured rubric based on a field's humus content—the amount of organic matter in the soil: A farmer who showed a minimum of 3 percent humus content could be deemed organic and receive a Rodale Seal of Approval. In 1972, the program's inaugural year, Rodale approved fifty-six certified organic growers.

A year later Rodale stepped away from his role in the agency in order to help others start similar ones. His leadership was passed to a group of California farmers and organic advocates based, not surprisingly, in Santa Cruz. They renamed the agency California Certified Organic Farmers—CCOF—and set out to redefine the standards a farm needed to meet in order to earn the "organic" label. CCOF threw out the humus content idea, as it addressed very few of their interpretations of the meaning of organic, and instead developed a set of regulations based on prohibited inputs, encouraged practices, and annual inspections.

❧ 32 ❧

O n the last day of my grandparents' stay in El Dorado County that summer, I drove to my mother's for a final visit. I found my grandmother and my mother sitting on the back porch, sipping from matching teacups. My grandmother, I knew, would be drinking her usual cha: black tea boiled with milk and fennel and cardamom, a spoonful of sugar stirred in, which, if my mother had made it, was probably less heaped than she'd have liked. My mother's own cup would be filled with strong green tea, no milk, no sugar. I took a seat across the table and listened to them chat in Punjabi, trying to guess the content of their conversation. I could distinguish hardly a word until my grandmother said "Ludhiana," and I recognized the name from a news article I'd read earlier that week. Without really meaning to, I repeated it aloud. "Ludhiana?"

My grandmother stopped talking and turned to me. "Haanah," she said, amused. "You know it?"

I shook my head. "No, not really. I've just heard of the place." The article I'd read was about a new collaboration between the USDA and the International Maize and Wheat Improvement Center focused on developing climate-resilient wheat varieties. Using "advanced genetic manipulation technologies," breeders were working to create new wheat varieties capable of producing high yields under the warmer and drier conditions predicted to come with climate change. The program was focusing its initial efforts on South Asia, where, the article stated, 20 percent of the world's wheat is produced and where, according to some predictions, yields would decrease by 10 percent with every one-degree rise in temperature. The first field trials were set to be conducted at the Borlaug Institute for South Asia—named, of course, after Norman Borlaug—located in Punjab outside of a city called Ludhiana. Reading the article, I'd repeated the name aloud a few times, attempting different versions of pronunciation. And so I was surprised to hear the name again now, enunciated confidently in my grandmother's voice.

"Ludhiana is very nice," she offered. "I have good friend there, very good friend. It is not far from my village." She leaned toward me. "You want to go? I will take you. Yes? You can come with me, please, I will take you!"

This was not the first time my grandmother had proposed that I go to India with her. Throughout my childhood my grandmother had traveled back to Punjab as often as she could afford, usually every other year. If I happened to be around when she was preparing for a trip, a suitcase splayed open on the ground, she'd pull me to her side. *Jackie, you come with me, haanah? Let's go, OK?* I would laugh and shake my head and stay pressed into her side until she remembered something more to pack and got up to fetch it. Each trip she brought two suitcases, one filled with her things, the other with gifts—rubber flip-flops, plastic dishware, clearance Halloween candy. When she returned, the extra suitcase would be emptied of its original contents and repacked with tailored salwar kameez, sacks of cardamom pods and black garbanzo beans, yards of fabric, and those mirrored shirts that ended up in my closet.

As a child, I daydreamed of joining my grandmother on one of her trips, imagining the exotic animals I might see—tigers or monkeys, elephants maybe—and faraway landscapes. I knew nothing about what Punjab was actually like—the scenes I imagined took their cues from the decorations on my grandparents' walls: photos of the Golden Temple and paintings of Sikh gurus sitting cross-legged against a backdrop of luminous mountains and sparkling blue rivers, flanked by baskets of fruit. I wondered what her village looked like. Who were these people my grandmother visited, these relatives she loved whose names I didn't even know?

My mother had never returned to India. Though she and my father traveled widely—to Thailand and Mexico, Laos and Nicaragua—she seemed to have no interest in visiting her birthplace, knew none of her relatives still living there. My grandmother was my only connection to our ancestral village, and as she and I both grew older, this fact gathered increasing weight. When my grandmother was no longer among us, that tenuous link would disintegrate and whatever part of my heritage existed in Punjab would be severed from me for good. While I found this thought unsettling, I also wondered: Would it matter? What was to be gained from digging up a past that had long ago been traded for a fresh start here in California? Why not simply allow whatever pieces of my family history that resided there to remain unknown?

I might have done just this had my grandmother not placed her palm on the table between us that afternoon and repeated, "Ludhiana, very nice. Only one hour from Pharwala, my village."

Pharwala. I repeated the name under my breath.

For a moment it seemed my grandmother was about to say something more. But then she settled back against her chair and resumed speaking to my mother in Punjabi.

For the rest of the day, that word—*Pharwala*—rattled around in my head. It was as if hearing the name had ratcheted my vague notions of an ancestral home out of the murky depths of speculation and into sudden, tangible, existence. There was a place, and it had a name.

Later that evening, back at home, I called my mother. "Did you hear what Naniji said? About going to India?" I asked.

"What about it?"

"Maybe we should." I ventured. After a moment of silence, I added, "Go with her, I mean."

My mother chuckled. "You can go," she offered, and changed the subject.

But over the ensuing weeks, we talked more about it. *Don't you want to see the place again? You might not have another chance. Naniji's getting pretty old.* This line of reasoning didn't seem particularly convincing, so I tried another: *I can't go without you. You're the only one who can speak both languages.* When that didn't work, I talked to my sister, who at the time had no permanent residence and spent most of her time traveling. I knew she'd be game to come along, and my mother wouldn't be able to resist the idea of a mothers-daughters trip, three generations of women. We booked the tickets, four round-trip flights from LAX to Delhi. Leaving in November, when the farm would be quiet, and returning just shy of a month later.

↫ 33 ↬

The first week of our third July on the farm, a heat wave barreled in and I learned I was pregnant. Ryan had left the farm at dawn that morning to drive to the Bay Area to pick up a load of harvest bins. He planned to stay the night with a friend and return the following morning. After he left, I walked down to our fields to begin the day's harvest in the already fleeting cool. By noon the tomatoes hung blood-warm on their vines, lettuce leaves wrinkled and drooped, and the thermometer on the barn hovered just above 100 degrees. My fingers were stained black with tomato resin. After tucking the harvest into the cooler, I walked out of the field and up to the house for lunch, carrying one plump tomato in each sticky hand.

In the kitchen, I switched on the radio and spread cream cheese across a slice of bread while a local zookeeper talked about the heat wave. All the animals eat blood-pops and fish-sicles to stay cool, she explained, only the panda bears get air conditioning. I slipped off my T-shirt, soaked it in tap water, then draped the wet cotton back over my skin.

For a week or two, something had been different about my body, a change had occurred that I was both certain about and found impossible to identify. What was once a whisper of a question had grown into a pounding on the door of my thoughts, and so, after lunch that afternoon, I walked to the bedroom, reached into the back of a drawer, and dug out a pregnancy test.

In the bathroom, I tore open the package and peed on the strip. I set the test on the windowsill and walked outside to wait for a full two minutes just like it said on the box. From the porch, my gaze caught on a tiny redwood tree in my front yard. A friend had given me the tree the previous winter. It had been her Christmas tree for two years and had become root-bound in its five-gallon pot. The tree might've had a chance somewhere else, further up the Sierras perhaps, or in a shady canyon. But I'd planted it in exactly the wrong place—into the red clay of my south-facing yard—at exactly the wrong time—the third year of what would become the worst drought in California's recorded history. No matter how often I watered it the foliage remained more brown than green, and eventually I gave up and left it alone. Now the tree had gone coppery and crisp except for three small green limbs at the base of the trunk. I'd been meaning to cut it down, wishing vultures would come carry it away as if it were a road-killed deer.

In the bathroom, I lifted the test from the windowsill and looked at the plus sign for a long time, until my fingers began to shake. Then, unable to think of anything better to do, I returned to the kitchen and washed my lunch dishes. The water sloshed down the basin and slapped against the plastic bucket below the drain of our still unplumbed sink. I scrubbed every dish I could find, then picked up the bucket full of dirty water and carried it outside. I usually dumped the dishwater off the edge of the porch near a honeysuckle vine and a bed of herbs planted there. But that day, I slipped on my boots and walked to the redwood, then knelt in the dust and slowly poured the bucket onto its roots.

⟿

Some weeks later, after Ryan and I shared the news with my parents, I gathered the nerve to call my grandmother. She replied exactly as I'd guessed she would: "But you are not married."

I stumbled through the assurances I'd prepared, explaining that she should think of this detail more like a technicality, not a reflection on the level of commitment in my relationship. "We've been together for five years, and we've lived together nearly the whole time," I told her enthusiastically. I heard a muffled clinking in response, and only then did it occur to me that this information might only make my grandmother more anxious.

"And we've been business partners for more than two years," I added, though I could hear the confidence draining from my voice.

It did not occur to me to try to explain why Ryan and I weren't married, or why we had no plans to become so. I could hardly articulate my reasoning to myself, back then. I knew only that I'd never—not as a girl or an adult—wanted to be married. I'd never dreamed about a wedding day or longed to see myself in bridal adornments. The thought of such things only called up dreary images of the institution's patriarchal foundations, its long history of constraining women, and I wanted nothing to do with the title "wife." All of this seemed to me then too far outside the limited range of language that my grandmother and I shared.

I listened to the sound of my grandmother's breath against the phone until she at last cleared her throat and spoke. "OK, Jackie," she said, "thank you. Goodbye."

I didn't want to hang up but I could think of nothing else to say. I held the phone against my ear, willing her to say more. A moment passed and, to my surprise, she did.

"Jackie?" she said abruptly.

"Yes, I'm still here."

She murmured something in Punjabi I couldn't make out, then, enunciating each word firmly, said, "Good luck." I started to offer a shaky thank-you, but my grandmother interrupted. "No, no, that is not it. What I want to say is, *congratulations*. Yes, congratulations, Jackie."

I let out a breath I hadn't realized I'd been holding. "Thank you," I said, and heard the click of her phone hanging up.

Without setting down my own phone, I dialed my mom and begged her to please call her mother and explain things. "I tried to reassure her, but I'm not sure it really came across in English. I don't want her to worry," I said, and couldn't help but think of my father's phone call three decades earlier, of the ensuing calamity. Had he implored my mother with a similar request?

Later that evening I drove to my parents' house for dinner. I found my mother in the kitchen chopping tomatoes for salsa. "So," I asked, "what did she say? Is she upset?"

My mother laughed. "Actually, she's fine. She only asked if I thought Ryan was a good person. Mostly we talked about the trip to India. I told her if anyone asks, we'd all just say you are married, since that's pretty much the truth anyway. That way, I told her, she wouldn't have to worry about what people might think."

My mother stopped chopping, set the knife down, and looked at me. "And do you know what she said? She said, 'Who cares what anyone thinks?'" My mother shook her head and chuckled, then repeated the line, pronouncing each word separately. "*Who cares what anyone thinks? I mean, can you believe that?*"

❧

Via a relay of phone calls over the next few weeks, my mother, sister, grandmother, and I debated whether or not to cancel the trip to India. I'd be nearing my third trimester by then, and there were some concerns about the long air travel, poor sanitation, contaminated drinking water. But I'd talked to my doctor, who affirmed it would be fine to travel, even a good time in the pregnancy to do so, and I had done just enough online research to confirm there were no dangers I couldn't avoid by drinking only filtered water and being careful about food. I was adamant we go as planned.

After my first ultrasound, my doctor had given me a small printout of the picture. I took it home and stared at the black-and-white photo, at the tiny life form the technician had pointed out, a peanut of white space. But even with the photo in hand, it was difficult to make the fact of this child seem real. The fetus looked more like an orb of light in a celestial landscape, a distant sun among a swirl of stars and dark matter.

I didn't think about the everyday details of motherhood—things so foreign to me I could not then imagine them: breastfeeding and sleepless nights, swaddling and changing diapers. Instead I stared at the tiny orb and thought: *descendant*. I would soon have a descendant. And with this came the realization that I would no longer be solely the recipient of a heritage, but also the giver of one, tasked with the duty of passing something on. And for this I felt grossly unprepared. So with a renewed sense of urgency, I yearned to better understand my own inheritance.

❦ 34 ❧

By the time the sweltering days of August 2014 arrived, Ryan and I had been living at the farm for a little over two years and were midway through our second full year in operation. By now we'd garnered many devoted local customers, wholesale accounts with restaurants and the food co-op, and popularity among the summer river-rafting crowd who liked to stop by our farm stand to pick up melons and tomatoes and bread. Locals complimented us on the progress we'd made, told us how glad they were that we were here growing food on this land. I was grateful for the robust support, for the enthusiasm so many in our community felt for what we were doing—in many ways all this added up to success. But I knew, too, that over the course of the last two years, I'd drained most of my savings, nearly $10,000. I also knew that, despite the apparent prosperity of our farm—harvest bins heaped with produce, fields striped with tidy green rows, our name listed on the menus of fancy restaurants around town—what really kept our farm afloat was not the income we earned selling vegetables, but money we made through means outside of farming: Ryan working as a carpenter and me as a baker.

I pulled out all our records, our notes on the inputs each crop required—labor, soil amendments, irrigation supplies, tractor usage, packaging, cooling—and the income each brought in. As I did periodically, I entered everything into the complicated excel worksheets that had accompanied *The Organic Farmer's Business Handbook*. I tested hypothetical scenarios—What if we grew only cut salad mix and potatoes? What if we closed the farm stand and focused instead on a produce box subscription program? Or were we better off continuing to do without the produce box program, as we'd done this last year, and doubling down on the farm stand and wholesale accounts?—trying to find an equation that might increase our income.

Over the past two years, certain facts had emerged clear enough:

Keeping up wholesale accounts with restaurants that ordered barely enough produce to make it worth the delivery was not profitable, no matter how proudly they listed our farm on their menu. And while CSA produce box subscribers liked the *idea* of receiving a box full of whatever was bountiful and in season, most actually preferred choosing their items, and many people had no use for mustard greens, carrot tops, or *so many beets.*

We'd made changes from the first season to the second. Instead of the traditional CSA produce box subscriptions, we offered a prepaid farm stand credit. This way we still benefited from receiving payment at the start of the season, when the majority of our expenses came around, but customers could choose their own produce. We stopped delivering to restaurants unless the order met a minimum. We sold a few select specialty items to the local food co-op—salad mix, melons, summer squash—but otherwise focused all our efforts on the farm stand, where we were able to retain more of the profit margin by selling directly to customers.

Even with these changes, the forecast the spreadsheets offered up didn't look hugely different. The next, and most obvious, strategy to increase our farm income was to produce more. But that would require more labor, and here I ran up against a problem. The cost of paying a single employee a living hourly wage—never mind providing health benefits, year-round work, paid sick leave or vacation time—would negate most of the gains made.

In those years, everywhere I looked there seemed to be evidence of thriving small organic farms: The grinning vendors behind the bountiful booths at the farmers market, where lines of shoppers filled their baskets with baby kale and beets. Banners stretched across grocery store aisles depicting happy farm families against a backdrop of grazing cows, couples cradling bundles of carrots, children holding watermelons in their laps. News stories of tech-engineers-turned-organic farmers. Social media photos captioned with witty quips: "Love what you do and you'll never work a day in your life! #organicfarming #locallygrown #living-soil." How were all those other small organic farms doing it? What was I missing?

When I began to look closer at some of these other farms, a few factors became clear. Many supplemented their farm profits with significant outside income streams: a spouse's paycheck, another job, inheritance, rental property. Others functioned as nonprofit organizations and subsisted on donations and grant funding. Some had no land payment because they'd inherited their farmland. Across the board, one practice stood out: nearly everyone depended on unpaid or underpaid labor of one kind or another.

Farmers who didn't have employees, like us, often exploited their own labor. Small organic farms that did have workers commonly used "interns"—who could be paid a stipend, sometimes in the form of produce and temporary housing, in exchange for what was often full-time work. Some used WWOOFers—travelers who camped out on the farm or stayed in an extra bedroom in exchange for labor. Others relied fully upon volunteers. Larger, more industrial organic farms often exploited cheap labor in ways no different than conventional farms.

Outside of the family members and friends whom we'd occasionally roped into helping us with especially tedious tasks—garlic planting, beet thinning—the only outside labor we had used so far was our four work-trade CSA members, during our first season. These people had signed up to work one morning each week in exchange for a weekly box of produce or a share of farm stand goods. They were neighbors, local gardeners, and food enthusiasts who enjoyed the opportunity to spend time outdoors and take part in the workings of a local organic farm. Even after we stopped the produce box program, two of them continued to volunteer time. They had their own gardens at home and asked for nothing except the occasional melon or bag of salad greens or loaf of bread.

I knew our volunteers enjoyed coming to the farm, I knew they found the work meaningful and fulfilling, and I was grateful for their help and their companionship. But whenever the subject came up in conversation, I always found myself hesitant to admit to using work-traders or volunteers. I recalled the days when Ryan and I had been looking for farm jobs ourselves, how frustrated I'd been when each lead turned out to be an "internship" of some sort. Part of my shame about this came from a sense that it was cheating—if the success of our business depended on free labor, did it really count? But there was something else at the root of this discomfort that I couldn't then identify, a murky sense of unease I tried my best to ignore.

⌒

It wouldn't be until several years later, while reading about the early days of California wheat farming, of those giant estates flush with Sonora and the laborers who came to "plow and sow and move on with their blankets," that I'd encounter the words to name the source of that unease.

In his 1949 book *California: The Great Exception*, Carey McWilliams writes of how the unique labor needs of California's tremendous nineteenth-century wheat farms gave rise to the enduring character of farm labor in the state. These giant estates, often managed from afar by absentee landlords, did not require consistent, year-round labor. Instead, seasonal workers were needed in the fall to plow fields and sow the seed. Then, for the remaining six or seven months of the growing season, there was nothing to do but wait. None of the constant work inherent in diversified farming—picking, weeding, irrigating, planting—was required. Then, come harvest time in late spring, extensive crews of laborers were needed, briefly and at once, to cut and thresh the wheat. To accommodate this, a migratory labor movement emerged in California in which thousands of workers squatted temporarily near farms to supply the required seasonal work and then were expected to move on when the task was done.

During the heyday of California wheat farming, from 1850 through 1880, these seasonal laborers were often dispossessed Native Americans—who were paid, at best, half the rate of white workers—and Chinese immigrants. After 1880, many of those large farms shifted from wheat to higher value specialty crops—citrus, grapes, vegetables—but the practice of exploiting migrant seasonal workers persisted until it had become such a standard practice in California agriculture that it seemed unavoidable, inherent. In turn, the state's farmland ballooned in value, based on the profits a farm owner could expect to make by exploiting labor. "By 1900," writes McWilliams, "a situation had been created in which the elimination of cheap labor would have involved a readjustment of land values and the entire capital structure of California agriculture."

Over the course of the next century this situation remained

unchanged. Only the groups of people supplying the cheap labor shifted, moving from one disenfranchised and vulnerable population to another, including, at times, Native Americans, Chinese immigrants, Japanese immigrants, Indian immigrants, Dust Bowl migrants, prisoners, Black migrants from the South, schoolchildren, German prisoners of war, Central American immigrants, Southeast Asian immigrants, and Mexican immigrants.

"The actors keep changing," McWilliams writes, "but the plot is always the same."

Unlike most of the people who have historically supplied cheap labor for California's farms, the workers on small-scale organic farms like mine—"interns," traveling WWOOFers, or self-exploiting proprietors such as myself—were often middle-class, highly educated American citizens. We were not coerced into providing undercompensated labor via a denial of rights or exclusion from economic opportunities. We chose to do so. We supplied our own farm labor for an unlivable wage and scraped by instead on an inherited cushion, or a better paying side job, or a spouse's income. And in doing so, we capitulated to the industrial agriculture system's insistence on the exploitation of cheap labor.

Here was the source of discomfort I had felt at the prospect of using "interns" or confessing that Ryan and I did outside work to subsidize our own uncompensated farm labor: If I did so, I'd have to admit that I, too, had failed to alter the plot. I hadn't thrown out the script, hadn't reinvented anything. Instead, I'd only made myself, my volunteers, my potential "interns" into the actors.

I could not, during my years on the farm, articulate the shape of this particular failure. Still, a nebulous awareness of its presence began to prod. Ryan and I declined to take on "interns." Instead, we made plans to limit our winter production so he could spend more time during that slower season working carpentry jobs, and I started baking twice as much bread, selling not 60 but 120 loaves at the farm stand each weekend.

⤜ 35 ⤛

U nder the scorch of the August sun, our Sonora stalks splintered and cracked. The seed heads, which should have been harvested months ago, lay powdered in dust and tangled in the mat of straw. One early morning Ryan and I bent between rows of summer squash, picking the fruits. Near the edge of the field sat our combine, as yet unused this year, its tires hung with morning glory vines and star-thistle. Ryan pointed to the machine.

"I think we should sell it," he said.

When I didn't respond, he reminded me that the combine was worth three or four thousand dollars, that it was a coveted machine among small-scale grain growers, that someone else would surely put it to better use. What he didn't have to say aloud: selling the combine would mean giving up on growing wheat. While Ryan had been excited about the possibility of incorporating wheat into our vegetable rotation, he wasn't invested in growing the Sonora for the same reasons I was. I murmured a *hmm, I guess you're right*, then stood and carried a bin of yellow pattypans to the truck.

A few days later, we posted the combine for sale on a forum for small-scale grain growers. The following morning Reed called. He'd come across our posting and was considering buying the machine himself. Though it was too small for his current fields, he could use this combine to custom harvest for a few other small-scale farmers he knew who had recently begun growing wheat. Our combine was small enough that it could easily be moved to different sites on a trailer. Reed could harvest, then take the grain back to his processing facilities where he had all the necessary equipment to clean and mill the product.

A few days later Reed drove out to our farm to have a look at the combine. We talked about the season, how the heat had settled in early this year and remained relentless. I asked how his Sonora had fared. He, too, had lost some to lodging due to that late-season storm. But more than half his field stayed upright and it had produced especially well despite the drought, giving him one of his greatest yields per acre yet.

I lifted a hand toward our own Sonora fields, and Reed nodded. "That can be a problem with Sonora," he said. "Tends to lodge." Then he looked out to where our Red Fife still stood, the stalks bronzed and swaying slightly in the breeze. Reed asked when we planned to harvest it—wouldn't we need the combine for that?

I kept my gaze on the field to avoid Reed's eyes. "We might not harvest it at all this year." I explained our hesitance to use the combine now that we'd listed it for sale, how we didn't want to risk a costly repair in the process of harvesting a crop we'd make no money on. Instead, we planned to treat the Red Fife like a cover crop—we'd mow it and turn it all back into the soil in time to plant fall crops in the same field.

For a moment Reed said nothing. I glanced at his face, searching for a hint of disappointment, a flicker of annoyance at our failure, our squandering of the seed he'd sold us. But Reed only nodded. "I understand," he said with a quiet chuckle. "Those machines have a way of breaking every time you use them. Still, it'd be a shame to lose it all."

We walked out to where the combine sat covered with a tarp. When we passed the Red Fife field Reed brushed his palm across the blades of wheat as if smoothing out a child's hair. "Looks good," he said. The last time I'd talked to Reed, he'd told me he wasn't certain he'd grow grains himself at all the coming year, with the drought predicted to continue. I asked him if he'd made up his mind whether or not to plant this fall. He put his hands onto his jean pockets and said he still wasn't sure, but that he had gone ahead and set aside enough of his harvest for seed. I was relieved to hear this. His commitment was comforting, though a part of me also wished he had decided to quit, so that if I gave up I wouldn't be alone.

As we walked out of the field, Reed told me about a community event he'd recently attended, a commemorative dinner to celebrate the local producers around his town. Michael Pollan had given a talk and a farm-to-fork meal followed. "I left the dinner feeling like everyone thinks I'm some kind of hero. People were thanking me for doing what I do, telling me I'm part of this great movement," he said, "and I went to bed thinking how can I quit now? But then I woke up the next morning and still I'm netting close to zero, still the numbers don't add up."

Reed drove away, and I went back to harvesting squash with his words echoing in my head.

◦

A few days later, Reed called with a proposition of sorts. He wanted to buy our combine, and he wanted Ryan and me to grow Sonora again next year, along with a few acres of Red Fife. He would harvest the Red Fife from our fields this year, give us from that the seed we'd need to plant two acres in the fall, then process and sell the rest of the harvest himself. We'd use the Sonora berries in our barn—the ones from the prior year's harvest that I'd been saving to grind into flour—to seed another two acres. Reed would then bring the combine over the following summer to harvest our crop and truck it back to his facilities to clean the wheat and mill it into flour. We would share the profits—if there were any.

The plan made sense: Reed already had all the equipment and we had available, certified organic acreage. If it turned into another drought year and we didn't get a harvest, no one had much to lose. I liked the idea. I took comfort in the collaboration, the notion that we were in this together, that the risks and the gains both would be shared. We agreed to his plan and readied the fields for planting, turning under the bolted broccoli plants and summer squash vines, spreading compost, until there was nothing to do but wait for fall rain.

☙ 36 ❧

By September of 2014, the California drought was in its third year and breaking all records. Statewide restrictions prohibited using water to wash cars or driveways; residential sprinklers were allowed to run only on certain days of the week. People timed their showers and left their sheets on the bed for an extra week, turned in their neighbors for violations and cringed at the sight of a sprinkler overshooting its target to puddle a parking lot instead.

I stopped watering the patch of grass outside our house—it was hardly green anyway, and full of star-thistle and burrs. Our kitchen sink still drained into a bucket, and I used the wastewater to keep alive the sage and lavender bushes I'd planted around our house, doling out a bucket to the little redwood once a week.

On the farm, where Ryan and I had already tried to reduce our water use as much as possible, we had less excess to cut. We ceased all overhead irrigation. Where we'd once used long strings of aluminum sprinklers to irrigate fields of direct-seeded crops like carrots and beets, we switched to drip lines. And, after some hand-wringing, we decided to let our patch of blueberries go. In order to thrive in our hot, dry fields, each of the forty shallow-rooted plants would need upwards of five gallons of water a day. This, it seemed amid the pressure of those drought years, was too much.

Under drought stress, a blueberry bush will pull the water stored in its berries out to other parts of the plant in order to keep itself alive. The berries shrivel, but the plant lives, if only just a little longer. A few days after we shut off the irrigation to the blueberries, I circled the bushes hoping for a last handful of fruit. But the berries, once plump and shiny, were now shriveled and pale, each one like a tiny popped balloon.

❧

The summer blazed on, bleaching the grass-covered hillsides surrounding the farm to an ever-starker blond. The oaks and pines dimmed to something closer to gray. Only the star-thistle kept its color, a stubborn wash of blue among the parched landscape. When I stood on the hill above our house, looked east toward the Sierras or west toward the Central Valley, I could almost always spot smoke somewhere in the distance. Sometimes I'd see a low fog of brown haze, other times a column rising into the sky. Sometimes I knew its source, the name of the wildfire and where it was located—Sand Fire, Reed Fire, Bible Fire. Other times I couldn't tell. Road signs reading "Today's Fire Danger" followed by a color-coded gauge indicating the current level of risk popped up all over that summer, but the arrows never strayed from the red wedge marked "Extreme." Stories spread around town of cousins and ex-husbands, friends and acquaintances who had been evacuated from various places around the state.

Often, smoke settled after dark into the crook of land that held our fields, and many nights that summer I dreamt of our farm catching fire. I'd wake to the smell of smoke, walk to a window and lean my forehead against the glass, half expecting to see a glow over our fields below. Instead there was only the dark night, the bleached grass on the hillsides silvered in moonlight, the howl of a coyote nearby.

One hot September evening, after closing the farm stand for the weekend, Ryan and I drove the two miles down to the river to swim, as we often did after work. My morning sickness was beginning to ebb at last, but the combination of that summer's relentless heat and the slight body temperature rise caused by pregnancy meant the only time I felt truly cool was in the river.

I stayed in the icy water, submerged to my neck for as long as I could bear it. Afterward we drove back up the hill to turn on irrigation and clean up the farm stand. As we crested a rise, there, directly in front of us, was a great lone cloud of smoke—reddish brown and purple in places like a bruise. It looked like it was right over our farm.

I drove faster.

When I rounded the last rise before the farm came into view, half expecting to find our fields ablaze, I saw that the smoke cloud was in fact several miles east. It was also, I now realized, much larger than it had first appeared. Ryan and I parked at the farm stand, climbed out of the car, and gazed at the colossal plume of smoke.

It was called the King Fire, we soon learned, and was burning fifteen miles east of our farm. In the coming weeks the blaze grew to more than 97,000 acres. On days when the wind blew smoke our way, the light grew dim and everything took on an eerie orange glow. Ash dusted the skins of tomatoes, gathered in cupped squash blossoms, and pooled in the hollow nooks rimming bell pepper stems. Officials declared the air unsafe to breathe and advised everyone to remain indoors. But "indoors" meant inside a sealed structure with air conditioning to filter the air, not inside an old farmhouse with gaping holes around the window frames so that, even if the windows were closed—which would make it unbearably hot—the inside air would be no cleaner than outside. So on the worst of these days, Ryan and I did only the necessary farm tasks and then took shelter in the homes of friends or family. Or we drove west to the coast for a night and camped on the bluffs of Marin, breathing in the salty sea air, or sometimes east, high into the mountains if we could find a place the smoke had not yet reached. But mostly we stayed home, started work as early in the morning as possible, took cold showers, and waited for the fall rains to bring some relief.

Pregnancy, I've been told, enhances the mother's sense of smell. Perhaps that's why, that summer and fall, I could never seem to get a breath free of that particular acrid scent of smoke. It permeated everything: T-shirts and bedsheets pulled off the laundry line, the clay mugs I drank tea from each morning, the upholstery in our car and the pages of books. Even my own hands always seemed to smell charred, as if something was smoldering underneath my skin.

Even now, an unexpected whiff of smoke can instantly send me back to those days: the heat, the drought, the nausea, the sense of anticipation and unsettledness, the feeling that my world was built of kindling, so crisped and dried one stray spark could set it all ablaze.

❧ 37 ❧

The first fall rains finally arrived in late October, with my trip to India only a few weeks away. I'd hoped for an early and wet autumn, but forecasts predicted another dry winter, a fourth year of drought. My belly had grown round, but not so much that I couldn't strap the broadcast seeder to my chest and march across the fields to sow the cover crop and wheat seed. I watched the sky as I worked—it was ribboned with clouds that looked as if they were just as likely to pull apart and drift away as they were to bear rain—and hoped the precipitation forecasted for later that evening wouldn't vanish. The longer the seed stayed out before germinating, the more susceptible it was to being eaten by birds and rodents.

When I went to bed that night, the stars shone bright and clear, unmasked by cloud cover. I fell asleep before the rain started, heard nothing of it clinking against my roof in the night. But the next morning, despite a sky that was again a cloudless blue, puddles of rainwater collected in buckets, in our truck bed, in dips in the tarp that covered our woodpile. In the fields, the soil was damp and dark. It wasn't much, and with another cloudless stretch in the forecast, I hoped it would be enough.

Two weeks and one more rainstorm later, on a crisp evening in early November, I packed the last of my things into a backpack and sat on the porch steps with Ryan, watching the sun slip behind the farm. The next morning I'd leave for LA, where my family and I would spend a night and a day together before catching a red-eye to India the following evening. The sky overhead went pink, and below, across the Sonora field, I could see a wash of green spread over the soil.

Part 3

WINDOWS

☙ 1 ❧

The morning before our flight to India, I sat with my grandmother at her dining table drinking cha when my mother and grandfather returned from a trip to the grocery store. My grandfather nodded hello, then disappeared down the hall toward the bedroom to rest while my mother unloaded the groceries. She set two jars of almond butter on the counter—the latest product she'd been insisting her parents eat every morning. *It's good for your hearts,* she told them, *and you need the protein.* My grandmother stood and walked to the counter to inspect the goods as my mother emptied her shopping bag. Out came a bag of cashews, and four organic Fuji apples. "We can bring them on the plane," my mother said. At the sight of the apples my grandmother motioned to the three gleaming Granny Smiths already in her fruit bowl and said something to my mother in Punjabi.

"Oh, I bought these ones for Jackie," my mother said.

"Ah," my grandmother said, picking up one of her Granny Smiths and holding it out to me with a smile. "You don't need to buy, you can eat these. Anything you want! It is not for me. It is for you!"

I knew that, of course. I thought of her words that evening two years before when she'd offered me the pearl necklace in her sitting room: *If someone come here, and they hungry, and I have nothing? Then what? What can I do with empty cabinet?* But before I could say anything, my mother pointed to the apples she'd bought. "These ones are *organic,*" she said. "Jackie likes those ones, especially since she's pregnant." I hadn't asked my mother to get the apples, but she was right—I avoided conventionally grown fruits like apples, which I knew carried an especially high dose of chemicals. My doctor had even advised me to do this during a prenatal visit.

My grandmother's smile vanished. She looked down at the green apple in her hand. I imagined her picking it out from a heap in the produce aisle, lifting fruit after fruit to her nose to smell for sweetness,

219

running her fingers around each circumference to check for soft spots, until she'd selected the finest one. Now, my grandmother turned the apple in her palm as if looking for a blemish she'd missed, a bruise or worm hole. "Aahcha," she said slowly, then placed the apple gently back in the fruit bowl.

I wanted to jump up, pluck the apple from the bowl and eat the whole thing right then. *Thank you,* I'd say, *thank you.* I wanted to lift the plastic bag of puny organic Fujis and shove it out of sight beneath the sink.

But my grandmother had now turned her attention to the Fujis and was picking one of them up. "*Organic?*" she said, repeating the English word my mother had used, pronouncing it slowly as if for the first time. She turned the apple over in her hand, then reached for a paring knife and spun the apple against the blade. The skin lifted off in curls. She sliced the fruit into eight even wedges and placed them on a plate, carried it to the dining table where I sat. Taking her seat next to me, she lifted one wedge and took a timid bite. She chewed slowly and her brow furrowed slightly. I looked at the apple. It had likely been shipped up from South America or down from Washington State. A bruise darkened part of the flesh; it didn't look crisp. My grandmother took another bite, then frowned, folded the paper towel around the remaining apple and pushed it aside with a shake of her head. She took a sip of cha as if to wash away the taste. "Jackie, you like these apples?" she asked. "You do not like those?" she said, pointing to her fruit bowl.

I looked down into my cup of now cold cha, considering an answer, but my grandmother didn't wait. She pulled her chunni up over her head and stood. "I'm going to go do padth," she said, and walked toward her temple room.

I watched her disappear down the hall, then shot a glare at my mother, who just shrugged her shoulders and reached for a slice of apple. "She's right," my mother said after a bite. "It's not a very good apple."

❧ 2 ❧

For dinner before our flight, my grandmother made a pot of yellow dal, fried okra, and a stack of buttered roti. Her close friend Paul, who had also immigrated to LA from northern India, came by to see us off and we all sat around the table to eat—my mother, sister, grandparents, Paul, and me. Between bites Paul offered advice on traveling: *Don't drink the water, always get the cell number of your driver, never give money to beggars.*

I asked Paul if he missed India. He shook his head. Then, dabbing his lip with a napkin, added, "I will tell you this: Once a person leaves his country of origin, he will never belong anywhere again." I glanced at my grandmother, wondering if she too felt this way. But she wasn't listening. Instead she filled Tupperware with okra and wrapped a stack of roti in tin foil for the long plane ride ahead.

"And you?" Paul said. "Why do you want to go to India? What do you plan to see? The Taj Mahal? The Golden Temple?"

I swirled a spoon through my bowl of dal, not sure I could explain what compelled me to make this trip, how I hoped that if I traveled to my family's homeland—if I felt the ground beneath my own feet and the air moving through my body, if I took in the views with my own eyes—I might forge a connection to that place. If I sipped cha with neighborhood women and learned the names of distant relatives, maybe I could shrink the chasm between myself and my Punjabi heritage. And, though I knew it was not likely, perhaps there was a chance, despite the odds, that I'd find growing in the fields of my grandmother's village a stand of landrace wheat just like my own.

Even if I'd been able to find the right words to articulate all this, I wouldn't have dared say them aloud. Instead, I looked down at my plate and mumbled something about just wanting the chance to see the place my family was from, the village where my mother was born. Paul said nothing. He only grinned back at me, as if he knew I wouldn't find what I was looking for.

❧ 3 ❧

Our plane landed in Delhi, 250 miles south of the village of Phar-wala, where we were headed. Smog hung over the city, a lid under which the smoke of smoldering trash piles stewed with diesel exhaust and the smell of ripe bananas, of piss on hot concrete, of frying dough. A friend of my grandmother's had arranged a driver to take us on the six-hour trip. The man strapped my grandmother's three suitcases, packed full with gifts, to the roof of his white minivan and piled the rest of our bags into the back. I sucked in a breath, felt its sticky warmth slink down my throat, and climbed into the van.

On the road out of Delhi, traffic tangled to a halt, a gridlock of rick-shaws and cars, bikes and horse-drawn carts, motorcycles and pedes-trians. Honks whined and bellowed. On the sidewalk a street vendor tossed patties of dough into a wok. Beggars and peddlers wove through the traffic: one man selling plastic airplanes knocked his merchandise against shut windows, another walked car to car with a bundle of shawls. A child carrying a baby held out a cupped hand. Inside our minivan, hot air blew through the vents and I could smell my own sweat mixing with the odors of the street.

A girl, just twelve or thirteen I guessed, walked toward us. She wore a pink shawl and no shoes and moved her hand to her lips, asking for food. She knocked against our driver's window, but the man shook his head and the girl moved down the van. At my window, she pressed her palm flat against the glass. I focused my gaze straight ahead and tried to scoot away from the window, but my mother and sister were squeezed next to me in the back seat and there was nowhere to go. Out of the corner of my eye I could see the girl cup one hand around her eyes and rest her forehead against the pane. Though she spoke loudly, her words easily penetrating the glass, I could understand nothing she said. I stared ahead as if there were no girl standing outside my window.

Maybe she noticed the tightening of my lips, the reddening of my cheeks. The girl curled her hand into a fist and pounded it against my window, one steady thud after another. I willed the traffic to move, the cars to shift just enough to let our van squeeze past.

The girl raised her voice a notch louder. If it weren't for the glass between us I would have felt the heat of her breath on my cheek. I no longer noticed the horns, the grumble of engines, only the girl's fist on the window, her face pressed against the quarter-inch pane of glass separating my world from hers.

I knew just one of the Punjabi words the girl shouted: Didi—sister. Over and over, "Didi," she said, "Didi, Didi."

Outside a three-legged dog, her swollen teats swinging beneath her belly, darted through traffic. The sound of the girl's fist on the glass shuddered through my head, my own hot blood quaking with each pound. At last I flung my head around to face the girl to shout, *No! I have nothing to give you!*

But before I could open my mouth she'd already turned away. The tail of her pink shawl flapped in her wake as she disappeared between cars. All that remained were three smudged lines on the glass where the girl had dragged her fingertips, a smear from her forehead, the stain of her breath.

✥ 4 ✥

A few hours north of Delhi, the landscape began to oscillate between industry and agriculture. Clusters of brick and cement buildings thrust spindly lines of rebar upward from their rooftops. Crops fanned out from the highway, and I recognized some of them—mustard greens, marigolds, sugarcane. As the distance between towns widened, the fields filled with short green grass: wheat. Acres and acres of wheat stretched as far into the distance as I could see, the fields cut into squares by a grid of irrigation ditches.

Soon we passed a sign with the English words "Borlaug Institute for South Asia." The sign stood at the entrance to a long, tree-lined driveway that led away from the main road and through a hefty gate. I turned in my seat, searching the landscape for a sign of the trial fields that I'd read about. Which of these green stalks, I wondered, all of them reaching up toward that same hazy sky, might be the new "climate-resilient" varieties?

As we traveled farther from Delhi, I waited for the smog to clear. But hours passed and it never did. It only thinned slightly, as if it were milky tea and someone had poured in a bit more water. We reached Pharwala in late afternoon, and my grandmother directed our driver into the village's labyrinth of brick streets. Soon, the roads grew too narrow for the driver to continue and he shut off the engine. A dog curled atop a concrete stoop lifted its head to examine our vehicle, eyed the three suitcases strapped to the roof. A toddler stepped out of an open door, cocked her head to the side, giggled, and disappeared back inside.

Then a flurry of Punjabi broke the quiet. Two women—one older, one younger—were bounding down the road toward us. At the sight of them, my grandmother flung open her door and heaved herself out of the van. I followed, uncertain how to greet these people, but the older woman gave me no time to hesitate. She wrapped a palm around my shoulder and pulled me close, embracing me into the woodsmoke and mustard seed scent of her shawl. The younger woman offered a more formal greeting, giving me two firm hugs, first right cheek to right, then left to left.

My grandmother introduced me to the older woman, Simran, and told me to call her Mamiji—Auntie—though she was technically my grandmother's niece. The younger woman was her daughter, Jeeta, my second cousin. Simran and Jeeta loaded their arms with our luggage and led us into their home. The house was mostly outdoor space, an open courtyard walled in by four small rooms and a kitchen. A cook fire occupied one corner of the courtyard; a few plastic chairs and a woven bench sat in the center. Jeeta showed us our room. Two small mats had been pushed together to form one large bed for my mother, sister, and me to share. In the opposite corner a single bed was made up for my grandmother.

I studied Jeeta's face, trying to ascertain her age. She reminded me of a drawing I'd seen as a child. The sketch was an optical illusion of sorts, which when examined one way revealed a pretty young girl, but with a shift of perspective became an old lady. Jeeta wore a traditional salwar kameez made of silky blue fabric with a paisley pattern around the hems. Her long black hair was coiled into a bun at the base of her neck. She spoke softly in a singsong voice. Her face was polite—plain almost. It might have been an easy face to forget if not for her eyes, round and dark and unflinching, at once both severe and childlike.

After our things were put away, Jeeta poured us cups of cha and offered a plate of biscuits. As I sipped the creamy tea she lifted her fingertips to touch my hair, which was short and hung loose and curly, so unlike her own tidy bun. Jeeta pulled a curl straight, released it and watched it spring back to shape. A giggle escaped from her lips, flitting out into the yellow-walled courtyard.

Though Jeeta was technically my second cousin—the granddaughter of my grandmother's sister—she called me Didi. Jeeta had once shared her house with her grandparents, her parents, and her younger brother, Tal. But her grandmother had passed away several years ago, and her father had died a year before. Now only Jeeta, her mother, and Tal remained in the house, along with her elderly grandfather, a rail-thin man whom I rarely saw except early in the morning when he would push an old steel bike strung with carpentry tools through the courtyard on his way out to work.

Of all the Pharwala family members, Jeeta spoke the most English. She'd learned some in school, which she'd attended through the ninth grade, but with no place to use it, the language had fallen into the crevices of her memory. Over the three weeks my family stayed with her, she dug it out, stringing the words back together.

The evening we arrived, Jeeta showed my mother, my sister, and me around her village: Here, the town shop where one could buy lentils and cardamom, sewing thread and gingerroot. Here, the flour mill where women carried sacks of wheat kernels to be ground into fresh atta. Here, the dairy where she walked each afternoon to pick up a tin of fresh milk. The houses leaned on one another, sharing walls so that it was impossible to tell where one began and another ended. Fields of newly sprouted wheat encased the village like a sea. The wheat stood just a few inches tall, the same height my own wheat would now be back home in California. Gazing out at the fields that first evening, I felt like I'd run into an old friend in a foreign city.

Jeeta introduced us to the neighborhood women, calling each one Auntie. The women invited us into their homes for cha, talked in Punjabi to my mother while I listened to the melody of their voices. The week before I'd left home, my doctor had informed me that the five-month-old fetus inside my belly was now able to hear sounds outside the womb. Sitting among these women I felt a certain contentment knowing that many of the first voices to fill my child's ears would be speaking the language our family had used for all the generations before me.

"My village, do you like?" Jeeta asked me after showing us around that first evening. She and I were standing on her rooftop, gazing out at the houses below. Laundry lines stretched across each roof, seeming to stitch the town together. I was mesmerized by the simple beauty of the village, by the tidy stacks of cow-dung patties, the clay cook stoves, the clusters of little boys dressed in white linen, flying kites from street corners. I didn't notice, that first evening, the heaps of garbage piled on the outskirts of town or the ubiquitous empty fertilizer bags reused to hold kindling or fabric scraps. I didn't look into the open sewage gutters that traced each brick street, the sludge shimmering blue-black like fish scales. Nor did I pay much attention to the shade of the sky, dulled by the constant haze of woodsmoke and burning trash.

"Yes." I said, "I like your village very much." Jeeta's eyes squished into two crescents and she let out another skittering laugh. I noticed her teeth were yellowed and pitted with rot.

❧ 5 ❧

At the time of our visit, Jeeta had just turned twenty. Like many women in the village, she worked as a tailor sewing salwar kameez. She sewed in a corner of the courtyard, spreading fabric across the concrete floor and using a Singer sewing machine powered only by her foot. While she worked, she played Punjabi pop songs from the crackly speaker of her cell phone, the same model I'd owned a decade earlier. Her sandaled foot rocked back and forth to the beat, driving the sewing needle up and down. She knew every word. Now and then she paused, looked to me, and said, "So romantic, I love romantic song." Next to her chair, an old fertilizer bag stuffed with scraps of fabric leaned against a wall.

Each morning I woke at dawn to the pleasant chatter of Jeeta's sewing machine, her voice singing softly outside my bedroom window. I wondered how long she'd been up working by the time I pulled a shawl over my shoulders and stepped into the murky light of daybreak. Already the cook fire had been burning for hours, bath water heated, laundry washed. Soon Simran would be squatting over the flame in the corner of the courtyard, frying muli parathas—flatbreads filled with shredded daikon, hot peppers, and ginger—for breakfast. Jeeta would stop sewing to bring out the matching set of plastic plates bought specially for our visit, setting them on a coffee table in her brother's room because the house had no dining room. When the parathas were done, Simran would herd everyone into the room and we'd take seats around the makeshift dining table. I would fold bits of bread between my fingertips, scoop up a smudge of yogurt and a sliver of pickled lemon with each bite. When I'd try to help with the dishes, Simran or Jeeta would shoo me away.

During the days, Jeeta took my sister and me into the homes of various relatives and friends. She called everyone Auntie, and my sister and I smiled, thanked each person for the cha she offered, the plate of biscuits or cup of soda. Jeeta watched both of us with what seemed to be an insatiable curiosity, but it was my sister to whom she gave her closest attention. I was pregnant and, for all practical purposes, married. Other than the fact that I was relatively old by village standards to be having my first child—twenty-seven—there was nothing especially surprising about this. But in my sister Jeeta saw a single woman, entirely unencumbered: no children or husband, nor any plans for such things. Here was a woman who wore her hair in a brazen bun on the top of her head, laughed in loud, open-mouthed bellows, wore her clothes a little too tight, spent hours drawing in her notebook. A woman who, it must have seemed to Jeeta, did just exactly as she pleased.

⌁

In the evenings, we ate vegetables or dal with roti and yogurt, and after dinner Simran boiled what remained of the day's milk to make a fresh batch of yogurt. She poured the hot milk into a tin canister and let it cool to the temperature of blood, testing it with the tip of a pinky, before inoculating it with a spoonful of the prior day's batch. Then she buried the canister in her bin of flour to keep it warm overnight. Simran always left a bit of milk in the pot and, after the yogurt was put away, she dropped in two pods of cardamom and simmered the milk until it was infused with spice. Then she poured the steaming liquid into two cups, one for me and one for my sister. Sometimes, at our insistence, she poured a third cup for herself.

↫ 6 ↬

Outside of the village, a few large houses stood alone, surrounded by fields. These houses were unlike the others in the village—they were brightly painted, had ornate molding around glass windows, and were surrounded by concrete walls with intricate metal gates. One had a giant shining eagle sculpture perching on its rooftop. When I pointed, Jeeta explained how the eagle concealed a water tank inside.

Jeeta led my mother, my sister, and me past this house one afternoon on our way to buy mustard greens from a friend who grew a patch of vegetables. "Who lives there?" I asked. Jeeta shook her head. "No," she said, "no one is there. They live Canada." She waved at the wheat fields surrounding the house. "Here, have kheth." *Farm.* I nodded and Jeeta pointed to another house, similarly extravagant and isolated. "They go London, maybe. Maybe Chandigarh."

"Really? These houses are empty?" I asked. Jeeta looked at me without saying anything, then raised her eyebrows as if to say, *You don't get it, do you?*

Instead, she let out a laugh and shook her head. "I'm sorry," she said, "I don't understand."

In the fields behind one of these houses, several women with sacks hung across their backs walked in parallel lines through the ankle-high wheat. I watched as they took fistfuls of white pellets from the sacks and tossed them rhythmically out on the ground in front of them. "Fertilizer," Jeeta explained.

When we reached the farm with the mustard greens, Jeeta called to a woman crouched among a row of some leafy green thing I did not recognize. "Sat Sri Achall, Auntie," she said warmly. The woman stood and greeted my mother, sister, and me with hugs. Cows milled around tidy stacks of dung patties with long ropes tied to their collars, one with a calf at her side. The woman led us to a section of the field where mustard greens grew thick and leafy. She filled a plastic bag with greens, then handed it to Jeeta, and we walked back, past the elaborate empty houses and into the cobbled streets of the village.

⇔

Most days I watched Jeeta sew, or sat with the many women who came to visit my grandmother. The women, old friends and relatives, rubbed mustard oil into my grandmother's hair, filled her in on local gossip, drank cha. My grandmother seemed at ease in a way she never did in Los Angeles. Here, the slight look of bewilderment she usually wore had vanished. I studied her face, how her muscles had relaxed to reveal a different pair of eyes, a new nose, an easy grin.

And yet when I asked her that afternoon, while I scrubbed my worn clothes in a bucket of soapy water, "Do you miss living here, do you ever think about moving back?" she shook her head without a moment's hesitation.

"No," she said, then repeated, "no. It is not good time in Pharwala now. Very bad, bad time." Girls could not safely walk alone anymore, she told me, and there were problems with theft, drug abuse. "It did not used to be so bad. When I was young, we have some problem, but not like now." She shook her head, pursed her lips. I waited for her to say more, and when she did not, turned back to my laundry.

"You know, I used to walk all the way to next village, to go to school?" She raised an arm to point in the direction she had walked all those decades ago.

"Past the fields we walked by today, where those big houses are?" I asked.

My grandmother nodded, "Haanah, but back then, no big houses like those. Back then, everyone lived here, in the village. Even, how do you say..." Her forehead furrowed and she called to my mother across the courtyard, who was filling a pot of water to heat for bathing. After a quick back and forth in Punjabi, she turned back to me. "*Landowner,*" she said, "back then, even landowner live here in village. Now? Now where are they? Now they go to Canada, London. They go to America. They have big nice house outside village, very nice house, you see? You see big gate, water tower? No one even there!"

At the sound of footsteps—rubber chappla slapping against heels—our attention turned to the courtyard door. Two women my grandmother's age stepped through, and my grandmother's face brightened. The women pulled up plastic chairs beside her, kissing her cheeks. They nodded warmly to me, then after my grandmother offered an introduction I could not follow, stood to offer me the same kisses on the cheek.

I hung my laundry and sat with the women, listened to the three of them talk, trying my best to pick up a word here and there. One of the visiting women reached across the circle of our chairs and placed her hand on my belly. Looking sincerely into my eyes, she said something in Punjabi. My grandmother translated: *Your baby is a boy. I can tell because you carry it on the right side.* I'd chosen not to find out the sex of my baby simply because I liked the mystery. I didn't know then that in India, female feticide was so common that prenatal sex screening was prohibited by law. I smiled at the woman, looked down at my belly. It did indeed seem larger on the right.

ᛞ 7 ᛞ

I t wasn't long after my grandmother and her family immigrated to California in 1971, leaving Pharwala for the last time, that the ill effects of the Green Revolution began to show up in Punjab. Despite their name, the "high-yielding varieties" of wheat only delivered on their promise when used in tandem with a package of inputs. Borlaug himself declared in his Nobel lecture: "If the high-yielding dwarf wheat and rice varieties are the catalysts that have ignited the green revolution, then chemical fertilizer is the fuel that has powered its forward thrust." Poorly suited to dry farming, the new seeds also required regular irrigation on top of heavy applications of fertilizer.

In addition, their short stature and genetic uniformity—in contrast to the tall and genetically diverse local varieties they had replaced—rendered the plants especially vulnerable to weed competition, pests, and disease. Chemical pesticides became essential, triggering a treadmill effect: as pests adapted to tolerate the pesticides, farmers needed stronger doses or different chemicals. A constant pipeline of new "improved" seeds was also needed to replace older varieties as they lost their competitive edge or succumbed to pests.

The necessity of these inputs meant that the high-yielding varieties only benefited farmers who had the extra capital to purchase them. Farmers who lacked such funds found they could no longer compete using traditional methods. Some left farming, while others borrowed the money needed to pay for the inputs. In the ensuing years, landlessness increased—by the end of the 1970s, small holdings in Punjab would decline by nearly 25 percent. Many of the small farmers still in operation found themselves caught in a cycle of debt.

In turn, excess nitrogen began to collect in drinking water, incidents of pesticide-related illness cropped up, and water tables dwindled. As the new seeds displaced local varieties, the great wealth of genetic diversity once held in this region vanished from farmers' fields. Some seeds were lost forever; others were whisked off into the coffers of international seed banks, where their genes became the raw material for new high-yielding varieties. On top of all this, hunger remained persistent; "because all along hunger had been primarily a matter of distribution, not aggregate physical supplies," writes historian John Perkins. "People without access to adequate land or income remain ill fed."

While it was becoming increasingly clear that the switch to high-yielding varieties was not helping its supposed beneficiaries—poor peasant farmers and hungry people—no doubt remained that the agro-chemical and seed industry did, in fact, have much to gain. Chemical companies (including Esso, a subsidiary of Rockefeller's Standard Oil, which invested $200 million in fertilizer plants in India during these years) increased production to fulfill the newly created demand for their products. The tendency for the new seeds to lose their effectiveness after a few seasons meant farmers were compelled to purchase new varieties regularly, rather than save seed from their own harvest. In this way, seeds were transformed into commodities, and the door was flung open for capitalism to further extend its reach into agriculture. After the United States passed the Plant Variety Protection Act in 1970—which gave breeders patent-like intellectual property rights to the seeds they developed, making it illegal for a farmer to save seed from her own harvest of such strains—agrochemical firms began to steadily acquire seed companies. The new biotech corporations born from these mergers embarked on a pursuit to develop products that created an increasingly inextricable link between seed and chemical.

Meanwhile, in California, my grandmother and her family attended to the tasks of settling into a new life. My grandfather at last found a job for a local machine shop, and my grandmother began working in a women's underwear factory, where she spent her days sewing the same piece of padding into the same lacy bra over and over again. My mother finished high school and started college at UCLA. There she played tennis, worked in the university labs, and studied toward a science degree. She wore bell-bottoms and paisley shirts, tennis skirts with baggy sweatpants pulled over the top until she was far enough from her parents' house to slip them off. When she got accepted to pharmacy school in

San Francisco she moved north, but returned to her parents' house each summer. One of those summers she took a clerical job at a property management company, arranged for her by one of her parents' Punjabi friends.

There, in the corridors of the office, she met my father—a tall, soft-spoken white man who wore his blond hair long. She told her parents she was meeting with friends to study or play tennis, then instead drove around the canyons of LA in my father's Beamer with Joni Mitchell and Neil Young streaming from the speakers. He introduced her to his hippie friends, took her to Griffith Observatory, and wrote her love songs he strummed out on his acoustic guitar. They talked of moving up north together, far from my mother's family and the crowds of LA, to the freedom and open space of Northern California.

I don't know if my parents sat together that summer and paged through my dad's beloved copy of *The Last Whole Earth Catalog*, as I did recently. If they did they might have noticed, among the descriptions of geodesic dome kits and marijuana growing guides, Wendell Berry's enthusiastic book review of *An Agricultural Testament* by Sir Albert Howard.

By that time, the organic food movement in California had begun to spill into the mainstream. Organic restaurants and markets could be found all around the state. CCOF had added dozens of certified farms to Rodale's original list, and eleven other certification agencies had cropped up across the country. Some were nonprofits while others operated as private for-profit companies, and each certifier had set slightly different standards for what counted as organic. The discrepancies had begun to create confusion for consumers and loopholes that could be taken advantage of by fraudulent producers. Industry leaders and organic advocates began to push for unified standards and state oversight.

In 1979, California legislators passed the Organic Food Act, which codified a legal definition for "organic," officially recognizing the differences that set these foods and farms apart. It did not, however, endorse organic agriculture or offer any support for its development—no subsidies for organic farmers or funding for organic research—nor did it tighten regulations regarding harmful chemicals or prohibit ecologically destructive agricultural practices. Instead, the law only legitimized the organic label, upholding its integrity and bolstering the price premium

attached to it. During these years, other states and countries passed similar laws, and advocates began to push the USDA to adopt a national
organic standard.

As the food geographer Julie Guthman writes, the organic movement's decision "not to ask for direct state support but rather to ask that
the state honor and uphold an industry-created definition of organically
grown . . . would have far reaching effects on practices and participation
in the sector." This incentive-based, market-driven strategy cemented
the organic movement's shift away from the goal of overhauling the con-
ventions of mainstream agriculture and toward the altogether different
aim of creating a marketable alternative to it, one that would not inter-
fere with the status quo but could instead operate alongside it.

Thus, even as organic foods and farming began to proliferate in some
corners of the world, the Green Revolution model of agriculture barreled
ahead unfettered.

❧ 8 ❧

Jeeta wanted to make salwar kameez for my mother, sister, and me to take back to America, so one morning we all took a bus to a nearby town to buy fabric. I watched out the window as we drew nearer to the town, the space between villages shrinking until we were on the edge of a small city. At each stop along the way, I noticed the same poster tacked up among a clutter of flyers, written partly in English and partly in Punjabi. I could read the English word "pesticide" but had to ask my mother to translate the rest. "It's something about pesticide poisoning," she said, "a hotline to call."

In town, we sat in shop after shop as men unspooled reams of fabric in front of us, tossing each aside at the shake of our heads. They brought out shawls and pashminas, watching as I ran my fingertips over the intricate weaves. I declined the men's suggestions of shiny fuchsia satin or fiery red cotton, choosing muted colors instead—a creamy white covered with delicate flowers, a heather gray dotted with turquoise and golden circles. Jeeta watched me with her usual wide eyes, her mouth curling into a near smile. Finally she lifted her hand to her mouth to cover a giggle she no longer bothered to restrain, then whispered, "Didi, these ones"—she pointed to the fabrics I'd picked—"they are not for young woman. They are for old lady, for grandmother!" I laughed but stuck to my choices, unable to imagine myself wearing the glittery alternatives.

After enough fabric stores, we stopped at a sweets shop where my sister and I shared a dish of rasmalai, two plump cheese dumplings floating in sweetened milk, and my mother chose pistachio burfi. Jeeta ordered strawberry ice cream. When the waiter came to clear the table, she tilted her bowl to pour the last pink drops onto her spoon before letting the man take her dish.

In the afternoon, Jeeta showed us where we could find souvenirs, guiding us from shop to shop. We wanted authentic Indian things— kajal paste for our eyes, bailnah (small wooden rolling pins for making roti), shawls that we rubbed carefully between our fingers and held up to the light to confirm they were in fact real wool and not polyester. Jeeta bought nothing for herself. My mother asked her at each shop, would she like anything? But always, Jeeta shook her head until at last we entered one final shop. Here, Jeeta pointed to a stack of American style T-shirts wrapped in plastic behind the counter. One by one the shopkeeper unfolded each shirt and spread it across the counter just the way the other men had displayed the fabric. Some shirts had tacky hearts stitched across the fronts, others spelled out words like "lucky." One had the Apple logo printed on the breast pocket. Jeeta examined the shirts just as I had inspected the shawls, running her fingertips across the threads. She chose a stretchy blue T-shirt with short sleeves and a row of plastic jewels along the hem. "Blue is my favorite color," she said, looking to my mother for approval, "sky blue." My mother shrugged, took the shirt and paid the man without even bothering to bargain. On the bus ride home, Jeeta hugged the bag close to her chest.

↤

That evening I climbed to the rooftop to watch the sunset. The day had been warm, but evening brought a strong breeze and I was glad for it. After the sun slipped below the horizon I heard the slap of Jeeta's sandaled feet coming up the steps. She smiled and stood next to me, following my gaze out past her village toward a horizon streaked pink. A cat slunk along the edge of a neighboring rooftop and she pointed to it. "Billi," she said. "Cat," I replied in English. We'd been trading words, trying to learn bits of each other's language.

"Cat," Jeeta repeated. Then she looked up at me. "Didi," she said. "Can I ask? Your marriage, is it love marriage?"

Before we left California, my mother, grandmother, and I had agreed it would be best not to mention the fact that Ryan and I were not technically married. It would be easier, we thought, than trying to explain our committed but unmarried domestic relationship.

"Yes," I said, "love marriage."

Jeeta beamed, then stepped closer and I felt her shoulder brush against mine. "Your husband, he loves you?"

I nodded.

"Do you know," Jeeta said, "I am married too?" I shook my head, wondering if I'd misunderstood. "For me, not love marriage," she said. "Arranged."

The night sky pushed the blue dusk to the edges of the horizon and the moon emerged, a crescent hanging low over the wheat fields. The crackle of Simran's cook fire snapped below us, sending a trail of smoke above the courtyard walls. In all directions, similar smoke trails rose above rooftops, twisting and curling together into the night.

Here, in the settling dark, Jeeta told me her story. She spoke softly, extracting her words carefully, one after the other, as if pulling shards of glass from her skin with a pair of tweezers. The story began with her father's death, one year before our visit. Jeeta was nineteen, the youngest of three sisters and the only one still unwed. Simran hurried to arrange a marriage for Jeeta before the family—now without its patriarch to bring in an income—slipped further into poverty and Jeeta became a less desirable bride. She found a groom from a nearby village. His family had seemed nice enough, respectable, but the man was rumored to have problems with drugs, to be violent. Some urged Simran to reconsider the arrangement, but she was adamant.

Jeeta didn't say if she protested, if she begged her mother to look for another groom, to wait just a little longer. Perhaps she too felt the urgency to be wed before it grew too late. The wedding took place a few months later in the gurdwara down the street, Jeeta in a red salwar kameez, arms laced with henna, gold rings through her nose. Four times she walked with her groom around the Guru Granth Sahib.

After the wedding, Jeeta left her home to live with her new husband and in-laws. It was not easy, but she thought things would surely get better, with time her husband would grow kinder, learn to love her. She tried to stick it out, cooked mutter paneer and saag, rolled out fresh paratha each morning. Still, he hit her, spoke to her as if she were a dog, allowed his friends to mistreat her.

After six months of marriage, Jeeta walked out of her husband's home and returned to her family's yellow-walled, blue-trimmed courtyard, swearing she would never go back. "Marriage," she said, "is prison." Her husband's family refused to allow her an official divorce, or to return the dowry.

"Didi," Jeeta said. "Before I marry, I was like you. I was slim, happy. But now..." She paused, looked down at her bare feet, and tugged at the hem of her shawl. When she looked back at me her eyes shone black and liquid. "Can you change me?" she asked.

I stared at Jeeta, wishing I could speak her language but also relieved that I could not. What words could I offer?

Jeeta looked away, flicked a lock of hair behind her ear. Then she lifted her gaze to the horizon, pointed to the moon. "Chand," she said, her smile returning.

"Moon," I said, a whisper.

❧ 9 ❧

The next morning I awoke to a changed place. Jeeta's story had washed away the rosy lens I'd placed over life in the village and, like that trick image, I was beginning to see the old lady in place of the young girl. I watched Simran squat over the cook fire, flipping paratha as she did every morning, and saw that she winced each time she stood. She caught me watching and pointed to her knees, grimaced, and said something I couldn't understand, but I got the gist: her body hurt. At dinner, before serving herself, Jeeta arranged two roti, a heap of carrots, and a bowl of yogurt on a plate and set it in front of her younger brother, who refused—and was never expected—to get his own food. Though I'd observed this daily routine before, that evening I couldn't help feel a prick of anger at such blatant patriarchy. I knew that this teenager, as the only son, would one day inherit the house and any wealth the family had accumulated while Jeeta and her sisters would get nothing.

During that same meal, Simran leaned across the table and told me that my child would surely be a boy—the third woman in the village to say this to me. I looked up from my food, realizing for the first time what should have been obvious: she, like the other women, was not saying so because of some gut feeling or superstition. She was saying this in the same way an American might assure me that my child would be born healthy—it was only polite. Simran reached her hand out to pat my shoulder, smiling, saying yes, she was sure of it. This time I didn't smile and say, *you think so?* Instead I looked down at my stomach and folded my hands over the curve of my growing child like a shield.

⇜ 10 ⇝

One day my grandmother and I found ourselves alone together in the courtyard, having just seen off a group of Aunties who had come to visit. Their voices trailed behind them, ricocheting down the narrow streets, growing quieter. When I could no longer hear their chatter, I cleared my throat.

"Naniji," I asked, "how did your sister die?" I knew my grandmother had been close to her sister, Jeeta's grandmother. She had visited her here every few years, in this very house, until her recent death. Watching my grandmother talk and laugh with so many other women in the village, I found myself wondering about Jeeta's grandmother—which room had been hers? Had she shared my grandmother's easy grin, her unflinching gaze?

My grandmother's chunni hung unevenly around her neck, the long tail pooling in her lap. She rearranged it neatly around her shoulders before answering me. "Cancer," she said, then turned to brush a fly off her shoulder. "Her son, Jeeta's father, same."

I nodded, though my grandmother was no longer looking at me. She gazed instead toward the courtyard gate, as if waiting for someone to appear there. A moment later a stray dog wandered in and trotted eagerly toward the cook stove, claws clicking on the concrete. My grandmother shouted something in Punjabi and he froze, perked his ears toward us, then turned and fled.

Weeks later, after returning home, I would read one news story after another about the alarming cancer rates among Punjab's wheat-producing villages. The articles described how the problem was so pronounced that the train from Punjab to the nearest public cancer hospital, located in a city 220 miles away, had become known as the "Cancer Express." Nearly all of the articles pointed to the increased use of agricultural chemicals as the most likely culprit, often citing a 2009 Greenpeace report that found 20 percent of drinking water wells in Punjab contained nitrate levels above the WHO's safe limit. Other studies linked heavy pesticide use to increased cancer rates. But causal relationships in these situations are nearly impossible to prove. Reading though these articles, I'd think back to this afternoon in the yellow courtyard in Pharwala and wonder about my grandmother's sister, about Jeeta's father. Had they once been passengers on that train? Had they, too, referred to it by that blunt nickname? But later, when I asked my grandmother about this, she only shook her head. "No, my sister, for her—no treatment."

From the many stories I read about the cancer train, one line remained lodged in my mind. In a piece for the *Washington Post*, journalist Rama Lakshmi spoke with two passengers aboard the train, a farmer and his wife heading to Bikaner so that she could receive cancer treatment. The farmer told her yes, he applied pesticides several times a year on his crops, and that he was aware of the potential health impacts of these chemicals, but without them his farm productivity would decrease and he'd not survive the profit loss. Lakshmi turned to the farmer's wife, Jasveer Singh, to ask her what she thought.

"It is all because of the poisoned water," she said, then added, "and my destiny."

❧ 11 ❧

I n the years that Jeeta and I were growing up on opposite sides of the
globe, the organic movement and the Green Revolution continued
to unfold in parallel. High-yielding varieties of wheat, rice, and maize
spread to countries around the world while natural food markets like
Whole Foods and organic coffee shops began to appear in affluent urban
neighborhoods. In 1987, regulators gave biotech corporations the green
light to begin the first field experiments of genetically modified food
crops just as readership of Rodale's *Organic Farming and Gardening*
magazine surpassed one million. Biodiversity in the world's agricultural
fields plummeted as mixed plantings of local cultivars were displaced
by mono-crop fields of genetically homogeneous seed. Meanwhile, individuals concerned by this loss, like Monica Spiller, found that many
of the traditional varieties no longer in cultivation were held in the cold
storage vaults of the USDA and other international seed banking systems. They procured samples and began the slow process of propagat-
ing enough seed to supply small organic farmers with the seeds to plant
fields destined to become $10 loaves of "heritage grain" bread. In 1997,
Monsanto's "Roundup Ready" varieties—seeds genetically engineered to
resist the company's herbicide glyphosate (Roundup), thus enabling a
farmer to indiscriminately spray an entire field and kill the weeds but
not the crop—were approved by the EPA for commercial release with
scant public pushback. That same year, the USDA released its proposed
draft of what would be the first national standards for certified organic
production. The draft rules allowed for the "big three": GMO seeds, ir-
radiation, and sewage sludge. Outraged activists and consumers sent the
USDA more than 275,600 oppositional comments, the most ever to be
received by a government agency, and the drafted rules did not move
forward. In 1998, CCOF celebrated its twenty-fifth anniversary, having
grown from Rodale's 52 growers in 1972 to nearly 650 certified organic

farmers in California alone. Over those same years, pesticide use in the state climbed to its highest level, and the use of known carcinogens more than doubled.

In 2002, the final revised USDA organic standards were approved after much debate. Activists had succeeded in demanding the removal of the "big three" from the standards, but less sensational points were ceded. Proposals to address social issues in the organic definition—to include rules on scale, ownership, and workers' rights—were ultimately rejected (just as they had been earlier by California and CCOF) in favor of an exclusive focus on growing methods, with particular emphasis on inputs. By this time, the more radical ambitions once held by some organic food advocates had largely eroded from the mainstream movement's priorities, but the narrow USDA standards—adopted by federal, state, and international agencies—marked a categorical relinquishing of those larger goals.

⊖

By the time I started college in 2005, multinational biotech corporations had grown into some of the richest and most powerful entities in the world. Four companies controlled more than half the global proprietary seed supply. The world was losing 75 billion tons of soil each year. Nine out of ten acres of soybeans in America were being planted with Roundup-tolerant seeds, and 75 percent of the diversity among agricultural crops had disappeared. Pesticides could be found in the cord blood of nearly every newborn baby, and biotech corporations were beginning to outpace the federal government in funding agricultural research at public US land-grant colleges. Climate change had risen to the top of the list of wreckage wrought by the industrial food system.

In Santa Cruz, however, vibrant farmers markets buzzed with people several times each week, and natural foods stores proliferated—an organic version of almost anything could be procured, for enough money. Babies wore onesies reading "I'm Organic," egg cartons sported strings of icons denoting their moral attributes, farm-to-fork restaurants served local micro-greens, and many forearms bore a beet tattoo. Alan Chadwick's organic garden project had grown into the thirty-acre farm at the center of the UCSC campus where as an undergraduate I'd wander one

fall morning, freshly overwhelmed with the news of contemporary ecological devastation, and sit at a sunny picnic table. There I'd watch that
group of apprentices fill crate after crate with wine-colored beets and I'd
indulge, for the first time, in a dreamy vision of becoming an organic
farmer myself.

ᘓ 12 ᘔ

In Pharwala the morning sun hung low, casting long shadows over the cobbled street as my grandmother led my mother, my sister, and me into the room of a small house next door to Jeeta's, where a distant relative now lived. Here, my grandmother told us, was where my mother had been born. She sat atop a slender bed, the room's only furnishing, and fanned one hand out as if to say, *here it is.* The walls and floor were concrete now, but at the time she'd given birth, my grandmother explained, the room had been made of mud.

I tried to imagine my grandmother, seventeen and married for less than a year, lying in this room nearly six decades ago. With her husband back in Nairobi, it would have been her mother and older sister who'd helped her care for the newborn. I remembered her telling me of the anguish she'd felt after my mother's birth, her bafflement at what to do with the baby—an unlucky girl child. But none of that fear and despair showed now. She only smiled, triumphant, it seemed, to show us this windowless room where she had first become a mother, to reveal a piece of what her life had once been, or maybe to show us exactly how far she'd come.

She did not tell me that morning the details of my mother's birth. But years later she would describe how on the day my mother was born a cold front had pushed the temperature in the village to a record low. To keep my grandmother warm while she labored, a pan of hot coals had been set beneath her bed. No one noticed when the bottom blanket began to smoke. Moments later, the cloth burst into flame. And although the attending women managed to smother the fire before it grew, my grandmother would always remember the birth of her daughter accompanied by the smell of smoke, singed cotton, a sudden rush of flame.

ᘔ

Later that afternoon, I accompanied Jeeta to the edge of town, where she was headed again to buy greens for saag. As we walked farther from the village center, the wheat fields drew nearer until they lapped at the edges of the road. I remembered my first evening here in Pharwala, how Jeeta had led me and my family down this same road and I'd felt a wash of warmth at the familiar sight of those fields. But on this afternoon, I no longer felt comforted by the sight of the wheat plants. Instead, an unsettling dissonance had begun to swell in its place.

Jeeta asked questions about my life at home: "Do you drive car? Have house?" I answered her as best I could, picking around our language gap, until she asked: "You have job? What you do for job?"

I looked out at the wheat fields flanking the road, and considered how to answer. Should I just lift a hand and point to the woman in the distance, bent away from us and tossing fistfuls of fertilizer across the wheat field? I knew the Punjabi word for farm: kheth. But how could I convey the difference between my life as a farmer and this woman's? My job did not expose me to pesticides, my drinking water was not contaminated with nitrates. My customers were, in large part, wealthy foodies who pulled up to my roadside stand in shiny SUVs and BMWs. They took photos of themselves against the backdrop of my wheat fields, my rows of zinnias and tomato vines, and posted them on Instagram. I'd *chosen* to become a farmer—I'd gone to college, held a degree, had plenty of other career options I could pursue. I could walk away from my farm anytime I wanted.

Even if I could've explained all this, I wouldn't have. I wasn't sure what embarrassed me more: the thought of admitting to Jeeta that I was a small farmer, growing crops on land I didn't own like many of the poorest people in this village, or the fact that my life as such was so unlike the lives of these farmers. I couldn't explain these differences, nor could I tolerate the idea of letting Jeeta believe that what I did for a living, and what the women in the fields beside us did, were in fact the same.

I turned from the fields to Jeeta and felt a surprising relief at our mismatched languages. My lack of Punjabi, which had for so long been an obstacle I struggled to ford, became in that moment a moat keeping me safely separate. I offered a sheepish smile, a shake of my head. "I'm sorry," I lied, "I don't understand your question." She looked at me for a moment, then touched her fingers to my wrist, laughed softly and said, "It is OK." Then, "I so happy to meet you. Please, please come stay again soon."

On the way back to the house that afternoon, Jeeta pointed to a doorway leading to a concrete room that housed the village's flour mill. I could hear the steady hum of a motor growling within. "For the atta," she said. I asked if we could look inside, and she led me in. There, in a room lined with sacks of grain, stood a stone mill constructed to almost exactly the same design as the mill sitting in pieces in my barn at home. Two hefty stones, each about two feet wide and eight inches thick, stacked atop one another. The bottom stone remained still while the top one spun. A trapezoid-shaped steel hopper fed grain into the mill, and a spout spewed the freshly ground flour into a sack. A young man moved around the room, checking the progress of the mill and heaving sacks of grain from stack to stack. I motioned to the bag filling with flour and asked Jeeta if I could look inside. She said something to the man and he dipped a hand into the bag and retrieved a fistful of flour. The cream-colored powder clung to the hairs of his arm like pollen. I held out a cupped hand and he poured some into my palm. I rubbed the flour between my fingertips, feeling its warmth on my skin.

When we returned to the house, Jeeta asked my mother if she could see a picture of my father, "the white man." My mother stepped into the bedroom and returned with an iPad she'd brought to use on the flight. In Jeeta's house there were no computers, no internet. My mother clicked opened her collection of photos and Jeeta looked over her shoulder. "There," my mother said pointing to my father, who in this photo stood in front of a lake, his long blond hair lifted by some unseen wind, an oversize T-shirt hanging low over plaid shorts. Jeeta laughed, that fluttering giggle I'd grow so used to.

Jeeta asked to see another picture, and my mother began scrolling through her photos. And suddenly there was my world in front of us all to see, the one I'd allowed myself to forget I had. A world of tiled kitchens and gas stoves and towering refrigerators. Of lying out in bikinis alongside rivers, of bowls heaped with fresh-picked strawberries, of swimming pools and sleeveless dresses and shorts, of a piercing blue sky. Jeeta's eyes were latched to the screen, the images flashing in her pupils. I felt like I'd been caught with a smudge of frosting on my lips after swearing I'd not had any cake, and I wished my mother would close the screen, let us forget the distance between our lives in America and Jeeta's life here.

Jeeta didn't ask about the mountain vistas, the indoor plumbing, the backyard swimming pools. She mentioned only our clothes. "I like this dress," she said, pointing to a photo of my sister laughing outside of a café, a tiny cotton dress draped over her thin body. "I like shorts, baseball hat."

When the photos at last ended, my mother took the iPad back to the bedroom and Jeeta turned to examine herself in the mirror. She stared at her face, twisted her hair between her fingers. "I like short dress," she said, grabbing a fistful of fabric from the billows of her pants as if she might rip them apart. "If I could wear short dress, I would be very happy."

She looked back into the mirror and I followed her gaze until I could see both our faces in the glass: two great-granddaughters of the same ancestors. But I saw little resemblance between us. Instead it was our differences that glared back at me, the confines Jeeta had inherited that I'd escaped.

Paul's words from the night before we left LA echoed in my mind: *once a person leaves his country of origin, he will never belong anywhere again.* At the time, I'd seen only tragedy in this sentiment, but watching Jeeta in the mirror now I wondered if perhaps Paul had meant something different. Perhaps he was alluding to the freedom of not belonging, of escaping the bounds of one's home.

For a moment Jeeta didn't notice me behind her in the mirror, her gaze fixed hard and cold on her own face. When she looked up to catch me watching, we both turned away and stepped toward our rooms. I laid on the bed that my mother, my sister, and I all shared, and closed my eyes. Later, in the dim light of evening, I woke to the shuffle of Jeeta's sandaled feet as she spread a shawl across my goose-pimpled skin.

Ɬ 13 Ɬ

The next afternoon I watched Jeeta make yet another kameez, drawing diagrams in my notebook, instructions I could follow to sew my own at home. My mother shelled peas for dinner with Simran, whose voice squawked and chirped through the courtyard as they worked. I couldn't understand what she was saying but noticed when her voice lowered, softened, then let out a quick quiver as if she might cry. I glanced in her direction. In one hand, Simran held a pea pod split down the middle. With her other hand she gripped my mother's shoulder. Her eyes, dark and round, just like Jeeta's, were locked on my mother's face.

Lying in bed that night, I asked my mother what Simran had said to her. "She asked me if I could get Jeeta to America," my mother told me. Then she rolled over to face the wall before adding, "I said I'd try." Outside the bedroom window, a hush of fog had settled over the village. Only the tsk-tsk of Jeeta's broom murmured softly in the gathering dark. I wanted to believe my mother could bring Jeeta to California with us. But long lines of Indians were denied visas to the United States each day—wealthy Indians who spoke impeccable English, held advanced degrees, wore Western business suits. I suspected Jeeta had little chance of getting a visa—a girl with no passport, no money, little education, and only rudimentary English.

The next morning, while watching Jeeta sew, I imagined her in a pair of jeans and a T-shirt, or maybe a black pencil skirt and low-cut white blouse on her way to work for a company somewhere in Los Angeles, perhaps a fashion firm or a marketing agency. Jeeta threaded her needle, singing softly, and began to hand-stitch the finishing hem of a neckline. Her slender fingers fluttered mothlike along the fold of fabric, leaving a trail of perfect hatch marks in their wake. Something about my image of her in LA—buying milk in a plastic carton from Safeway, T-shirts from Target, fabric from JoAnn's, the yellow-walled courtyard empty of her singing—struck me as sorrowful. I flicked the thought away. I knew my ability to romanticize the ordinary facts of Jeeta's life was a luxury afforded to me because I'd grown up with privileges and opportunities she might never know. I could extol the virtues of the village—the closeness of community, the richness of tradition—because I was exempt from its bounds.

Later, Jeeta asked if she could try on some of our Western clothes. She pulled on a pair of my boot-cut Levi's with an elastic waist to accommodate my growing belly, and my mother's V-neck orange T-shirt, and admired herself in the mirror, turning this way and that, perhaps pretending for a moment that she was someone else. Jeeta caught me watching and let out a gleeful giggle. "I look changed?" she asked. I nodded. The clothes fit her well enough—I could have believed they were hers.

❧ 14 ❧

I was sitting with my mother, Simran, and my sister in the midmorning sun when Jeeta burst in through the courtyard gate and let out a sharp wail followed by a few swift lines of Punjabi. My mother and Simran stood and, leaving my sister and me behind, followed Jeeta back out of the courtyard and down the street. Through the gate came a sound like a cat howling. The sound grew louder, thicker, like a chorus of singers. A moment later Jeeta reappeared. "Sonia's grandfather expired," she told us, her eyes brimming with tears. Then she spun back around and disappeared down the alley.

My mother returned and explained that the old man who lived in the breezeway—a distant relative of ours—had died. Incontinent and incoherent, the man had lived in a covered space between two houses where he spent his days sleeping on a heap of blankets. People brought him trays of food, changed his blankets daily. "The women are wailing," she said lifting a hand toward the howling sound, which was now loud enough to be clearly human and was growing louder still. My grandmother, stirred awake from a nap, stepped slowly out from her room and glanced in the direction of the wailers. Without asking for details she muttered, "Thank God."

My grandmother told me she had prayed for him to pass away swiftly. "It is his time," she said. I nodded—he had looked to me like the oldest person I'd ever seen. But later, when I asked my grandmother his age, she told me: Seventy-five. A year younger than herself.

I followed my grandmother to the breezeway where women crowded around the dead man, their voices lifting and falling in a chorus of wails as they prepared the body to be carried to the pyre. I looked up from the body to notice a woman staring at me. Our eyes met and she looked away, then stepped toward my grandmother and spoke softly into her ear. My grandmother glanced back at me, and the two women began talking. Another joined in, and another. Simran and Jeeta, too, began talking. I could understand nothing, as usual, only recognized the back and forth tempo of argument. At last my mother informed me the women were debating whether or not I should attend the funeral. "It's because you're pregnant," my mother said, dismissing the discussion with a flick of her hand. "Some superstitious thing about bad luck."

We left the women and returned to the house. A few minutes later, Simran rushed through the door to say that it had been decided that I should attend, but I would need to perform a particular ritual to prevent ill fortune from slinking into my child's future. I agreed and she beamed, then disappeared into her room. She returned holding a strip of white cloth. With great care, she knelt on the courtyard floor and tied the cloth snuggly around my big toe. Then she stood, gripped both my hands in hers, and in a long, breathless outpouring of Punjabi began to explain what I needed to do. When she was done, I nodded assuredly and gave her hands a firm squeeze. Then I looked desperately to my mother.

"She says you are to wear the string on your toe while you walk to the pyre. Then remove it using only your left foot, and hand it to her and she'll put it on the pyre with the body to be burned." I glanced back and forth between both women, Simran nodding enthusiastically, my mother shrugging. How, I wondered, had my mother translated in a few short lines what had taken Simran many more to explain? What else had been said, what had I missed?

Simran gave my hand a final squeeze, then turned to rejoin the women wailing. My mother followed, but I stayed behind a moment to attempt alone the balancing act of removing the white cloth from my right toe with my left foot. After a few rehearsals, I hurried to catch up.

When I reached the breezeway, the old man's body lay cleaned and wrapped in white cloth atop a stretcher. Women stood on one side, men on the other. Someone draped a deep red shawl over the top of the body while a man read from the Guru Granth Sahib. Then four men, one at each corner of the stretcher, lifted the body onto their shoulders and began walking. Everyone else followed. The crowd filled the width of the streets, and I could see nothing of where we were going, only the jig-sawed cobbles and blue-black gutters underfoot. The procession wound down one street after the next until I lost all sense of direction.

When at last we emerged into the open space at the edge of town, we were in a place I'd never been. A cluster of shacks huddled together along the road. Behind the homes was a heap of trash, and beyond that the flat expanse of wheat fields. Outside one of the shacks a woman squatted to winnow wheat, pouring the berries back and forth between two bowls and letting the breeze carry away the chaff. Our procession moved past, but she did not look up. This, my grandmother later explained, was where the poorest of the village lived. As is true the world over, many of the poorest people here were landless farm laborers, like the women I'd seen tossing fertilizer pellets onto the wheat fields.

The pyre came into view around a bend and Simran scurried up to the men leading the procession, then back to me. She pointed to my toe, whispering frantically, always hopeful that I might yet understand her words. I looked around for Jeeta, but she had disappeared into the crowd. The procession paused, and my cheeks burned under the gaze of so many onlookers. Slowly, I slid my feet out of the rubber chappla I was wearing, borrowed from Jeeta, then used my left foot to remove the tie from my right toe. When the scrap of fabric fell loose and dropped to the ground, I bent to pick it up and placed it, no longer white but dusty red, into Simran's waiting palm. She squeezed my arm gently, then rushed to the stretcher and tucked the stained fabric into a fold of shawl covering the dead man. A ripple of nods passed through the crowd, and I let out my breath.

At the pyre, the men lowered the dead man to the ground then began stacking long logs over his body. Someone spilled an armload of old clothes and blankets into the pile. All around me women sobbed and wailed, but none louder than Simran. Her own husband had died a year prior—the anniversary of his death, I later learned, was the next day.

Once the pyre was stacked tall with wood, two boys flung armloads of dried grass on top. Another poured a liquid in generous streams over the mass. Someone struck a match and the grass began to crackle. A moment passed, then the pyre erupted with a great rush of air and roar of flame. Men walked through the crowd dispensing fistfuls of parshad into cupped hands. A man read from the Guru Granth Sahib, his voice loud and rhythmic like the one that poured from speakers across the village every dawn. Then his voice went silent and all at once everyone bowed in unison, touching fingertips to the ground. My sister and I followed, a beat too late.

Afterward, I found my grandmother sitting beneath the canopy of a great sprawling tree. I sat in the shade beside her, leaned back against the trunk, and together we watched the fire burn.

"This tree, you know it?" my grandmother said after a moment. She turned to face the trunk and placed her palm flat against the bark. The trunk, too wide for me to wrap my arms around, was not a single pillar but a bundle of sinewy bands twisting around one other, the way a length of sturdy cord is made of a hundred threads. "It is a pipal tree. You know pipal tree?" I shook my head, but my grandmother didn't seem to notice. "My mother, long time ago, plant this tree," she said, and traced her gaze up the length of the trunk to where the bands untwined into leafy branches. "After her own child died. She wanted shade, you know? For the families of the dead."

I followed her gaze, watched the leaves flutter in the breeze. Smoke drifted into the tree's highest branches and I turned to face the fire, imagined that strip of white cloth catching flame, blackening and shriveling, joining the plume and swirling up through the leaves overhead. My grandmother and I sat there with the tree until people began leaving, then we stood and stepped slowly out of its shade.

↫ 15 ↬

J eeta and I returned from the flour mill one morning with a new sack of atta to find my mother, Simran, and my grandmother sitting in the courtyard, a bowl of peas they'd just finished shelling between them. When we stepped into view, the murmur of their voices came to a sudden halt. "Sat Sri Achall," Jeeta said warmly. She shifted the sack of flour to one arm, reached for the bowl of peas with the other, and turned toward the kitchen to bring everything inside. But before she could take a step my grandmother called her name, and Jeeta spun back around. "Yes, Auntie-ji?" she said. My grandmother cleared her throat then spoke quietly in Punjabi, her voice solemn but not unkind.

When my grandmother stopped speaking, Jeeta only looked down, focusing it seemed on the toes of her bare feet. Then she muttered something apologetic and fled toward the kitchen. The rubber sole of her flip-flop caught on the concrete and she lurched forward, the bag of flour slipping from her hands to the floor with a thud. The paper sack split along the side and a little waterfall of flour spilled out. Jeeta knelt and swept the flour into her palm, poured it back inside the bag, and hastily carried it into the kitchen. A moment later she returned with a dustpan and broom. No one spoke as Jeeta moved the broom in a few quick flicks across the concrete. She dumped the dustpan's contents into the ashes of the cook fire, then disappeared into her room.

In the charged quiet that filled the space, I took a seat on the woven bed at the opposite end of the courtyard from my grandmother, watched her pull out her prayer book and begin to read. Simran slipped out of sight into the kitchen and my mother, who had been sitting very still, stood suddenly and crossed the courtyard to join me. On her face, I could see a look of exhaustion beginning to supplant one of rage, a kind of resignation I'd rarely seen her allow herself at home.

She sat next to me on the woven bed and leaned back against the wall, sending a tumble of flies swirling into the air. "Can you believe that?" she said. I had to remind her I hadn't understood the exchange.

She didn't explain right away. Eventually she dropped her gaze to her lap, rubbed her palm across her face and spoke quietly enough not to disturb my grandmother. She told me they had been talking about Jeeta, about Simran's plea to get her to America. The only way anyone knew to do this was via a marriage to an American citizen. Simran had been urging my mother to take a photo of Jeeta so that she might show it to prospective grooms. My mother paused as if she might stop. Then continued, her voice a notch lower.

"Your grandmother told Jeeta she should try to lose some weight, that she looks unkempt, *unappealing*." Repeating the words in English seemed to rekindle my mother's rage and she shook her head in disbelief.

I thought of Jeeta on the rooftop the other night, of everything she'd told me, of her unflinching eyes. *Marriage*, she'd said, *is prison*. I glanced across the courtyard at my grandmother, who was still reading from her book of prayer, and felt my own skin grow hot with anger.

I wanted to confront my grandmother. Perhaps she'd listen to me, for she'd never told me such things—never commented on my own often "unkempt" appearance, my boy-style short haircut, my lack of makeup, my never-polished nails or jeans-and-T-shirt wardrobe. I imagined settling into the empty chair next to her, beginning to speak. But what would I say? That Jeeta was a vibrant and capable young woman, that she was beautiful and healthy and strong, that she shouldn't be disparaged for not being model-thin? Or would I say that appearance didn't matter anyway, she didn't need to waste her time attending to the slimness of her figure or the shine of her hair, she wasn't beholden to such nonsense and could look and act and be however she wished?

I imagined my grandmother peering curiously back at me as I said all this, not protesting or taking offense, only setting her jaw and waiting. Then, I imagined, she'd clear her throat and it would be Monica Spiller's words from that fall day on my farm that would slip softly from her lips: *You don't know. How could you?*

I glanced toward the doorway to Jeeta's bedroom. Perhaps it was she I should talk to. Only a curtain covered the opening. I could slide it aside, step through and take Jeeta's hand. I could point in the direction of my grandmother, roll my eyes. *She's old-fashioned*, I'd say. *She's wrong. Don't listen to her.* And Jeeta would look at me and nod. *Yes, I know,* she'd say, and we'd peek out the door at my grandmother praying furiously in her plastic chair, share a conspiratorial laugh, then emerge together, still giggling, into the bright light of late morning.

The image of that doorway remains burned in my mind—that narrow passage, that length of thin cotton separating the room inside from the courtyard where I sat, how easily I could have pushed the fabric aside. But I didn't.

Instead I climbed the stairs to the rooftop, sat alone on the concrete ledge, and watched a pair of white birds step silently through the wheat fields, their legs unseeable in the fog.

⟨ 16 ⟩

On the last day of our stay in Pharwala, Jeeta and I stood together once again on her rooftop. I'd come up to take in one final view of the village, Jeeta to dump her dustpan after sweeping the courtyard. We gazed quietly out over the rooftops and wheat fields. Then she reached out to smooth flat the hem of my sleeve where it had folded over. "Your kameez, it look very nice, haanah? You like?" I was wearing the suit Jeeta had sewn for me, made from creamy white cloth covered in a bright floral pattern with short sleeves and a scooped neckline that was, she told me, called a "sweetheart." As she'd promised, Jeeta had made a salwar kameez for my mother and sister as well—all three were deftly sewn and perfectly fitted to our frames. I told her how much I loved the outfit, thanked her for all the time she'd put into it. She laughed, shook her head, and said, "Good!" Then, her voice softer, she asked, "You like my village? You will miss it?"

I wanted to tell her that I liked her village very much, that in my own town I knew few of my neighbors, was not invited in for tea in the afternoon. Other than my parents, I had no relatives nearby, no one to call Auntie. I bought my yogurt from the supermarket in a plastic tub, ultra-pasteurized and exactly the same as the tub behind it. My clothes weren't tailored but came from a factory somewhere overseas, always ill-fitting. Freshly milled flour wasn't available; I hadn't even managed to mill my own wheat. I wanted to tell her that here, in her village, something existed that I craved in my life in America. But even if I'd had the Punjabi words for this I would've felt foolish saying it—she, I guessed, would trade these things in a second for the freedom to wear a short dress, take a solo walk into town, smile at a boy passing on the street, attend college or learn to drive a car.

I nodded at Jeeta. "Yes," I said. "I will miss your village."

Jeeta grinned, then turned and carried the empty dustpan back downstairs. I listened to the slap of her sandals echoing through the concrete passageway and wondered if I had been wrong to come to this village 8,000 miles from my home. I felt like a voyeur, peeping into the lives of people whom I knew would likely never have the same chance to look in on my own life. I'd claimed these women as my family for these weeks, called them sister, Auntie, enjoyed the charms of their everyday lives—cooking over a fire, bathing from a bucket, scrubbing clothes by hand—all the while knowing I'd soon return to gas stoves and hot showers, indoor plumbing and fresh air.

But what if I hadn't come? What would I have to offer my child when they ask where their ancestors came from or what was left behind in that place? *What does the town look like?* my child might ask. *Do we still have any family there?*

I walked to the corner of the rooftop where Jeeta had emptied her dustpan. After sweeping the courtyard Jeeta always carried the pan up to the rooftop to dump it where birds could snatch up the discarded bits of food. Among the small heap of dirt were a few black lentils, two potato peels, an onion skin, and a speckling of stray wheat kernels. I knelt next to the pile and picked out a half teaspoon of kernels. I rubbed my fingers over the berries until they shone free of dust, then examined the mound in the center of my palm. This wheat was nothing special—just the modern high-yielding variety most farmers in the region had grown that year, the wheat Jeeta and her family carried to the mill to be ground into flour, then ate every day in roti and paratha. But if I wanted to return home with wheat from my family's village, this was it. I found a scrap of fabric the size of a playing card buried in the pile and pulled it loose, then folded it around my palmful of kernels. I carried the tiny package downstairs and tied it closed with a piece of Jeeta's sewing thread, then tucked the bundle inside the pocket of my passport case and slipped it into my bag.

⌀

When the driver arrived later that morning to take us to Chandigarh, where we'd catch a train, and then a flight home, Simran sobbed and sobbed. She lifted the edge of her orange shawl to her face and wiped her tears into the wool, then balled the fabric in her fist. A white dog curled on the street corner lifted his head to watch us all hug goodbye. Overhead, a kite circled upward. I loaded my bag into the minivan and, one by one, we climbed inside. Jeeta's eyes remained wide as if trying to take in every last bit of us before we drove out of sight. I could see they were glossy, the rims brimming with tears, but Jeeta didn't allow a drop to fall.

The driver slid my door shut and I pressed the button to roll the window down, but nothing happened. I moved the button up and down, jamming it harder each time, but the window remained closed. The driver started the engine and I looked up through a film of dust at Jeeta and Simran, then pressed my palm to the glass. The van grumbled forward, picking its way down the cobbled street until we turned and Jeeta and her mother were no longer in sight.

The van continued south away from the village. Wheat fields covered the distance between me and the yellow-walled house, and Simran's fist wrapped around a ball of tear-soaked wool, and Jeeta's unflinching eyes. The fields unspooled behind us until I could make out nothing of the village in the distance, only a smooth carpet of green fraying into fog.

⨭ 17 ⨮

O n the plane home, my mother and I tore bits of roti from a roll we'd packed for the flight and used them to pinch up bites of curried vegetables. "You want to know the strangest part?" my mother said. "After my family settled in LA my mom had the chance to sponsor another family from India to come to California. She chose her sister, Jeeta's grandmother." My grandfather had filled out all the paperwork, gathered the required documentation. The sponsorship was granted and my grandmother sent the paperwork to her sister. I imagined my grandmother's anticipation of bringing her sister's family to LA, transplanting a small piece of her village there. Perhaps with all of them together the foreign city could become more like home.

But the paperwork never reached my grandmother's sister. The package, it would later come out, had landed instead in the hands of another relative. Spiteful to have not been the one my grandmother chose to sponsor, this relative slipped the papers into the trash pile to be burned. At the time, everyone assumed something had fallen through with the process—the sponsorship had been declined, perhaps, visas refused. No one was very surprised. It had all seemed too good to be true. And so they did not try again. Instead, my grandmother's sister and her family remained in Pharwala. Not long after, her son and daughter-in-law bore their third baby, a third unlucky girl child. They named her Jagjeet, but she would always go by Jeeta.

My mother wiped her lips with a napkin, wrapped up the food, and switched off her overhead light. I leaned my forehead against the window and looked out. I could see only the wing lights blinking into the black night.

At the customs checkpoint in LAX I slid my passport across the counter to the man behind the kiosk. "Reason for your trip?" he asked, without looking up from the pages of the booklet. I stared at him for a moment, unable to answer.

"Just a visit," I said. The man closed my passport, pushed it back to me, and swept his arm to the side to signal I could pass. I walked toward the exit, a glass wall separating the street from the terminal. Two panels slid open and I stepped into the darkening California night. The freshness of the air seemed impossible and I sucked in gulp after gulp of sweet storm-laden air—greedily, desperately, as if I could never pull enough of it into my lungs.

❧ 18 ❧

I t was dark when, after the long, rain-drenched drive up from LA, I got home to the farm the following evening. Inside our house, Ryan had the wood stove burning. A cast-iron pan sizzled on top and the house flickered with firelight. I took off my shoes and walked through the living room toward the west window, listening for the familiar thud of my socked feet on the pine boards, running my fingers over our bookshelves to feel the warble of saw marks. I didn't have to glance at the skillet to know it was heaped with collard greens frying in garlic.

At the window, I looked out into the night. Rain tapped gently against the glass, the cloud cover so thick no moonlight filtered through. I could make out nothing of our fields. I squinted for a glimpse of something recognizable, but I couldn't see past the mulberry branches dripping in the yard. At last, a car approached on the road, its headlights glinting off the tin side of our barn, and for a moment I could see a swath of foliage, the wink of an irrigation header, our greenhouse lit like a lantern. Then the car dipped down the hill and, just like that, everything vanished.

Part 4

GEESE

❧ 1 ❧

I unpacked my bag in a daze of jet lag, tossing my clothes in a laundry basket and pulling out the yards of fabric and the two wool shawls I'd bought. In the bottom of my backpack, I found the kameez Jeeta had sewn for me. I spread the dress out across my bed, the silky fabric cool against my palm, and ran my fingertips over the dainty flowers that covered the cloth. The midsection curved outward with two petite pleats to fit my rounded belly. In a few weeks I'd outgrow the dress, and once I was no longer pregnant it would be far too large. I might never wear it again. I folded the garment into a square the size of a paperback and placed it on the highest shelf in my closet.

The last thing I unpacked was my passport. As I slid it into a drawer, the case caught against the wood, and I looked down to see a bulge in the pocket. Only after running my fingers over the lump did I remember the wheat kernels I'd taken from Jeeta's rooftop. I pulled out the thimble-size bundle, tugged gently on the thread that held it closed. But before the knot slipped loose I changed my mind, decided to leave it as it was. I didn't want to see what lay there: a few dozen mundane wheat kernels stolen from a distant rooftop. Nor did I want to admit that I'd no idea what to do with them.

I considered shaking the contents into the dirt outside my window; surely some birds would find the seeds there, carry them away as Jeeta had intended. Or perhaps I should simply toss the bundle into the trash with the crumpled boarding passes and airplane napkins. But I could bring myself to do neither. Instead, I tightened the thread and dropped the package into the bottom of a mason jar on my desk, where I might forget about it among the clutter of pens and paperclips.

⊷ 2 ⊶

For weeks I craved hot paratha each morning, warm milk with cardamom before bed. I tried to make yogurt, heated a pot of milk on the stove just as Simran had done each evening. I stirred in a spoonful of the prior day's yogurt, poured the liquid into a jar and wrapped it in a dish towel to rest in the oven overnight. In the morning I'd find the milk transformed, but something about my yogurt was never quite right—the flavor too sour, the shade too white, lacking the creamy sweetness of Simran's batches.

During the days, I busied myself with wintertime farm tasks—harvesting for wholesale orders, filing taxes, mixing potting soil, starting onions and broccoli in the greenhouse. Our Sonora field was flushed bright green, but the plants were hardly six inches tall, much shorter than the foot or two they should have been by now. We were entering a fourth consecutive year of drought, and new growth had yet to come to the grasses on the surrounding hillsides. The Sonora field was a swath of tender green shoots in an otherwise still-grayed landscape. Flocks of hungry geese had found the field right after the seedlings emerged and flocked to it all fall and winter, keeping the wheat stalks bitten short and allowing the weeds to get an early foothold. I walked past the field each day, waiting for the Sonora to surpass the weeds as it always had before. But this year, the geese kept it mowed short.

Though the farm occupied my thoughts during the day, at night I dreamt of India. Sometimes I'd find myself in a fabric shop, sometimes on the rooftop of Jeeta's house or walking the streets of her village. In the mornings, I'd often wake to the patter of her sewing machine, or her voice singing along to a Punjabi pop song crackling through an old cell phone speaker. But after a moment, the threads of reality would restitch themselves around me: It wasn't Jeeta's sewing machine I heard but the tap of branches against the house or the clink of Ryan stirring milk into coffee. Not Jeeta's voice, but the honks of geese or the meow of a cat in our backyard. I was not in the yellow-walled house in Punjab, but in my own bed in California.

Sometimes, on those murky mornings, I closed my eyes and tried to recall the details of the courtyard, the village, Jeeta's face. Other days I rose quickly, slipped into the bathroom and splashed cold water across my face as if I could rinse clear the residue of such dreams.

↤

One of those mornings, after washing my face and drinking a cup of strong black tea, I drove four hours west to the resort town of Pacific Grove on California's Central Coast to attend the annual EcoFarm Conference. Founded in 1981, EcoFarm is the oldest and largest organic farming conference west of the Mississippi. I'd been asked to participate in a panel discussion on the topic of leasing farmland from a land trust. As I neared the town of Salinas, the air grew salty and cool. On either side of the road, mono-crop fields stretched for miles: salad greens, strawberries, spinach. And between rows I could see the bent backs and bandana-covered necks of farmworkers.

In the Salinas Valley, as in Punjab and other industrial agricultural communities across the world, farmworkers and residents face a disproportionate risk of pesticide- and fertilizer-related health disorders, including cancer, autism, and birth defects. Nearly all the farm laborers in this area are immigrants, many of them undocumented. A lack of social and economic resources and the ever-present fear of deportation leave many of these workers particularly vulnerable to exploitation. Their jobs are consistently ranked among the top three most hazardous occupations.

But this is not where I was headed—I was only passing through on my way to the coast. At the Asilomar Hotel and Conference Grounds in Pacific Grove, there were no fields in sight. Instead, the ocean gleamed turquoise in the late afternoon sun, and the grassy grounds were milling with hundreds of smiling conference-goers joyous to spend the weekend talking about the work we all loved. I checked in and found my way to my room. There were floor-to-ceiling windows facing the sea, crisp linens on the bed, tiny pastel soaps in the bathroom.

That evening I scanned the conference program. The panels covered topics from practical skills ("On-Farm Poultry Processing") to marketing ideas ("Chinese Medicinal Herbs: An Emergent Organic Market") and business planning ("Get to Know Your Farm: Planning Tools to Achieve Financial and Personal Goals"). There was something called "Practical Earth Magic," an artisanal beer-tasting event, and a seed and scion swap. After a welcome reception, a band played and people danced into the night. But I was seven months pregnant by then, and didn't feel much like dancing anyway. Instead I took a walk on the beach, sat in the sand to watch the white-capped waves silver against the darkening sky.

The next morning I delivered the presentation I'd prepared, sharing details about our lease arrangement and answering as best I could the questions from farmers looking for land. No, our rent was not subsidized by the nonprofit, we paid market rate. Yes, it was sometimes difficult to negotiate with an entire board of directors rather than a single land-owner. I tried not to sound discouraging, but even simply describing the challenges of our situation—our inability to build equity, the nag of uncertainty, the high rent payments—felt at odds with the celebratory mood of the conference.

A month ago I wouldn't have dared admit that our farm was sur-viving because of the supplemental income we made through side jobs: baking and carpentry. Talking about money felt taboo in farming circles, especially talking about not having enough of it, an offense akin to com-plaining. But earlier that week I'd looked into the national statistics, and what I found surprised me. According to USDA data, intermediate-size farms like mine, which gross more than $10,000 but less than $250,000 per year, obtain only 10 percent of their total household income from the farm. The other 90 percent comes from an off-farm source. Farms smaller than ours actually lost money farming, earning 109 percent of their household income from off-farm sources. Only the largest farms, which represent just 10 percent of farming households in the country, earned the majority of their income from farm sources (income that in-cludes government subsidies). The median farm household income in the United States for that year was projected to be *negative* $1,626. These stark numbers—and their dissonance with the ubiquitous valorization of America's small farmers—had so nettled me that I shared my own farm's financial weaknesses there on the stage. Other farmers on the panel and in the audience then chimed in, naming their own off-farm income streams: outside work, inheritance, a spouse's job, savings from a past career.

After my presentation, I sat at the back of another lecture hall to hear a last talk before driving home. A middle-aged woman next to me leaned in and gestured to the packed hall. "All these people," she said, flicking the end of a long brown braid over her shoulder. "I've been coming here for years, and it's always inspiring, always so many incredible projects." I nodded but noticed that the woman wasn't smiling. She looked at me a moment longer, then said, "But do you know what? You know how much farmland is actually organically farmed?" I shook my head. "Less than one percent. Not even *one single percent.*"

The speaker began to talk, and partway through the presentation the woman next to me stood up and left early. I didn't see her again, but later I confirmed what she'd said to be true: both worldwide and within the United States, only 1 percent or less (respectively) of farmland was being cultivated organically.

I drove home that afternoon with images stuck in my head of those attractive conference-goers dancing in their cowboy boots, the glittering Instagram feeds associated with various speakers I'd clicked through, those tiny soaps. Meanwhile, outside my window endless fields of salad greens flanked the highway, workers crouched between rows. The dissonance between the reality outside my car window and the one inside the resort gnawed at my thoughts, and by the time I returned home I had a pounding headache.

I sat at our dining table and paged through an organic seed catalog looking for the last few items I still needed to order. Outside, I could see the Sonora field in the distance, slicked gold with the light of the setting sun. If I cupped my hands around my eyes, squinted slightly, I could imagine I was back in Pharwala, watching the sun set over wheat fields from Jeeta's rooftop. But as soon as I let my hands fall to my sides, blinked my eyes clear, the similarities dissipated. My thoughts turned to Jeeta and her mother. I thought of the empty fertilizer bags repurposed around their house to hold fabric scraps and kindling, of the "cancer train" and the pesticide poisoning hotline posters, of those kernels of wheat I'd taken from their rooftop—high-yielding varieties nothing like the Sonora in my own fields. I thought, too, of the scenes of the Salinas

Valley I'd passed through hours before, and of that stranger's words: *one single percent.*

I gave up on the seed order, put the catalogs away for the day, and instead dug my sewing machine out of the closet. I spread a square of fabric from India across my kitchen table, began to mark the lines, cut the shape of my shoulders just as Jeeta had done, but I couldn't quite remember—*did she fold the neck here? Did she stitch along the side?* I pulled out my journal to examine the notes I'd taken there, the complicated diagrams and arrows, but I couldn't follow any of it now. My machine squealed electric complaints, the jerky power of it so unlike the even patter of Jeeta's foot easing her pedal up and down. My thread tangled, the bobbin jammed. I gave up, tossed my half-assembled dress into the corner of the closet to be cut up for rags.

That night, I dreamt again of India: I was in the back seat of a car. It was the white minivan, of course, unmoving in a tangle of traffic. The girl in the pink shawl appeared at my window, began her pounding. In the dream, I turned quickly to face the girl and caught her leaning against the pane. But it was Jeeta's face I found staring back at me, her eyes dark and liquid as ink. *Didi,* she said, her breath on the glass between us, *Didi.*

↩ 3 ↪

B y the time I attended that EcoFarm Conference in 2015, organic
foods had grown into a $100 billion global industry. Organic prod-
ucts could be found at mainstream box stores like Walmart and Target,
at gas stations and fast-food restaurants. The word had become a household term. Even the White House had an organic vegetable garden. All
this appeared to provide evidence the organic movement had achieved
spectacular success. And in some ways, it had: National and international government bodies that had once dismissed organic farming as "a
hoax" had come around to acknowledging its legitimacy via their official
state standards and certification systems. Unprecedented numbers of
people counted themselves as supporters of the organic movement, and
public awareness of the ills of conventional agriculture had increased
tremendously.

Yet these more visible triumphs obscured underlying failings. Much
of the growth in the organic sector came after 2002, when the USDA
finalized its national organic standards, making it possible for Big Ag to
enter the organic market. Large corporate farms found they could meet
the federal organic standards without transforming much of anything
about their industrial production model. They substituted allowed organic inputs (less noxious biological chemicals) for those banned under
the USDA standards, but did not change their fundamental growing
practices to attend to the health of the soil and broader ecosystem, or
to the well-being of their workers. Instead, they maintained industrial
practices: mono-cropping, exploitation of labor, dependence on purchased off-farm inputs. Their products, however, bearing the same official organic label as farms that practiced a fuller interpretation of organic
principles—the use of cover crops and green manures, diversified rotations and careful tillage, fair labor practices—became indistinguishable
in the marketplace.

In the ten years between the passage of the USDA's organic standards and the day Ryan and I started our farm in 2012, large agribusiness corporations steadily folded certified organic production into their operations. Using the advantages of economies of scale and highly industrialized production systems, these companies effectively drove down the price premium for organic produce. Just as had occurred decades earlier on conventional farms, smaller organic growers were squeezed out of the market and wealth became concentrated in the hands of a few powerful firms. Many successful independent organic farms and processors—those that had made names for themselves prioritizing the health of the soil, fair labor, seed-saving, compost production, diverse mixed-cropping, direct-to-consumer sales, minimal off-farm inputs—were bought out by corporations that then conventionalized their practices to meet the lowest enforceable organic standards but retained the original brand name and logo. (In a few especially egregious cases, the new firms dropped organic practices entirely and quietly removed the word *organic* from the product label, a change that went unnoticed by all but the most observant consumers.) Those that weren't bought out lost what little economic viability they'd briefly enjoyed. Some of these farms disappeared altogether, some pivoted to niche boutique crops resistant to industrial production, such as tender heirloom tomatoes. Others survived on a customer base of especially privileged consumers willing to pay a steep premium. Many found outside jobs or other income streams to keep their farming businesses afloat.

By the time Ryan and I started our farm, large firms had come to dominate the organic industry. As sociologist Brian Obach details in his 2018 book *Organic Struggle,* many of the most powerful agribusiness companies—Cargill, Kellogg's, ConAgra, Coca-Cola (all companies that had committed atrocious violations in the areas of human rights, environmental health, and public safety)—were now involved in "organic" farming. Their entry into the organic sector increased the visibility of organic foods, expanding their availability into national chains like Safeway and Walmart (though even in these stores organic products are sold at a higher price than their conventional counterparts). But it also conferred control of the organic market to agribusiness, whose interests are firmly wedded to maintaining the structures upholding the industrial food system.

As climate change, dietary-related diseases, social inequity, and increasing ecological wreckage began to direct more and more public scrutiny to that very system, scholars and activists argue that the availability of certified organic "alternatives"—many produced by the same companies responsible for worsening those maladies—has served as a convenient pressure release valve. "By providing a small segment of highly motivated consumers with a means to reliably secure the goods that meet their desires," writes Brian Obach, "the incentive for these relatively privileged individuals to demand broader systemic change is diminished." Rather than advocate for major reforms aimed at the structural underpinnings of the food system—strong labor protections and fair wage standards for farmworkers, federal subsidy programs that support low-input biodiverse farming instead of mono-crop chemical-intensive industrial production, funding for sustainable agriculture research, stronger antitrust laws, bans on carcinogenic pesticides and those known to cause ill health effects, strict regulations and high taxes on synthetic petrochemicals, land reform to conserve agricultural land for farmers—concerned individuals with enough discretionary income can choose to protect their personal health and support "alternative" agriculture by buying certified organic foods. Meanwhile, a food system based around chemical-intensive industrial farming can continue unabated.

And that is exactly what it has done: Despite the impressive increases in the availability of organic food, the use of synthetic fertilizers and toxic chemicals has continued to climb. Farmworkers remain the poorest workers on earth and suffer 385 million cases of acute pesticide poisoning each year. Rates of soil degradation and biodiversity loss have not slowed. While the organic food industry has kept a scant percentage of toxic chemicals and synthetic fertilizers out of the environment and given some individuals access to foods grown without harmful substances, these modest gains have come at the high price of widened social disparities and the undermining of a movement to promote systemic change for all.

❧ 4 ❧

On a clear February morning, not long after returning from the EcoFarm conference, I was sitting at my desk in the dark of pre-dawn when an article on the United Nations Food and Agriculture Organization website caught my eye. The article featured a photo of a wagon heaped with sacks of US-AID fertilizer, surrounded by men in salwar kameez. The scene, of a farming community in Pakistan, was familiar: flat plains in the background, dusty streets and concrete structures, fertilizer bags very much like the ones in my grandmother's village. The article stated that the global use of synthetic nitrogen was on track to rise 25 percent over the decade spanning 2008 to 2018. After a few more clicks leading me from one article to the next I read that pesticide use, too, was climbing both globally and nationally.

They were plain facts—unsurprising, really. And yet I felt a slow burn spreading at the back of my throat, a feeling like being the last one let in on a joke. I read the article over a few times, waiting for the burn to subside. When it didn't I closed the computer and stepped out onto the porch. Below, my fields lay blue-tinged in the first light—dark soil striped with lines of snap pea seedlings, cover crop waist high, rows of mustard gone to flower and left for the bees, the field of wheat bursting green. I glared out at all this, trying to recall what it had once looked like to me, to see again all the potential I'd once believed these fields held. But that morning, no matter how hard I stared, I could no longer see it that way.

Instead I noticed a tangle of bindweed curling up the steel tines of an idle tractor implement, a patch of star-thistle already growing tall along the fence line, and I wondered: how long would it take for the landscape to erase my farm if I simply walked away, if I quit farming today? If no one dragged a scuffle hoe through the rows of onions or mowed the thistle, if no one harvested the wheat, no one seeded cover crop next fall? The thistle would flower, each bloom dropping a dozen seeds into the soil. Ground squirrels would make quick work of the rows of carrots and potatoes. Birds would wait for the figs to ripen, then dart their sharp beaks through the leathery skin and carry away the fruit's ruby insides. The neat edges of each half-acre block would fray, weeds creeping in until the ten acres appeared once again undivided, just a fallow field as it had been when I'd arrived.

I noticed, too, the geese. Though the sun had not yet crested the eastern horizon and the farm lay in shadow, I could see them clearly enough. A flock of forty or so birds, necks bent downward, grazing busily in their usual place in the Sonora field. I imagined their nimble beaks efficiently plucking the tips off each blade. I imagined the weeds growing strong and tall between the slender wheat stalks, gaining more height on my Sonora each day.

Soon, I knew, the thistle would surpass the wheat. It would swallow my field, likely rendering the wheat impossible to harvest. There wasn't much I could do to stop it now. And though I wanted this to matter, in truth it didn't. No one was counting on this harvest, on these two acres that might have yielded a couple thousand pounds of flour. If Ryan and I mowed it down and turned the straw and grain all back into the soil, the wheat would still serve as an enriching cover crop. The field would be better for it, ready for winter plantings by the end of summer. No significant loss. We could plant again next year. If there was a next year.

By the time I stood on my porch that spring morning, nearly a century had passed since the days Sir Albert Howard and my great-grandfather had walked the same wheat fields in the plains of Punjab. A century since the two movements—organic farming and the Green Revolution—had intersected there, unfolding in disparate directions to shape the landscapes of his great-granddaughters' lives.

That day on my porch I wasn't thinking of any of this. I was thinking instead of how I'd gotten myself here, wondering what I'd once believed I might achieve by starting this farm, by growing this wheat, and what it would mean if I failed.

It is only now, years later, that I recall that winter morning on my porch and think backward through time. I follow the organic movement's trajectory in reverse to land upon that other moment, in those other wheat fields, where my great-grandfather sharpens the curved blade of a scythe while, not far away, Sir Albert Howard puzzles over the task set before him as imperial botanist: How to wrest harvest after harvest of wheat—and of cotton, tea, sugar—from India's increasingly depleted fields?

The answer Howard devised, his organic farming method, was designed to accommodate the particular parameters of the colonial agriculture system for which he served—the lack of animal manure, the high price of chemical fertilizer, the imperial need to maintain political control while extracting wealth from India's fields and farmers—and made no attempt to question the dictates of that system. Like the Green Revolution's package of high-yielding seed and synthetic fertilizer that followed, Howard's organic techniques offered a way to sidestep growing demands for fundamental social change by providing instead a technological fix to increase crop yields. Both fixes sought to mitigate the problems afflicting agrarian communities and food production systems while avoiding questions of sovereignty, land ownership, labor relations, and the unequal concentration of wealth and power.

In the decades between Howard's time in India and that morning I stood watching the geese nibble away my wheat, the organic movement that he'd started and I'd joined had, at times, come to examine those questions and criticize the historic and structural forces undergirding them. But the bulk of our efforts and achievements—market-based solutions focused on the creation of certification programs, labeling initiatives, and alternative food and farming businesses—remained directed not at confronting and dismantling those systemic forces, but at carving out a way to exist within the bounds of their logic.

In recent years organic methods have begun to garner more attention than ever. As the climate crisis escalates and the vulnerabilities of conventional food production are further exposed, a growing body of research has examined the potential role organic agriculture techniques might play in creating a more resilient food system. These studies have resoundingly affirmed many of Howard's assertions, and those long held by farmers the world over: organic methods can offer a solution to soil loss, maintain greater biodiversity, protect ground and surface water from contamination, and produce foods containing less pesticide residue. In addition, recent research has shown organic farming uses 45 percent less energy and produces 40 percent less greenhouse gas. On top of all these environmental and public health gains, yields generated via organic farming can match—and under stress conditions such as drought, have been shown to surpass—those of conventional methods.

Until we confront the structural forces that constrain agriculture, however, organic practices and their fruits are likely to remain relegated to the fields and tables of the few. Perhaps we might conceive of the health of our food system in the way Sir Albert Howard inspired so many to view the health of a plant: not as an isolated entity but as part of a broad web of relations to be examined as "one great subject and not as if it were a patchwork of unrelated things."

⌁

That morning on my porch, I stood beneath the clear winter sky until the sun edged over the horizon. The first rays seared the hilltops to the west of my fields, but down below, in the bowl that held my farm, the geese remained in shadow. I thought of the woman's words at EcoFarm, *less than one single percent*; of Jeeta's fingers pressing a scrap of fabric into an old fertilizer bag; of my dwindling savings account and the child moving in my belly; of the geese nibbling steadily at my wheat. I tried to turn away, to go back inside, make another cup of tea and forget my wheat, the birds' swift beaks, the sack of flour I'd never give my grandmother.

But I couldn't quite turn away. I watched the geese in the field until I could stand it no longer, then took a step down the hill toward the farm. I picked up a handful of gravel from my driveway and start to jog. The geese lifted their long necks as I neared, and I hurled rock after rock at them. "Go away," I shouted, but the birds stared motionless and my voice seemed only to dissipate into the stillness of the morning. I reached the edge of the field and flung the last few rocks into the wheat. A ripple passed through the flock as each goose stretched open a pair of wings. Then, with a sound like a gust of wind, the birds lifted in unison into the air above me. I dropped to my knees, tilted my head back and watched their white bellies flame pink as the geese flew up out of shadow and into the blaze of the rising sun.

❧ 5 ❧

A few days before the start of spring 2015, my daughter was born. Indy came into the world alongside apple blossoms and wild lupines, into a season brimming with new life. My grandmother called a few days after the birth to ask how the baby and I were doing. Indy lay asleep atop a sheepskin spread out beside me on the couch, and I traced my fingertips along the curve of her head, through wisps of dark hair. I thought of the birthing room my grandmother had shown us in Punjab and told her we were both doing just fine. My grandmother asked if Indy was eating enough and I assured her that she was. Satisfied, she said goodbye, then added, "Congratulations." If my grandmother was disappointed that I'd had a girl, she let no hint of that into her voice. Over the following weeks she called often to check in on Indy and me. If Indy was bothered by gas, my grandmother advised me to grind a pinch of asafetida into a paste and feed it to her. If the baby was plagued by hiccups she assured me it was only a good sign that she was going through a spurt of growth.

Consumed with the demands of a newborn, I spent the first few weeks of that spring breastfeeding, washing diapers, and walking my daughter to sleep. Friends and family came to help with the farm, planting seedlings, rolling out irrigation lines, hoeing the eruption of spring weeds. I set up a crib in the greenhouse so I could seed flats while the baby slept. If the weather was clear and warm, I carried a blanket out into the fields and laid Indy on her back while I worked, watched her track the geese flying overhead, clouds bunching and stretching across the sky.

Now, as I recall those days of harvesting cut flowers with the baby on my back, of pulling young carrots from the field for her to gum, I try to remember the particular moment when I first seriously considered giving up our farm. When did the stray musings calcify into a pressing, specific desire? I can locate neither. The shift happened the way the mulberry trees lost their leaves each autumn: I'd never see the first leaf fall, not the second or third, but one day I'd notice the ground covered in yellow and look up to find the branches already half bare.

By the time Indy was two months old, the thought of leaving was constantly on my mind. I found myself once again perusing the internet in search of other options. At first I looked only for local work, a job I could take outside of the farm to supplement our income, a part-time gig as a substitute teacher or an adjunct community college instructor, or something for the state park down the road. But at some point my search criteria expanded until I was looking at full-time positions, then jobs in other states. Ryan, too, found intriguing possibilities across the country and every few weeks we'd get excited about something and start putting together the materials to apply. But a day later I'd be harvesting flowers at sunrise with Indy asleep in a carrier on my back, the sky over-head ribboned with coral-colored clouds and rows of chest-high zinnias on both sides, and the thought of leaving this place would seem utterly inconceivable.

On my computer desktop, adjacent to a folder marked "Resume/ Cover Letter," our proposal to lease more acreage for wheat waited, ready to send off to the conservancy.

One late spring morning, my mother came over to watch Indy for a few hours while I harvested for a wholesale order. I squatted next to a row of carrots, attempted to pull up a bundle by hand. This was usually an easy task this time of year, but that morning the tops snapped off and the roots remained clenched in the hardened soil. I used a digging fork as I did in the summer months to pry the roots up from the dry ground.

In the back section of the farm our Sonora had grown to its full height, finally abandoned by the flocks of geese. But the damage had been done: the field was thick with star-thistle. Even from a distance I could see the blue hue of their stems woven through the bright green Sonora stalks. When a breeze washed over the farm, the wheat did not ripple gracefully like the surface of a lake as it had in past years.

I didn't know if it was harvestable at all. The thistle would jam the combine—I had witnessed that already, and knew the thickest patches would have to be relinquished. But in some places the thistle was thin, in a few sections absent altogether. Perhaps a few hundred pounds could be salvaged still?

When I returned to the house with a bucket of carrots too small for the order but perfect for roasting, I heard my mother cooing softly from another room. At first her words sounded like baby talk, just nonsense babble, but after a moment I realized she was speaking Punjabi. I stepped into the room to find Indy lying across my mother's lap, looking up at her. At the sound of my footsteps my mother startled. She flashed me a brief glance, then returned her attention to the baby and announced that she'd resolved to speak only Punjabi to Indy. "That way she'll just pick it up, you know?" My mother stroked a finger across Indy's cheek and continued muttering lulling sentences, the words falling so effortlessly from her lips. "And then," she added without meeting my eyes, "you can learn with her."

I leaned against the doorframe and listened. Indy stared up into my mother's face, her brows two crescent moons above blue eyes held wide open. I closed my own eyes, focused on the words coming from my mother, trying to pull some meaning from the sounds. At last I recognized something: *Kheth*, farm. *Gajar*, carrot. *Kaanakh*, wheat.

⇜ 6 ⇝

Later that spring, when Indy was not yet three months old, my grand-parents made the trip to El Dorado County to meet her—their first great-grandchild. Ryan and I drove with Indy over to my parents' house to join them for dinner. From the driveway I could already hear voices on the back porch, the crackle of something simmering on the big propane burners. With Indy in my arms, I followed the voices into the yard.

For a moment, no one noticed me approaching and I watched the scene from a distance: My grandmother sat in a plastic chair and sliced an onion over a bowl in her lap, my mother swirled a spoon over a cast-iron pan, my aunt rolled out balls of roti dough. A chatter of Punjabi bounced between the three women, their voices hardly distinguishable.

My grandmother looked up and her face split into a grin. She put the onions aside, then flung the tail of her silk scarf over her shoulder and stood. "Ah, the baby is here," she said and held her hands out toward me. I placed Indy in her arms.

My grandmother cradled the baby close against her chest, then held her out to take in her face. She spoke to Indy in English, told her how beautiful she was, what fat cheeks she had. Lowering her voice to a near whisper, she murmured, "I'm sorry. I'm so sorry, I cannot talk to you. I don't speak much English, you see." My cheeks swelled with heat and I glanced away. I wished I could pluck my grandmother's words from where they hung in the air, expunge her apology. I wanted to tell my grandmother the depth of my regret over the fact that I'd never know what she sounded like when speaking her own language but knew her only in translation, her thoughts squeezed into ill-fitting containers. I watched my grandmother cup my daughter's head in her palm, then said, "Speak to her in your language—she's learning. Speak in Punjabi."

My grandmother turned to her husband and carefully passed him the baby. The two looked like a set of opposites: My daughter, brand new, all creamy skin, blue eyes, and chubby cheeks. My grandfather in what would be the last decade of his life, skin wrinkled and thin, dark eyes pillowed in bags, the bones of his face unconcealed by extra flesh. Indy stared up at her great-grandfather and he looked down at her—two pairs of eyes locked on each other.

When he spoke his voice was a near whisper. "Hello gol gappa," he murmured, calling her the name of an Indian snack, a ball of deep-fried dough filled with tamarind juice. My daughter smiled, let out a soft coo. "Hello little gol gappa," he said again, and a smile curled the corners of his own mouth.

I could not, on that day, imagine my grandfather decades earlier, young and strong and ready to murder my parents—could not reconcile that figure with the man standing before me, those big hands so full of gentleness. Nor could I imagine how, in the coming years, my daughter and my grandfather would come to adore one another, that I would watch her place a doll into his lap so he could pick it up and stroke its plastic head, that I would see him pretend to eat a roti she'd made from play dough, or that he would call her gol gappa until she was old enough to say the name herself.

⌐⊃

When I said goodbye to my grandmother that evening, she handed me two Tupperware packed full of leftover okra and dal and a stack of roti rolled up in aluminum foil. Then she slid two bills into my hand, $21— always an odd number, for good luck. I tried to refuse the money but my grandmother insisted. "It is for Indy," she said. I relented and put the bills in my jeans pocket. My grandmother placed her palms on either side of Indy's face and kissed the baby's forehead.

"Jackie," she said, her voice quieter now. "Let me tell you one thing." She paused, then apologized for her inability to express exactly what she needed to say in English. For a moment I thought she'd given up, but she cleared her throat and began again. "You must not tell your daughter 'you can not do this' or 'you can not do that.' Do you understand?" Her right hand clutched my elbow and, without waiting for an answer, she continued. "You must let her have . . . how do you say? Freedom? Yes, freedom. Give her freedom."

Surprised by the force of her words, I could manage only a nod. For a long moment she kept her gaze on me, scanning my expression as if searching for some assurance that she had made herself clear. "You *must* give her freedom," she said a last time, then released my arm. She kissed the baby again on the cheek. "OK, OK, goodnight." Her voice was soft and cheerful again, and she tucked a wisp of hair behind my daughter's ear before stepping past us and down the hall toward her room, the tail of her chunni trailing behind her.

ᐊ 7 ᐅ

One Wednesday afternoon, our slow day on the farm, I put the baby to sleep in her crib and went to sit on the old couch in the back porch we'd recently screened in. Ryan carried out a cup of coffee and took a seat beside me.

There was almost always a breeze on the porch, but in the midday hours even the breeze blew hot. That July afternoon it felt to me less like wind and more like someone breathing too close.

Beyond the porch steps, the garden I'd planted around our house— salvias and rosemary, lavender and geraniums—looked parched. A fuzz of red dust laced the screens. In the distance, I could see the heat rising off the baked earth. In the foreground, a line of laundry stretched across the yard. We never seemed to have enough clothespins, and I noticed a sock had blown off the line into the crisped weeds below. I stepped off the porch to pick it up. Covered in prickles of all kinds—burrs, foxtail stickers, thistle tines—it looked like something that had been left out for a season. I made a half-hearted attempt to shake it off, then held it up to Ryan.

"Throw it away?" he said, and we both laughed. I sat back down next to him, the sock between us, and we began plucking each stubborn sticker from the wool.

"We should probably send out that letter before the weekend," Ryan said, his eyes on the sock.

We'd spent the last few weeks drafting an email stating our intention to terminate our lease at the end of the year. The letter suggested some ideas about how to deal with the infrastructure we'd added to the farm. One option was for Ryan and me to piece things out to sell or take with us: the tractor and implements, our two hoop houses, hand tools, miles of irrigation tubing, produce display boxes, harvest crates. Alternatively, the conservancy could purchase everything and then lease the property for a higher rate. That way the farm would be ready to go in the spring, the only missing piece being the farmers. Then there were all the things we couldn't move: the bread oven, the walk-in cooler, the farm stand, washing stations. We'd pored over the fine print of our lease, trying, unsuccessfully, to determine if we could be compensated for these improvements.

"Yeah," I said to Ryan. "I guess you're right."

A noise came from the far side of the yard. For once I hoped the sound was coming from the baby in the bedroom so that we could leave this conversation for another day. I waited for a second cry. But a moment later one of our cats emerged from around the corner, meowing softly, and I returned my attention to the sock.

Ryan got up and stepped inside, returning with our laptop. He passed it to me and I flipped the screen open. On the desktop was a Word document titled "Letter." I clicked it open, copied everything, and pasted it into an email.

"Do you want me to read it aloud?" I offered.

Ryan shook his head. We'd already read it a dozen times, tweaking words here and there, though I'm not sure what difference any of our changes made.

"Just send it."

I pressed the button. Hardly a sound was generated—only the soft click of the touchpad, but I felt as if I'd dropped a beloved piece of pottery, and when I recall this moment now it is as if I can feel the clay slipping though my fingers, hear the smash of a hollow vessel against the floor. My fingers seemed to burn and I felt an instant flare of regret followed by the slow rise of something akin to relief, like a long-awaited exhale: Hadn't I known this moment was coming, hadn't I known this thing couldn't last?

I closed the email window and stared at the desktop. There, on the screen next to "Letter" was another document. "Additional Acreage Lease Proposal." I dragged the icon to the trash, then flipped the computer shut.

When I looked up, Ryan had the sock in one hand, free of debris. "There," he said, "it's done." He passed the sock to me. "I think we got them all."

I ran my fingers over the wool; the sock appeared clean enough, and I hung it back on the line. But I'd spend years rubbing at my ankles, teasing apart the wool to dig out hair-thin spines. I'd never get the itch out.

ᶒ 8 ᶓ

O nce we'd finalized our decision to leave, I'd no idea how to start ex-
tricating myself from the land. I did small things at first. I pruned
the perennial herbs to keep the plants healthy through the fall but left
the weeds to spiral around the bottoms of the thyme and sage. Instead of
sorting our garlic harvest and setting aside enough to use for seed in the
fall, we sold it all. Where I would have sown a new succession of carrots
and beets for winter, I left the field vacant. I tried my best to remove
myself from the farm the way I'd often disentangled the root ball of one
tomato seedling from another—separating the two while attempting to
keep both intact.

I wrote Reed to tell him of the status of the Sonora—that most of the
field had been more or less swallowed by star-thistle. Maybe a third of it
could still be harvested, I guessed, though I knew that was an optimistic
estimate. He said he'd bring the combine over soon, when he had a window of time, and see what he could do.

A few days later, in the last week of July, a high of 106 was forecast.
Ryan and I took the afternoon off to drive up to the mountains where
we camped for a night with Indy, hoping she might sleep better in the
cool alpine air than in the soupy heat of our house. Early the next morning, I got a message from Reed saying he was on his way over with the
combine. I told him to let himself into the farm, that we'd be back in the
afternoon.

As we approached our farm later that day, I could see our old red
combine hunched over in the far corner of the fields. Sections of wheat
had been harvested, swathes of mowed stalks striping the field. It looked
like a half-acre of the Sonora had been cut. The Red Fife remained
untouched.

Reed was gone when we arrived at the farm, but he had sent an email
updating us on his progress. The thistle had clogged up the combine
pretty good, but he'd managed to harvest four or five hundred pounds

of Sonora. He'd started on the Red Fife when the lift cylinder on the combine broke and he could no longer run the machine. He'd taken the Sonora seed back to his place to clean. After all the weed seed and chaff had been sifted out, the harvest had shrunk to around 350 pounds. We were welcome to pick up our share whenever we wanted.

↤ 9 ↦

A few weeks later Reed had managed to fix the combine and return to harvest what he could of the Red Fife. Between the two varieties, several acres remained tangled in thistle, uncut. Ryan and I planned to mow the field in the fall, then disk everything back into the soil, but one late September afternoon, a neighbor who raised sheep came strolling up to my farm stand. Hat in hand, he asked if he could graze his flock through the remaining wheat. All hints of green had vanished months ago from the surrounding pasture where his sheep roamed. Rather than buying grain or hay, the neighbor could feed his sheep off our field for a few weeks.

I agreed, and the next day he strung an electric fence around the Sonora field. After he moved the livestock in, I walked out to see the animals. The sheep looked up at me as I neared, their blocky heads held motionless except for the rhythmic grinding of their jaws. Satisfied that I was no threat, the animals resumed grazing. Unbothered by the thistle spines, they pushed their way gracelessly through the wheat, breaking the stalks against their woolly bodies and nibbling off the berries. It wouldn't take them long to flatten the Sonora to the ground. I stood still for a moment, watching. Then I turned around and walked away until I could no longer hear the stalks snapping beneath the sheep's two-toed hooves.

The next morning, I carried Indy around the farm as the sun crested the eastern horizon, pouring a buttery light across the fields. A trace of dew dampened the soil beneath my feet and jeweled the edges of the last of the beet greens and lettuce heads. I walked slowly between the rows of late summer vegetables, along the block of perennial flowers—sage and echinacea still blooming—and out past the greenhouses, empty now for the first time. I whispered in Indy's ear the names of crops. Here a row of sweet peppers, here collard greens, here winter squash and pumpkins. I wanted to show her everything. Though I knew she was far too young to retain any of this, I wanted to fill her eyes with images of the farm. I wanted to steep her in mornings like this one, hoping that something of this place might remain with her, a sliver of memory banked somewhere in the corners of her mind.

Before heading back to the house, I carried Indy out to the wheat field on the far side of the farm. At the west edge of the field, one small patch of wheat, missed by the combine and outside the sheep fence, still stood chest-high, sipping at the morning sun. This lone patch of stalks, twenty or thirty in all, still held heads plump with grain, crisped and bleached by the summer sun. A swell of wind poured down the far hillside and across the valley floor, swirling through the brittle wheat. I listened to the stalks brushing against one another, then lifted Indy's hand and ran her fingertips across a braid of berries. "And this," I told her, "is Sonora wheat."

⊷ 10 ⊷

In early November Ryan and I made one last drive down to Reed's house, this time to pick up our wheat. We'd agreed that Reed should keep most of the harvest, as it wasn't much use to us now that we were leaving the farm. We'd take only enough to use ourselves, around 30 pounds of each variety, which Reed agreed to mill into flour for us.

When we pulled into the driveway a gust of wind lifted a swirl of oak leaves into the air, and the wheat farmer stepped out of his house, smiling. In each arm he held a sealed plastic bag full of flour. I reached for the Sonora and turned the bag over in my hands. The flour was cream-colored, tinted gold like rich butter, and peppered with darker bits of bran. I opened the ziplock and rubbed a pinch between my fingertips, then lifted it to my nose to smell the slight caramel aroma of the freshly milled flour. We said goodbye to Reed, thanking him for all his help, then climbed back into our car and drove home. With the bag of Sonora heavy in my lap, the others stacked in the back seat, I rested my head against the window and fell asleep.

When we reached the farm, I carried the flour up our porch steps to find another package waiting there on our doorstep, this one bearing a note in my mother's handwriting: *From Pharwala*. The bundle, a cotton sack printed with Punjabi characters and wrapped snuggly around itself, revealed no postage, and I later learned it had not come through the mail but via a series of handoffs, passed from Jeeta to a neighbor headed to Delhi, then to a friend of my grandmother's, then to a son headed to LA, then to my grandmother, my mother, and at last to me.

Inside, I set the flour on our kitchen table and unwound the cotton bag to reveal a tidy square of folded cloth. I lifted it from the bag and the fabric fell open: a toddler-size salwar kameez, bright blue satin with gold and green trim, and a gauzy chunni to match. I turned the neckline inside out and there were Jeeta's stitches, tiny hatch marks perfectly in line.

In the months following our visit to Pharwala, there'd been talk of trying to bring Jeeta to California, some vague possibilities relayed back and forth between my grandmother and other relatives, but nothing worked out and the idea was eventually dropped. Then one day I heard news that Jeeta was engaged to be married again. She'd at last received an official divorce and a new marriage had been arranged. This was good news, everyone said, but I couldn't forget Jeeta's words that night on her rooftop: *marriage is prison.* What about her coming to California? I asked. *Oh, no, she doesn't want to come to America,* my mother said, my grandmother and aunt too. The idea was so swiftly and unanimously dismissed I wondered if I'd imagined the urgency of Simran's plea that evening in Pharwala, if maybe it was not desperation I'd heard in her voice that day. Perhaps Jeeta had never wished to leave her home, to trade her yellow-walled courtyard for a rootless life in a foreign city. Or maybe it had once been a real wish but now things had changed, new opportunities had arisen for her at home. Or maybe she'd tired of lusting after something unattainable and chosen instead to bury that particular desire.

At my kitchen table, I spread the small kameez smooth and traced my fingers along the seam, overcome with the urge to thank Jeeta, to express my appreciation for this gift of a perfect suit—those skillful stitches, the striking design, that brightest of blues, a color that, she couldn't have known, matched my daughter's eyes. I tried to think of a way to repay her generosity, her thoughtfulness. What could I give her? My eyes fell upon the bag of Sonora flour there on the kitchen table, and for a moment, I imagined offering it to Jeeta:

I'd set the bag in her hands, tell her to lean close and take a breath, smell its summer-corn sweetness. She'd look at me, eyes wide and searching, and offer that bemused smile I'd grown so used to. Perhaps she'd laugh, ask why had I not instead brought her a pair of jeans, a bottle of nail polish? A cell phone? A bus pass, a plane ticket, a passport? Or maybe she'd shake her head and go along with it: lean in, sniff. But then, I imagined, she'd pull her face back and her brow would surely be furrowed, her amusement vanished. *This?* she might ask, the bag of flour cradled in her hands. *This, of all things, is what you've brought me? What am I supposed to do with this?*

⁓

The next morning I dressed Indy in the suit, working her chubby eight-month-old arms through the sleeves, pulling the salwar up over her diaper. The pant legs ballooned out at her feet, the dress fell far past her knees. She wasn't near walking yet, but even if she was, the chunni draped around her neck would drag on the floor. It would be a year or two before it fit, and I couldn't help but wonder what occasion she would have to wear the salwar kameez. Would she wear it at all, or would the dress remain unworn in the back of her drawer, just like the salwar kameez of my own childhood?

I folded the tiny suit and packed it snuggly into a box with my own kameez from Jeeta, then slipped the box onto a shelf in my closet. An imagined day played out in my mind, some years into the future, in which a young girl, seven or eight, plays among the clutter of a different closet in some other house. This girl, my daughter, notices a cardboard box with a corner of shiny blue fabric poking out. She lifts it from the shelf and finds inside the toddler-size suit with a matching chunni, carefully folded and stacked atop an adult-size kameez with a pleated center for a pregnant belly. She wonders: *Where did these come from? Why do they not look like anything else in our house?* She calls me over, asks *Mama, what's this?*

Would I lift a kameez to my face and take a breath? Would I hold the fabric out to my daughter and ask, can you smell it? Can you smell the trace of cook-fire smoke, the hint of mustard oil, of cardamom? Would I run my fingers over the stitches and tell her of the young woman— her Auntie—who once held a measuring tape against my curved belly? Would I tell her of the yellow-walled courtyard, of the room nearby where her grandmother had been born, of the wheat fields surrounding it?

Would I tell my daughter her Auntie had waited in this courtyard for the news of her birth so that she would know which kind of suit to sew— one for a boy or a girl? She might have taken a bus to the fabric shop in a nearby city. There, she'd have looked at roll after roll of cloth until she found the bluest one. *Sky blue,* she would have said, and paid with money saved over many months. Or perhaps she'd not bought the fabric but squirreled away a scrap left over from another woman's order, a piece just large enough for a child's dress. Would I describe the kick pedal–powered sewing machine, the way Jeeta would have spread the fabric across the swept concrete floor, marked the length, the sleeves, the neckline, how she might have held the finished kameez up to admire her work—a suit made not to the specifications of a customer's order but a design all her own? How she might have imagined the small dress making its way down the cobbled streets out of her village, past its wheat fields and out of her country, across the Pacific Ocean, to America? Would I tell my daughter how this woman had once called me Didi, how she'd tried on my clothes, how she had taught me the Punjabi word for moon one evening while we stood together on her rooftop?

And if I did tell my daughter all this, what would I say next, when she looks up at me and asks: *Where is this Auntie now? When will she come to visit us?*

I left the box in the closet and shut the door, not sure if, when this imagined day arrived, I'd say any of this at all. Instead, I could look at the garments and shrug. "Oh, that stuff?" I could say, "That's just something I've been meaning to give away."

✧

That evening, after Indy fell asleep, I attempted to begin sorting and packing up our kitchen in preparation for our move in early December. But I couldn't seem to find anything that we wouldn't need to use in our remaining weeks here, so I gave up and instead filled the kettle with water and set it on the stove to boil. I leaned against the wall and my gaze settled on the bundle of wheat resting in a vase above my kitchen sink. I'd gathered the stalks the first year we'd grown Sonora, tied them together with a length of twine, and displayed them in my windowsill. Over the years the clusters of berries had faded from amber to pale blond, and the stalks had grown brittle. I reached for the vase and slipped the bouquet out. A layer of dust covered the wheat and I brushed it away, careful not to disturb the perfect geometry of the kernels.

The kettle boiled. I set the Sonora on the counter and poured water over a teabag. While the tea steeped I walked to my desk, dug my fingers into the mason jar of pens until I found the tiny bundle of wheat seed I'd taken from Jeeta's rooftop nearly a year ago now. I brought it into the kitchen and tugged at the end of the thread. The bow slipped loose and the fabric fell open. Inside, the chestnut-colored kernels looked just as they had the day I'd picked them out of Jeeta's dust pile.

I turned back to the Sonora bouquet and plucked a spikelet of seeds from one of the heads. Layers of chaff wrapped each kernel and I rubbed the spikelet between my fingertips until the chaff fell loose. With a puff of breath I blew it away, leaving only the naked kernels in my palm. I looked from these seeds to those resting on the fabric and yearned to see something there besides two small heaps of distinctly different wheat berries. Somewhere way back, I knew, the two varieties shared an ancestor. I wanted to understand how they were related, how their histories entangled and diverged, how each had made its way into a different farmer's field on an opposite side of the world. Instead, I poured the Sonora seeds onto the fabric along with the wheat from Jeeta's rooftop. The creamy Sonora kernels bumped against the nut brown of the others and I swirled a finger through the pile, then refolded the fabric and wrapped it tight with thread, binding the two varieties together in the only way I then knew how.

☙ 11 ❧

A short walk north of our farmhouse a hill rose just high enough
that I could stand at its crest and look down upon the entirety of
our ten acres: the grid of fields, the strip of wetland to the north, the two
hoop houses, the tractor and implements, the barn. From this distance,
the farm appeared perfectly cupped in a palm of land.

I often sought out this hilltop in the evenings or early mornings, never
tiring of its view. Sometimes I thought of the Nisenan people, indigenous to this place, and tried to imagine how the land might have looked
before roads and fences, before cattle or wheat or grapes, before those
flakes of gold and the droves of miners who sought them. Other times
I turned to look east toward the Sierras, to the thunderheads that often
gathered over the Crystal Basin range forty miles away, and thought of
those gold-hungry pioneers and eager settlers who, if they'd survived the
treacherous journey over those mountains, would have descended right
here, into this long-dreamt mother lode and its promise of reinvention
and prosperity.

It was upon this hill, too, that I'd stood the evening after the county
agriculture inspector informed me of my neighbor's plans to spray herbicides on her land next to the farm. Thinking of the "buffer zone" I'd
been told to create in order to maintain my organic status, I'd looked out
at the fence line, closed one eye, and held up my hand to block out the
swath of wheat I'd lose. The required 75 feet was two-fingers' worth from
where I stood.

Recalling this moment recently, that number—75 feet—struck me as
odd. I hadn't thought to question it at the time, but now it seemed both
too wide and too narrow, and I wondered how it had been determined.
Was the distance a standard requirement, and if so, whose?

I paged through my old copy of the CCOF rules handbook, then
looked in the National Organic Program regulations. I found no confirmation of a required 75-foot buffer zone. Instead I found a statement

declaring that, while organic acreage must have a buffer zone to protect it from non-permitted chemicals applied to adjacent lands, national regulations do not mandate a specific size. CCOF, too, declines to provide a standard width, stating instead that it uses a 25-foot baseline to be altered at their discretion, based on factors such as physical barriers or agricultural practices.

It's not really surprising that no one can seem to quantify the distance required to protect an organic space. In truth, contaminants don't pay heed to such borders. They slink past in the air and waterways, penetrating fence lines as easily as they seep through the boundaries of our bodies, traversing not only distance but time. Fourteen organochlorine pesticides, all phased out in the United States—including DDT, banned now for fifty years—continue to be found in the cord blood of newborns across America, along with more than 250 other chemicals. A recent study found detectable levels of glyphosate (Roundup) in nearly all commercial breakfast cereal products tested, including (though in significantly lower levels) those certified organic. Greenhouse gases emitted while manufacturing nitrogen fertilizer raise temperatures the world over, driving species of plants, insects, fish, and birds to extinction—a loss we all shoulder. Systemic exploitation of agricultural workers means all farms, including my own, must rely upon, or contend with, cheap labor.

The word *buffer* originates from an old English verb no longer in use—*buff*: to make a dull sound when struck, like that of a blow against a body. The noun *buffer*, then, in its most literal definition, means the thing that makes such a sound, the meaty tissues of the outer body, the muscles of a turned back.

The buffer zone surrounding a farm, of course, makes no such sound when encountering interlopers: pesticides drifting on the breeze, GMO seeds carried by birds or a strong wind, fertilizers and herbicides slinking down rivulets of rainwater. It is silent, too, when these trespassers slip heedlessly past.

The buffer zone, then, is a fiction, a kind of facade, a pretense. And yet, as is the case with many borders—the painted line delineating lanes of traffic, a partition separating one country from another, a frontier beyond which lies the possibility of reinvention—it is not the realness of the boundary that matters, but the belief in it. Because, while buffer zones fail at their supposed purpose, they succeed in something else: they enable us to conceive of the landscape as divisible, thus making it possible to believe that two conflicting systems of food production— one safe, the other toxic, one ethical, the other exploitive—can coexist. It's a belief that demands the rejection of its opposite: the reality that the world is interconnected, each space stitched to those adjacent and far-flung via wind patterns and ocean currents, the lineages of seeds and routes of migrations, the histories that bind each of us to one another.

And so, all these years later, it is not what the buffer zone fails to do that I find most unsettling, but what it achieves. I think now of that word—*buff*. The sound of a blow against a turned back. A buffer: the thing that produces the sound, the turned back. To buffer, then, is to turn one's back; forsake, wash one's hands of, deny, renounce, disown.

⌖

I can still close my eyes and recall the view from that hilltop, our fields held in that palm of land. When I do so now, I think of a passage from Joan Didion's book *Where I Was From*. Didion writes of the early years of California settlement, of the frontiersmen and women who in the mid-1800s crossed the country in pursuit of these gold-laden hills and fertile land. Didion examines the diary entries left by some of these early Californians, finding stories that lay bare another side of the quest for reinvention. They are not only tales of courage and tenacity, but of betrayal and abandonment. In one such story, described in the diary of Bernard J. Reid, a wagon train, unwilling to be slowed down, abandons a seventeen-year-old girl, Miss Gilmore, and her cholera-sickened younger brother in the High Sierra. Memories of choices such as these must have been difficult, Didion writes, "to reconcile with the conviction that one had successfully met the tests or challenges required to enter the new life."

"When you jettison others so as not to be 'caught by winter in the Sierra Nevada mountains,' do you deserve not to be caught? When you survive at the cost of Miss Gilmore and her brother, do you survive at all?"

<h1 style="text-align:center">❦ 12 ❦</h1>

I n November, my grandparents came up for one last visit while Ryan and I still had our farm. I walked them around the land as I'd done before, but this time there was less to show: no rows of winter greens, no garlic mulched with straw, no field of just-sprouted wheat. The barn was tidy, towers of harvest bins stacked against the walls, hoses curled on hooks in the washing stations, hand tools sharpened and organized. In the farm stand, the "South Fork Farm" signs were gone from the walls, wooden display boxes lay empty and upside down atop the shelves, the fridge stood cleaned out and unplugged.

On the last day of their visit, I drove to my mother's house for dinner. Inside, I found my grandmother sitting on the couch. With Indy in my arms, I bent to give her a hug and for a moment the familiar scent of masala and black tea, cardamom and milk, enfolded me. I stepped back but Indy clung to my grandmother's silk scarf so I set her on her lap. "Hello Indy, hello moatie-choatie," my grandmother said, patting the baby's chubby cheeks, squeezing her thighs. Indy pulled my grandmother's scarf to her face, and I wondered if the scent of the fabric would sear itself into my daughter's memory the way it had my own.

I left Indy with my grandmother and walked back outside to my car to retrieve the produce I'd brought: a box of carrots from cold storage, a couple pounds of onions, and a bag of my Sonora flour. I carried the food into the kitchen, where my mother and aunt were laughing and clanking pots as they began preparing a big meal, the last before my grandparents headed back down to LA in the morning. Their suitcases were already in the hall, lined up and ready to go.

My grandmother no longer did most of the cooking when she came up to visit. Nearly eighty now, she was easily exhausted by the long drive, the guest bed, the absence of her usual routine. Instead she coached my mother and my aunt from the couch, calling out directions as she lay draped in a shawl. *Cut the onion very thin, put in one pinch paprika for color.* Every so often, she pushed herself up and walked over to the kitchen to examine the consistency of a pot of dal or the shade of browning onions, adding a bit of this or that.

I set the Sonora flour on the kitchen counter and explained to my mother that I wanted her to use it to make the roti for the meal. She pointed to a bowl of dough resting on the counter. "We already made the atta." Maybe we could make some with Sonora as well, I suggested—that way we could compare the two. She agreed and filled another bowl with a heap of golden flour.

My grandmother carried Indy into the kitchen, passing her to my aunt. I lifted the bowl of Sonora, cupped a handful of flour in my palm. "Naniji," I said, "I brought this flour, it's made from the wheat I grew." My grandmother peered at the mound and nodded, not particularly interested. "It's this summer's harvest," I added, but she didn't seem to hear me. I poured the flour from my palm back into the bowl and dusted my hands. My mother turned her attention from the onions browning on the stove, pointed a spoon toward the flour and spoke to her mother in Punjabi. I recognized a few words: *kheth*, farm, *kaanakh*,wheat. My grandmother's eyes widened. "Aahcha?" she said, and turned to look again into the bowl of flour. "You grow this atta?" she asked. I nodded.

My grandmother had, of course, forgotten the field of wheat I'd shown her several years ago. She'd forgotten about the promise I'd made to bring her some atta from my farm when it was ready. I lifted the bowl once more and held it out to her. She dipped her fingertips into the flour, took a pinch into her cupped hand and spread it across her palm. "Nice," she said.

My mother poured water in the bowl of Sonora and mixed it into a smooth ball of dough. Then she set it aside to rest, and my grandmother lowered herself into a chair just outside the kitchen where she could still see the stove.

When the dough had rested long enough, my grandmother came slowly back toward the counter. My mother and aunt stepped aside, and my grandmother pressed her fingertips into the dough, nodded, then plucked a hunk from the mass. She rolled it between her palms, shaping a plum-size ball. Then she pressed the ball flat into a disk, dusted it with flour and rolled it thin. I watched the dough move beneath the wooden rolling pin, the diameter widening outward as the disk spun. "Ah!" she said, and turned from the bread to grin at me. "Very nice, haanah? You see how it spread, so thin, so easy? Yes, very nice atta!"

My grandmother's motions were so seamless, so utterly capable, that no one offered to help. She lifted the circle of dough and tossed it back and forth between her hands a few times to stretch it further, then slapped it onto the tuva waiting on the stove. The dough swelled and darkened instantly against the hot steel. Steam rose from the pan, and with it that faintly sweet scent of Sonora.

I found a metal tin in a cabinet, lined it with a fresh dishtowel. When the first roti was done, I held the tin out and my grandmother lifted the hot bread from the pan, swirled a spoon of butter across the blistered surface, and dropped it in.

⟜

Though it was November, the day had been warm. When Ryan arrived, he and I set up a table on the back porch. We carried out pots of dal, a subji of carrots and potatoes, roasted eggplant, jars of pickled lemon, a bowl of freshly set yogurt, and two stacks of hot flatbreads wrapped in dish towels. My aunt herded everyone outside and we all took seats around the table in the last warmth of the low-slung sun.

Indy picked up bits of potatoes and eggplant, smearing them around her tray and across her cheeks, directing the occasional morsel into her mouth. She sucked on the corner of a paratha my grandmother had made for her, balling it up in her fist. My grandfather picked slowly at a few tablespoons of eggplant, one buttered flatbread. My grandmother kept an eye on everyone else's plates, offering more food at the sight of any empty space.

Were they better, the roti made with Sonora? They were tender, flaky almost, and golden. The freshly milled flour lent a rich aroma to the dough, a hint of sweetness lacking in the others, which were chewy and bland in comparison. By the end of the meal, every Sonora roti had been eaten—only the ones made with store-bought flour remained.

When we could eat no more, we sat at the table and watched bats flit across the sky until it grew too dark and cold to stay. My grandparents retired to their bedroom and the rest of us began cleaning up. On the counter lay the sack of Sonora flour, a few pounds still inside. I poured it into a ziplock, then slipped the bag into a pocket of my grandmother's suitcase.

⇜ 13 ⇝

It was nearly winter when we left the farm at the start of December. In the back of our truck, along with bags of clothes and boxes of dishes, sat two bulb crates filled with what remained of our final harvest. One carried winter squash—creamy butternuts, mossy green kabochas, and flaming red kuris. The other was heaped with burlap sacks of onions and braided garlic, jars of canned tomatoes, and two gallon-size bags of Sonora flour. The produce wouldn't last us long, I knew—a few weeks perhaps and it would be gone. The flour, too.

We pulled out of the driveway for the final time, wound slowly up the hill, then paused once more at the top of the rise to gaze down at those ten acres. As promised, Ryan and I had done our best to steward the land through one last fall, to prepare the fields for whomever might arrive to take our place. We'd mowed the remnants of our last crops, then disked everything back into the soil. I'd waited once more for a forecast of rain, then zigzagged across the ten acres with the broadcast seeder slung over my shoulders, flinging cover crop seed. When I reached the field that had held our last crop of Sonora, I could see clusters of pearly kernels rattled loose by the mower and pressed into the soil, a handful of intact ears scattered about, and wondered how many of these seeds would germinate.

From the top of the rise that final evening, the farm looked tidy, everything in its place: tractor implements lined up, hoop houses cleaned out, irrigation tape wound on reels. There was no sign yet of the cover crop we'd planted, or those remnant wheat kernels harrowed under. The fields appeared empty in the November dusk. But I knew the seeds were there, just beneath the soil, waiting.

Part 5

GIFT

❧ 1 ❧

As it turned out, I was wrong about the blue salwar kameez. A few years after we left the farm, an occasion arose for my daughter to wear it. On a mid-December evening when she was three, my grandfather passed away. He died at home, in his living room, after complications following surgery. I was living in Oregon by then, with Ryan, Indy, and our infant son, Asa. We'd been preparing for a trip to Los Angeles to visit my grandparents when my mother called with the news of her father's death. We didn't even need to change our plane tickets to attend the funeral.

It was late morning when we pulled into my grandparents' driveway, and, except for the extra cars squeezed in, everything appeared just as it always had: swept concrete, peachy stucco siding, plastic blinds drawn over the windows. My grandfather's old Camry sat in its usual place and the sight of it sent a wash of memories over me—the car pulling into the driveway of my childhood home, its trunk packed with food, my grandfather behind the wheel, my grandmother in the passenger seat, and me watching from my bedroom window.

I stepped out of our car, hoisted my son onto my hip, clasped my daughter's hand, and together we all walked into the house. In the kitchen, a pot of cha boiled on the stovetop but the room was empty. I glanced around: colanders sat on the counter heaped with fruit, tubs of achar were stacked on a side table, a twenty-pound bag of basmati rice tucked underneath. I had the urge to open the fridge, to look in the garage and make sure everything was still in its place. But the slap of chappla against the hall tile stirred me from my wonderings, and I turned to see my grandmother walking toward us.

"Hello, Jackie, hello," she called, but did not usher me to the dining table, did not ask if I was hungry. She gave me a hug and I released my daughter's hand to wrap my arm around her shoulders. I wished I knew the right words to say to a woman who had just lost her husband of more than sixty years. Instead, I did only exactly what I'd always done: I rested my chin against my grandmother's shoulder and pressed my face into the folds of her scarf, inhaled. When I pulled away the baby was gripping the scarf and my grandmother's face was wet with tears. She took Asa's hand and carefully unwound his fingers from the fabric. She patted his cheek and shuffled back toward the living room, where friends and relatives sat drinking cups of cha.

My aunt emerged from the back of the house to help carry in our bags. I expected to follow her down the hall toward the guest room where I usually slept, but instead she led me toward those sliding glass doors opening into the temple room. Several months ago, she explained as we walked, my grandparents had decided they could no longer properly care for the Guru Granth Sahib. So they'd returned the sacred book to the gurdwara to be passed on to a different household, and the room was undergoing a kind of reverse transformation. Before I could fully take in this news, she pushed open the door and we were inside.

The sacred book that had lain open across a raised bed-like platform for as long as I could remember was gone. The dressings that had adorned the platform—shiny draperies and garlands of marigolds, intricately crocheted shawls and gold statues, vases of peacock feathers—had all vanished. The platform itself remained in its place and, I saw with rising unease, was now topped with a makeshift mattress made of several thick blankets. This was where Ryan and I were meant to sleep. At the foot of the bed, a foam futon had been set up for the kids. I thanked my aunt and she disappeared out the door. I took a step toward the bed, then lowered myself gingerly onto the blankets, unable to keep from wincing, as if my weight might injure some being hidden there beneath the covers. No one, of course, cried out, so I settled onto the platform and lay flat on my back.

Above me, brightly colored garlands still hung across the ceiling, shining in the lamplight. The same vinyl shades sealed the windows, blocking the outside light from seeping in. Gold-framed paintings of Sikh gurus, decorative jewelry, stacks of papers, and lacy table coverings that had once been neatly arranged about the room now sat piled along the walls, shoved into corners. I imagined the space transforming further over the coming months, the piles packed into boxes, the last garlands pulled from the ceiling, a floral couch brought in, maybe a TV, until the room no longer revealed anything of the temple it had once been.

Through the stack of blankets, the wood of the platform pressed hard against my spine. I stood up, dragged the blankets down and spread them instead across the carpeted floor. "Much softer," I said to no one, relieved for an excuse to avoid sleeping on the bed that had, just months prior, held the Guru Granth Sahib, with one grandparent or the other muttering softly beside it. I couldn't bear the notion of that book gone, and in its place the mundane weight of my own body.

Later I walked around my grandparents' neighborhood, down the streets my grandfather had walked each day. I thought of that note he left my mother all those years ago, signed "your doomed father," and it occurred to me that there was more than one possible meaning to those words. Now—too late, of course, to ask—I wondered if he'd meant that my mother's actions had consigned him to a certain future, or if he meant that he'd been destined all along for the particular kind of fate he was then confronting.

The only Indian funeral I'd attended was that of the old man in Pharwala. I didn't know what to expect now, how the rituals were to be enacted, but I'd been asked to speak on behalf of the grandchildren. On the morning of the funeral I held the page I'd written and listened to my aunt explain how the service would proceed, where I should be and when. I thought of that white string I'd practiced removing with my foot in the village in Punjab, and that same fear of getting it wrong began to well up.

It was a crisp winter afternoon in the San Fernando Valley when we pulled up at the funeral home—seventy degrees and sunny. A breeze fanning off the ocean blew the air clear, and in the distance dry mountain ridges rose in sharp relief. In the parking lot I attempted to nurse the baby in the car, negotiating the unfamiliar and stretchless fabric of my borrowed kameez. Indy had run off with my aunt toward the growing gathering of relatives and friends, most of whom were strangers to me. I watched through the car window as the wind rippled my daughter's blue salwar kameez, the one Jeeta had made, then caught the twin tails of the matching chunni. The scarf drifted up behind her, and for a moment I could hardly distinguish cloth from sky.

When I found Indy later, an old woman I'd never met was speaking to her in Punjabi. My daughter's face was pressed into the slippery fabric of my aunt's salwar as she looked sideways up at the older woman, nodding shyly. I assumed she was only nodding to please this stranger, hoping—as I'd always hoped when I was a child—that no one would notice how she hadn't understood. But then the woman asked a question and Indy replied without pause. Though my daughter had responded in English, it was clear she'd understood the Punjabi question. "Good girl!" the woman said. Indy beamed, then both of them broke out in laughter. And I remembered: my daughter did understand. Though I knew her comprehension was partial and might fade as she grew older, for now, at least, this language belonged to her.

The service began and everything was in Punjabi. I could catch only a sole word here and there until it was time for the eulogies. A friend of my grandfather spoke first, in English. He talked of the days when he and my grandfather met, shortly after they had both arrived in America in 1971. Back then, he told the crowd, there were only a few Sikhs in the valley. "We had no grocery stores, no restaurants, no temples, and no guarantees. And now—" he swept his arm across the packed room.

When my turn came my aunt nudged me forward. I stood and adjusted the chunni over my head, trying to make the movement look perfectly natural, like it was something I'd done a thousand times. From behind the podium I attempted to tell the crowd something of what my grandfather had meant to me, to share the moments most etched into my memory. I told, too, of his relationship with my daughter—his first great-grandchild—how he had given her the nickname "gol gappa," and how, though he hadn't had the chance to meet him, he was survived now, too, by a great-grandson. I described a recent morning, when I'd walked into my living room to find my daughter lying on the floor cupping her baby brother's chubby cheek in a palm, how she'd pressed her lips close to his ear and, in her three-year-old-voice, whispered *Hello gol gappa! Hello my little gol gappa!*

After everything had been said, we all filed past the casket to take a final look at the body of the man inside. When the lid was closed, we walked in a long snaking line out of the temple to where the cremation chamber was located behind the building. Here, my grandfather's wooden casket was placed in front of two steel doors leading to the firebox. My grandmother stood closest to the casket. My mother stood to her right, then me, and finally my daughter clutching my hand. We were lined up, I realized, in descending order, a trail of generations.

Someone opened the doors to the mouth of the firebox and slowly slid the casket inside. There was a clang of the steel banging shut again, then the sound of wood catching fire—at first just a crinkle like someone crumpling a paper bag, then a rush of flames followed by a surge of smoke from the chimney. I watched the smoke pour upward, thick and black against the bright blue sky, then closed my eyes and listened to the fire roar. I thought of the funeral in Pharwala, that same crackle and rush as flames engulfed the pyre. I recalled the heat on my cheeks, the trunk of the pipal tree against my back, once just a sapling pressed into the earth by my great-grandmother, sixty years later bearing me up. And I thought, too, of those other fires, those my grandfather had described to me, witnessed when he was just a boy crouched on a rooftop, a bell clanging overhead while the flames crackled below. I imagined that boy lifting his gaze past the fires, past his village, and into the fields beyond. Dappled with corn and vegetables, sugarcane and chickpeas, mostly these fields hold wheat, the stubble of the prior year's crop glinting in the fire glow. The fields unfurl into the distance, past caravans of people traveling on foot in both directions. Among these masses is the eight-year-old girl who will become, in not so many years, this boy's wife. The fields spread onward past rivers and roads, toward the new border, and past that too. They spread into the gridded and irrigated plains of west Punjab where a heap of tools, those my great-grandfather once used to mend plows and scythes, lies abandoned in the dust. Zoom out and the piece of land upon which these tools rest reveals itself to be wedge-shaped, bordered on either side by a river. Pan out farther still, not just through space but also time, and the tidy grid lines blur, canals disassemble, swaths of green turn brown: wheat fields become desert. Five rivers come into view, each growing wider before joining together in a palm and pouring down into the waters of the great Indus. Follow this river to the salty waters of the

Arabian sea, up the coastline, into the Persian Gulf, and overland north-west toward the Fertile Crescent. Here, 10,000 years into the past now, a stand of green emmer wheat sways in a breeze. Watch this wheat ripen and bronze under the summer sun, the seeds fattening until they reach maturity and burst from their ears to the ground below. But look closer and notice some seeds do not fall, do not scatter. They remain in their ears, kernels snug inside layers of chaff like gifts in tissue paper. And here, a pair of human hands, ready to unwrap them.

❧

One by one, we stepped away from the roar of the fire and made our way to the gurdwara for a meal. In the temple's dining hall I waited in the food line with my daughter. Behind the counter giant dishes held dal, subji, saag, rice, fresh yogurt, and khir. Last of all sat the roti, hundreds of breads heaped atop one another, glistening gold beneath the overhead light. With a pair of tongs, a woman lifted two from the stack and folded them neatly onto my plate. Then she turned to my daughter, smiled, and placed a third warm bread into her open palms.

❧

The morning after the service I found my grandmother at her kitchen table with a dried gourd-like vegetable in her hands. I pulled out a chair and sat beside her.

"Turai squash. You know it?" she asked.

I shook my head.

"It is like, what you call, zucchini? You know zucchini?"

I nodded, but the squash didn't look like a zucchini to me.

"When it is fresh, it is like zucchini. Now, it is very dry. You see?" She held the vegetable out and chipped off part of the peel. Inside the flesh was white and sinewy. "This you can use to wash, very good for scrubbing." I leaned closer.

"Oh! It's a loofah squash," I said. My grandmother shrugged.

"When it is fresh, you can make subji. Very good subji. You come in the summer, yes? I will make for you. Now, look," she said, holding out the squash, "I am taking the seeds, for next year." A friend had brought her this squash from his garden, and she hoped to grow a plant in her own yard next year.

She squeezed the squash and the skin crinkled, then tore, and she began to peel off the pieces. I watched as she rubbed away the last bits of skin until only the inside remained, a tight weave of fiber. She laid the naked squash flat on a napkin, sliced off one end, and tapped the open side against the table until the mesh released one black seed. She continued to tap and a heap accumulated on the napkin.

I reached across the table and plucked a seed from the pile. "Bija," my grandmother said, and I nodded: seed. It was a word I'd only recently learned. One afternoon my daughter and I were practicing Punjabi, pointing at things around our kitchen and trying to name them. Gunda, Lussin, Loon, Sunthra. She'd pointed to three seeds lying on the counter, picked out of an orange slice. When neither of us knew the Punjabi word, I'd called my grandmother. After she pronounced it for me, I looked it up to see how to write the Punjabi characters and read online that this word is used metaphorically in both Buddhism and Hinduism to mean "origin." The metaphor had seemed straightforward then: a seed is, of course, a starting point, the beginning from which the rest of the plant unfurls. But now, watching my grandmother tap loose those black seeds from the dried squash, I thought of how a seed was not just a point of origin, but also a kind of carrier of origins. Within a seed lies a promise for what's to come, but also a record of the past, the genetic memory of the lives lived before and the landscapes and relations that shaped each one. I turned the squash seed over in my fingers. Here, in this small capsule, both history and future resided, bound together in a single body.

I placed the seed back on the napkin and my grandmother folded the paper around the heap, then told me she was going to rest and carried the bundle down the hall into her room.

෴

I was bent over my backpack, packing things up for our flight home later that day, when I heard my grandmother call my name. I found her on the couch in her sitting room with a pillow-size plastic bag at her feet. I sat beside her and she lifted the bag. "Jackie," she said, "I have something for you. If you like, you take?"

She pulled out a bundle of cloth. It tumbled to the ground, then unrolled flat. A rug: navy and cream-colored yarns woven into an intricate pattern of saw-toothed lines and geometric shapes. "It's beautiful," I said.

My grandmother studied the pattern for a moment, as if she too was seeing it anew, then nodded slowly.

"You know, I make this? This rug, I make when I was fifteen."

Before I could voice my astonishment she added, "I make it for my dowry."

I ran my fingers over the tight weave, imagined my grandmother as a teenage girl, aligning one row of yarn against the next, pulling the fibers taut, weaving the very fabric that would secure her dreaded marriage and everything that would follow, each strand a yarn's width closer to that fate.

"But now," my grandmother said, nodding as if affirming something to herself, as if she'd always known she would one day say the words that followed. "Now, it belongs to you. For you to, how do you say? To remember me."

I turned to the rug, busied my hands with rolling it into a tidy scroll, then fitting it back inside the bag. When the sting in my eyes had receded, I looked up to thank my grandmother, but now she was offering me something else. Her fingers were closed around another gift, held out to me in a fist.

It was the pearls, I felt certain. After all these years, she was at last going to offer them to me again. This time I knew what I'd say.

But when she opened her hand, I saw a heap of seeds: six cherry-pit–size spheres, four oblong disks.

"Bija. From the limbri tree," she said, "and the turai squash. So you can grow at your home, haanah? Then, you have fresh limbri leaves whenever you need, and you can make very good dal!"

I held out my own upturned palm and my grandmother smiled. Then she spilled the seeds from her hand to mine.

ACKNOWLEDGMENTS

This project unfolded over the better part of a decade and was made possible by countless people whose mentorship, support, and research kept it afloat:

Immeasurable gratitude to Debra Gwartney, the first to believe in this book, whose rigorous critiques, ceaseless encouragement, and warm friendship nourished it into being.

Heartfelt thanks to Julie Guthman, whose UCSC classes planted the seeds of thought that would later fuel my inquiries for this book and who has contributed hugely to the body of research on organic farming and the alternative food movement. As an undergraduate, I lacked the experience and grasp of history to understand her work, but when I embarked upon the project of trying to make sense of my own farm's failures, her books were among the first resources I turned to. I owe a great debt to her deep research and unrelenting advocacy for a more just food system for all.

Gratitude and admiration for the extraordinary teachers who shared their wisdom on writing, farming, and baking: Michael Meyer. Philip Graham. Monica Spiller. Fulton Ford. Dave Miller. Reed Hamilton. Doug Mosel.

This book was informed by countless other books. I'm particularly indebted to the following writers for works that greatly informed this project: John H. Perkins. Joan Didion. Imran Ali. Carey McWilliams. Brian K. Obach. Julie Guthman. Raj Patel. Gregory A. Barton. Jack Ralph Kloppenburg Jr.

Many thanks to the institutions and journals that supported my work with fellowships and published essays that evolved into parts of this manuscript: *The Normal School, High Country News, The Ninth Letter, Salon, Fourth Genre, Orion*. The Elizabeth Kostova Foundation. Fishtrap. Community of Writers. Wildbranch Writers Workshop. Appreciation, also, to the Oregon State University library, which offers all Oregon residents free access to their wealth of resources, including many of the hard to find books I relied upon for this project.

Gratitude to the many people who cared for my children while I wrote: Tracee Highfield, whose wisdom and care has been a gift for our entire family. Julie Courtney and Margaret O'Connor, who brought such joy and warmth through the murky years of the pandemic.

For your good humor, conversations, and encouragement love and appreciation to: Jean Strandberg. Naomi Baker. Gloria Dominguez. Fulton Forde. Katherine Weeks. Ben Verhoven. Jacky Grey. Hannah King.

Thanks to Kate Garrick for her early enthusiasm for this project, and for her buoyant warmth and deft navigation through the process of finding it a home. To Catherine Tung, who made each page of this book better, and everyone at Beacon Press for the care and energy they brought to the process of bringing it into the world.

Love and gratitude to my family:

My grandparents, Gurmeet Kaur Saund and Sawarn Singh Saund, for their courage in opening their histories to my examination, for teaching me how to make roti and all the rest, and for showing me how much can be shared with so few words.

My family in Pharwala for their boundless hospitality, insights, and heart.

My ever-supportive parents, who encouraged this project and many other far-fetched endeavors: Jas Moyer, for generously offering her memories and trusting me with them, and for teaching me the art of strong-willed determination. Dan Moyer, for always nurturing my creativity and for introducing me to the musicians and songwriters who first kindled my love of language.

My sister, Aly Moyer, whose fearless pursuit of self-expression has been a lifelong inspiration.

Deepest thanks to Ryan, for the steadiest kind of support over the many years this project has lived in our house.

Thank you Indy and Asa, for your daily reminders of what it is to love this world. You are my guiding lights.

WORKS CITED

Prologue

John Percival, *The Wheat Plant: A Monograph* (London: Duckworth and Co., 1921).

PART 1: ORIGIN STORIES

Chapter 2

Daniel Zohary and Maria Hopf, *Domestication of Plants in the Old World: The Origin and Spread of Cultivated Plants in West Asia, Europe, and the Nile Valley*, 3rd ed. (New York: Oxford University Press, 2000).

Uncertainty persists regarding exactly when and where nonshattering emmer came into being. Signs of cultivated emmer have been documented near Damascus from as early as 7800–7600 BCE. I choose the year 8000 BCE as the date of this imagined scene, but the exact year and particular details are unknowable.

Chapter 4

Zohary and Hopf, *Domestication of Plants in the Old World*.

Abdullah A. Jaradat, "Wheat Landraces: A Mini Review," *Emirates Journal of Food and Agriculture* (2013): 20–29.

Chapter 6

Zoe Brent, "Farmland Preservation, Agricultural Easements and Land Access in California." Paper presented at Food Sovereignty: A Critical Dialogue International Conference, September 14–15, 2013, Yale University.

Chapter 14

USDA Census of Agriculture Historical Archive, "Selected Operator Characteristics for Principal, Second, and Third Operator: 2012," agcensus.library.cornell.edu /wp-content/uploads/2012-California-st06_1_055_055.pdf.

Chapter 16

Lorraine Boissoneault, "How Ancient Teeth Reveal the Roots of Humankind," *Smithsonian Magazine*, July 2, 2018.

Chapter 17

Monica Spiller has contributed immensely to the development of small-scale land-race grain production in California. She holds a wealth of knowledge about growing, sourcing, milling, and cooking with these grains, and her website is a trove of information: wholegrainconnection.org.

Chapter 18

Percival, *The Wheat Plant*.

Chapter 20

A few of the many heirloom grain millers, grower, bakers, educators, and general revivalists include: Anson Mills, Hayden Flour Mills, Whole Grain Connection, Dave Miller Bread, Mendocino Grain Project, Community Grains, Tara Jensen, Elmore Mountain Bread, Fritz Durst, Capay Mills, Camas Country Mill.

PART 2: GOLD HILL

Chapter 1

Data USA: El Dorado County, California, datausa.io/profile/geo/el-dorado-county -ca#economy (accessed March 2023).

Chapter 2

Carey McWilliams, *Factories in the Field* (Boston: Little, Brown and Company, 1939).
Monica Spiller offers an interesting theory of Sonora wheat's arrival to North America here: wholegrainconnection.org/sitebuildercontent/sitebuilderfiles/Sonora historyanotherlook2008.pdf.
Daniel Geisseler and William R. Horwath, "Wheat Production in California," for the Assessment of Plant Fertility and Fertilizer Requirements for Agricultural Crops in California project funded by the California Department of Food and Agriculture Fertilizer Research and Education Program, updated February 2014, cdfa.ca .gov/is/ffldrs/frep/FertilizationGuidelines/pdf/Wheat_Production_CA.pdf.
Alan L. Olmstead and Paul W. Rhode, "A History of California Agriculture," *Giannini Foundation Information Series* (University of California, December 2017).
Frank Norris, *The Octopus* (New York: Penguin Books, 1986).
Carey McWilliams, *California: The Great Exception* (New York: Current Books, 1949).

Chapter 3

Stephen C. Wagner, "Biological Nitrogen Fixation," *Nature Education Knowledge* 3, no. 10 (2011): 15.
John H. Perkins, *Geopolitics and the Green Revolution* (New York: Oxford University Press, 1997).
Alan R. Townsend and Robert W. Howarth, "Fixing the Global Nitrogen Problem," *Scientific American*, February 1, 2010.
Stefano Menegat, Alicia Ledo, and Reyes Tirado, "Greenhouse Gas Emissions from

Global Production and Use of Nitrogen Synthetic Fertilisers in Agriculture," *Scientific Reports*, August 2022.

USDA Economic Research Service, "Fertilizer Use and Price," ers.usda.gov/data-products/fertilizer-use-and-price.aspx (last updated October 30, 2019).

Chapter 7

"Summary of Public Service [after 2 September 1800]," *Founders Online*, National Archives, founders.archives.gov/documents/Jefferson/01-32-02-0080. [Original source: Barbara B. Oberg, ed., *The Papers of Thomas Jefferson, vol. 32, 1 June 1800–16 February 1801* (Princeton, NJ: Princeton University Press, 2005), 122–25.]

Jacob Allen Clark and Burton Bernard Bayles, "Classification of Wheat Varieties Grown in the United States in 1939," USDA, 1939, handle.nal.usda.gov/10113/CAT86200790.

Jack Ralph Kloppenburg Jr., *First the Seed: The Political Economy of Plant Biotechnology* (Madison: University of Wisconsin Press, 2004).

H. Garrison Wilkes, "Plant Genetic Resources over Ten Thousand Years: From a Handful of Seed to the Crop-Specific Mega-Gene Banks," in *Seeds and Sovereignty: The Use and Control of Plant Genetic Resources*, ed. Jack R. Kloppenburg Jr. (Durham, NC: Duke University Press, 1988).

Sharon Rempel, "Red Fife Wheat," in *The Canadian Encyclopedia* (Toronto: Historica Canada, 2009).

Chapter 9

Kloppenburg, *First the Seed*.

Perkins, *Geopolitics and the Green Revolution*.

Isabel Shipley Cunningham, *Frank N. Meyer, Plant Hunter in Asia* (Ames: Iowa State University Press, 1984).

Chapter 12

The US National Plant Germplasm System can be searched at: npgsweb.ars-grin.gov/gringlobal/search.

Geoffrey F. de Montmorency, "Chenab Canal Colony," in *The Agriculture Journal of India Volume III*, ed. the Inspector-general of Agriculture in India (Calcutta: Thacker Spink and Co, 1908).

Imran Ali, *The Punjab under Imperialism, 1885–1947* (Princeton, NJ: Princeton University Press, 1988).

Ravinder Kaur, "The Second Migration: Displacement and Refugees from Rawalpindi during Partition," *Journal of Punjab Studies* 14, no. 1 (2007): 89–120.

M.S. Randhawa, *A History of Agriculture in India, Vol. III [British rule from 1757 to 1947]* (New Delhi: Indian Council of Agricultural Research, 1983).

Perkins, *Geopolitics and the Green Revolution*.

Chapter 13

Sir Albert Howard, *The Soil and Health: A Study of Organic Agriculture* (New York: Schocken Books, 1972).

Gregory A. Barton, *The Global History of Organic Farming* (Oxford: Oxford University Press, 2018).

Albert Howard and Gabrielle Louise Caroline Howard, *The Development of Indian Agriculture* (London: Oxford University Press, 1927).

Chapter 14

Willard W. Cochrane, *The Development of American Agriculture: A Historical Analysis* (Minneapolis: University of Minnesota Press, 1979).

Guinness World Records, "Most wheat harvested by a single combine harvester in eight hours," guinnessworldrecords.com/world-records/68077-combine-harvesting-wheat-single-in-eight-hours.

Perkins, *Geopolitics and the Green Revolution.*

Chapter 16

Vaclav Smil, *Enriching the Earth: Fritz Haber, Carl Bosch, and the Transformation of World Food Production* (Cambridge, MA: MIT Press, 2001).

Barton, *The Global History of Organic Farming.*

Maria McGrath, "The Bizarre Life (and Death) of 'Mr. Organic,'" *New Republic,* August 2014.

J.I. Rodale, "Introduction to Organic Farming," *Organic Farming and Gardening,* vol. 1, May 1942, archive.org/stream/OrganicFarmingAndGardeningMay1942/Organic+Farming+and+Gardening+May+1942_djvu.txt.

Chapter 17

Geisseler and Horwath, "Wheat Production in California."

Chapter 18

Perkins, *Geopolitics and the Green Revolution.*

Cochrane, *The Development of American Agriculture.*

Chapter 19

The origins of the Green Revolution in Mexico are far more complex than can be addressed here. For a more thorough investigation of this period in the history of wheat improvement see Eric B. Ross, *The Malthus Factor: Population, Poverty, and Politics in Capitalist Development* (New York: Zed Books, 1998); Raj Patel, "The Long Green Revolution," *Journal of Peasant Studies* (2013); and Perkins, *Geopolitics and the Green Revolution.*

Advisory Committee for Agricultural Activities, "The World Food Problem, Agriculture and the Rockefeller Foundation," June 21, 1951.

Inaugural Address of Harry S. Truman, 1949, avalon.law.yale.edu/20th_century/truman.asp.

Howard, *The Soil and Health.*

Chapter 21

Perkins, *Geopolitics and the Green Revolution.*
Patel, "The Long Green Revolution."
Cochrane, *The Development of American Agriculture.*
Philip McMichael, *Development and Social Change: A Global Perspective* (London: Sage Publications, 2004).
Wilkes, "Plant Genetic Resources over Ten Thousand Years."

Chapter 22

Russell M. Wilder, "A Brief History of the Enrichment of Flour and Bread," *JAMA* 162, no. 17 (1956).
Ferris Jabr, "Bread Is Broken," *New York Times Magazine,* October 29, 2015.

Chapter 24

NACLA's Latin America and Empire Report, "The Food Weapon," 1975, tandfonline .com/doi/abs/10.1080/10714839.1975.11724007?journalCode=rnac17.
Perkins, *Geopolitics and the Green Revolution.*
Advisory Committee for Agricultural Activities, "The World Food Problem."
Ross, *The Malthus Factor.*

Chapter 25

Harry Cleaver, "The Contradictions of the Green Revolution," *American Economic Review* 62 (1972): 177–86.
Vandana Shiva, *The Violence of the Green Revolution: Third World Agriculture, Ecology, and Politics* (Lexington: University Press of Kentucky, 2016).
Susan George, *How the Other Half Dies: The Real Reasons for World Hunger* (Montclair, NJ: Allanheld, Osmun, 1976).
Perkins, *Geopolitics and the Green Revolution.*
Ross, *The Malthus Factor.*
McMichael, *Development and Social Change.*
Cochrane, *The Development of American Agriculture.*
Edward T. Breathitt, "The People Left Behind: A Report by the President's National Advisory Commission on Rural Poverty," 1967.

Chapter 26

Wendell Berry, *The Unsettling of America* (San Francisco: Sierra Club Books, 1977).
McWilliams, *California: The Great Exception.*

Chapter 30

Patel, "The Long Green Revolution."
Norman Borlaug, Nobel Lecture: "The Green Revolution, Peace, and Humanity," December 11, 1970, nobelprize.org/prizes/peace/1970/borlaug/lecture/.

Chapter 31

Wade Greene, "The Guru of the Organic Food Cult," *New York Times Magazine*, June 6, 1971.

Warren J. Belasco, *Appetite for Change: How the Counterculture Took in the Food Industry, 1966–1988* (New York: Pantheon Books, 1989).

Brian K. Obach, *Organic Struggle: The Movement for Sustainable Agriculture in the United States* (Cambridge, MA: MIT Press, 2015).

Julie Guthman, *Agrarian Dreams: The Paradox of Organic Farming in California* (Berkeley: University of California Press, 2004).

McGrath, "The Bizarre Life (and Death) of 'Mr. Organic.'"

Rodale, "Introduction to Organic Farming."

Chapter 34

McWilliams, *California: The Great Exception*.

McWilliams, *Factories in the Field*.

PART 3: WINDOWS

Chapter 7

Borlaug, Nobel Lecture.

Perkins, *Geopolitics and the Green Revolution*.

Shiva, *The Violence of the Green Revolution*.

Ross, *The Malthus Factor*.

Patel, "The Long Green Revolution."

Kloppenburg, *First the Seed*.

Obach, *Organic Struggle*.

Guthman, *Agrarian Dreams*.

Stewart Brand, ed., *The Last Whole Earth Catalog*, 1971.

For more on the relationship between hunger, food supply, and distribution see Amartya Sen, *Poverty and Famines: An Essay on Entitlement and Deprivation* (Kiribati: OUP Oxford, 1982). He writes:

> Starvation is the characteristic of some people not *having* enough food to eat. It is not the characteristic of there *being* not enough food to eat. While the latter can be a cause of the former, it is but one of many *possible* causes.

Chapter 10

Rama Lakshmi, "Passengers on India's 'Cancer Train' Share Stories of Pain and Hope," *Washington Post*, January 2, 2013.

Reyes Tirado, "Chemical Fertilisers in Our Water: An Analysis of Nitrates in the Groundwater in Punjab," Greenpeace India Society, 2009.

Chapter 11

Barton, *The Global History of Organic Farming*.

Kloppenburg, *First the Seed*.

Center for Human Rights and Global Justice, "Every Thirty Minutes: Farmer Sui-cides, Human Rights, and the Agrarian Crisis in India," NYU School of Law, 2011.

Food and Agriculture Organization of the United Nations, "Global Soil Partnership Endorses Guidelines on Sustainable Soil Management," 2016, fao.org/news/story /en/item/416121/icode/.

Guthman, *Agrarian Dreams*.

Obach, *Organic Struggle*.

Tom Philpott, "How Your College Is Selling Out to Big Ag," *Mother Jones*, May 9, 2012.

Andrew Olsen, "Cancer-Causing Pesticide Use Rising in California," Pesticide Ac-tion Network North America, 2000, panna.org/legacy/panups/panna-cancer -causing-pesticide-use-rising-california.

Patel, "The Long Green Revolution."

Kristina Kiki Hubbard, "The Sobering Details Behind the Latest Seed Monopoly Chart," *Civil Eats*, 2019.

PART 4: GEESE

Chapter 2

Patrick Rogers and Matthew K. Buttice, "Farmworkers in California: A Brief Intro-duction," California Research Bureau, 2013, latinocaucus.legislature.ca.gov/sites /latinocaucus.legislature.ca.gov/files/CRB%20Report%20on%20Farmworkers %20in%20CA%20S-13-017.pdf.

"Rural Families," Pesticide Action Network, panna.org/resources/rural-families/ (ac-cessed June 2023).

"Farmworkers," Pesticide Action Network, panna.org/resources/farmworkers/ (ac-cessed June 2023).

USDA Economic Research Service, "Organic Production," ers.usda.gov/data-products /organic-production/documentation.aspx.

Julia Lernoud and Helga Willer, "Organic Agriculture Worldwide 2017: Current Sta-tistics," Research Institute of Organic Agriculture, 2019, orgprints.org/id/eprint /33355/5/lernoud-willer-2019-global-stats.pdf.

IFOAM, "Global Organic Area Continues to Grow," 2020, ifoam.bio/global-organic -area-continues-grow.

USDA Economic Research Service, "Median Farm Household Income Forecast to Decline Slightly in 2014," 2014, ers.usda.gov/data-products/chart-gallery/gallery /chart-detail/?chartId=77687.

Chapter 3

For extensive and provocative discussions of the pitfalls of social change movements based around political consumption and the creation of "alternatives," see the work of Julie Guthman and Andrew Szasz: Andrew Szasz, *Shopping Our Way to Safety: How We Changed from Protecting the Environment to Protecting Ourselves*

(Minneapolis: University of Minnesota Press, 2007); Julie Guthman, *Weighing In* (Berkeley: University of California Press, 2011); Guthman, *Agrarian Dreams*.

Obach, *Organic Struggle*.

W. Boedeker, M. Watts, P. Clausing, and E. Marquez, "The Global Distribution of Acute Unintentional Pesticide Poisoning: Estimations Based on a Systematic Review," BMC Public Health, 2020, doi.org/10.1186/s12889-020-09939-0.

Chapter 4

Food and Agriculture Organization of the United Nations, "Fertilizer Use to Surpass 200 Million Tonnes in 2018," 2015, fao.org/news/story/en/item/277488/icode/.

Food and Agriculture Organization of the United Nations, *Pesticides Use, Pesticides Trade and Pesticides Indicators: Global, Regional and Country Trends 1990–2020*, FAOSTAT Analytical Briefs, no. 46 (Rome, 2022), doi.org/10.4060/cc0918en.

Catherine Badgley, Jeremy Moghtader, Eileen Quintero, Emily Zakem, M. Hahi Chappell, Katia Avilés-Vázquez, Andrea Samulon, and Ivette Perfecto, "Organic Agriculture and the Global Food Supply," *Renewable Agriculture and Food Systems* 22, no. 2 (2007), doi.org/10.1017/S1742170507001640.

Lena Brook, "Organic Agriculture Helps Solve Climate Change," Natural Resources Defense Council, 2022, nrdc.org/bio/lena-brook/organic-agriculture-helps-solve-climate-change.

C. Hyland, A. Bradman, R. Gerona, S. Patton, I. Zakharevich, R. B. Gunier, and K. Klein, "Organic Diet Intervention Significantly Reduces Urinary Pesticide Levels in U.S. Children and Adults," Environmental Research, vol. 171 (2019), doi.org/10.1016/j.envres.2019.01.024.

Obach, *Organic Struggle*.

Sir Albert Howard, *An Agricultural Testament* (Oxford City Press, 2010).

Chapter 11

CCOF, ccof.org/faq/what-buffers-are-required-organic-parcels.

Joan Didion, *Where I Was From* (New York: Vintage Books, 2003).

Environmental Working Group, "Body Burden: The Pollution in Newborns," 2013, ewg.org/research/body-burden-pollution-newborns.

Environmental Working Group, "Breakfast with a Dose of Roundup?" 2018, ewg.org/research/breakfast-dose-roundup.

ABOUT THE AUTHOR

Jaclyn Moyer grew up in the foothills of the Sierra Nevada in northern California. Her essays have appeared in *Orion, Guernica, The Atlantic, The Normal School, High Country News,* and other publications. She lives with her partner and two young children in Corvallis, Oregon.